Black Well-Being

UNIVERSITY PRESS OF FLORIDA

Florida A&M University, Tallahassee
Florida Atlantic University, Boca Raton
Florida Gulf Coast University, Ft. Myers
Florida International University, Miami
Florida State University, Tallahassee
New College of Florida, Sarasota
University of Central Florida, Orlando
University of Florida, Gainesville
University of North Florida, Jacksonville
University of South Florida, Tampa
University of West Florida, Pensacola

→ **Black** ← **Well-Being**

Health and Selfhood in Antebellum Black Literature

ANDREA STONE

UNIVERSITY PRESS OF FLORIDA
Gainesville/Tallahassee/Tampa/Boca Raton
Pensacola/Orlando/Miami/Jacksonville/Ft. Myers/Sarasota

Publication of this work made possible by a Sustaining the Humanities through the American Rescue Plan grant from the National Endowment for the Humanities.

Copyright 2016 by Andrea Stone
All rights reserved
Published in the United States of America

First cloth printing, 2016
First paperback printing, 2022

27 26 25 24 23 22   6 5 4 3 2 1

Library of Congress Cataloging-in-Publication Data
Names: Stone, Andrea, 1971– author.
Title: Black well-being : health and selfhood in antebellum black literature / Andrea Stone.
Description: Gainesville : University Press of Florida, [2016]
Includes bibliographical references and index.
Identifiers: LCCN 2015043064 | ISBN 9780813062570 (cloth) | ISBN 9780813069456 (pbk.)
Subjects: LCSH: American literature—African American authors—History and criticism. | African Americans—Intellectual life.
Classification: LCC PS153.N5 S76 2016 | DDC 810.9/896073—dc23
LC record available at http://lccn.loc.gov/2015043064

The University Press of Florida is the scholarly publishing agency for the State University System of Florida, comprising Florida A&M University, Florida Atlantic University, Florida Gulf Coast University, Florida International University, Florida State University, New College of Florida, University of Central Florida, University of Florida, University of North Florida, University of South Florida, and University of West Florida.

University Press of Florida
2046 NE Waldo Road
Suite 2100
Gainesville, FL 32609
http://upress.ufl.edu

For my parents, David and Edith Gray

> The Negro thrives under the shadow of his white master, falls readily into the position assigned him, and exists and multiplies in increased physical well-being.
>
> HENRY S. PATTERSON, M.D., "MEMOIR OF SAMUEL GEORGE MORTON"

> We should indeed regard them as wards and dependents on our kindness, for whose well-being in every way we are deeply responsible.
>
> WILLIAM HARPER, JURIST AND SENATOR, "MEMOIR OF SLAVERY"

> It is true, efforts have been made by wise and good men in almost every age, to enlighten and improve mankind; but these have been confined to individual instances, and have in general been devoted to the propagation of opinions only, in which each individual is in some degree at variance with every other; but the discovery to which we allude, is the practice of combining society itself in intellectual masses, for the purpose of attaining some certain, defined, and acknowledged good, which is generally allowed to be essential to the well-being of the whole.
>
> STATEMENT OF THE LIVERPOOL SOCIETY FOR THE ABOLITION OF SLAVERY

> Law has as much to do with the hideous monster, slavery, as medicine or any other respectable business.
>
> MARTIN DELANY, *NORTH STAR*, JANUARY 28, 1848

Contents

List of Figures x
Acknowledgments xi

Introduction. Human, Person, Self: Blackness and Well-Being 1

1. The Ruled and Regulated Self: Medicine and Race Science in the Black New World 27

2. Ancient Ideals and the Healthy Self: Mary Ann Shadd's *Plea for Emigration* and Martin Robison Delany's *Condition, Elevation, Emigration, and Destiny* 51

3. The Self in Pain: Colonialism, Disability, and National Identity—Mary Prince, Sophia Pooley, and Lavina Wormeny 84

4. The Protective Self: Slave Sexual Health, Crime, and U.S. Legal Personhood—Celia's Murder Trial and Harriet Jacobs's *Incidents* 121

5. The Promising Self: Sexual Expression, Heroism, and Revolution—Frederick Douglass's "The Heroic Slave" and Martin Robison Delany's *Blake* 155

Conclusion. Black Intellectuals, Black Well-Being: Questions about the Future of Black American Literary Studies 194

Notes 201
Bibliography 213
Index 229

Figures

1. "Likenesses of two Negroes," Nott and Gliddon, *Types of Mankind* 35
2. "Caucasian, Mongol, and Negro" skulls, Nott and Gliddon, *Types of Mankind* 35
3. Greek head and Negro head, Nott and Gliddon, *Types of Mankind* 36
4. "Tableau to accompany Prof. Agassiz's 'Sketch,'" Nott and Gliddon, *Types of Mankind* 37
5. Canada West, 1852 map 54
6. First edition of Shadd's *Plea for Emigration; or, Notes of Canada West* 56
7. Addenda to trial summary, *Missouri v. Celia, a Slave*, 1855 137
8. Addenda to trial summary, *Missouri v. Celia, a Slave*, 1855 139
9. Deposition bearing Celia's mark, June 23, 1855 146
10. Questions for testifying physicians, prosecution objections, and objections sustained, 1855 147

Acknowledgments

This book began at the University of Toronto with the help and guidance of George Elliott Clarke, Jeannine Marie DeLombard, and Alan Bewell. All were tremendously generous with their time and insights as the work navigated Canada, the United States, and the Caribbean, the worlds of slavery, law, health, and the body. They remain indispensable colleagues and wonderful friends. The book benefited from the support of the Social Sciences Research Council of Canada, Ontario Graduate Scholarships, and the Barbara Frum Award. A two-year fellowship in Health Care, Technology, and Place (HCTP), funded by the Canadian Institutes for Health Research (CIHR), offered not only generous financial support but also an intellectual home and access to the ideas and suggestions of Elizabeth Harvey, Gillian Einstein, Pat McKeever, and Margrit Shildrick. I'm also thankful for Jill Matus, Heather Murray, and Paul Stevens, as well as the friendship and support of Jody Mason, Eli McLaren, Triny Finlay, Jan Purnis, Brandy Ryan, and Ella Soper.

Participants' comments during the School of Criticism and Theory's six-week seminar on "Black Intellectuals," especially those of my great friends and colleagues Thomas Aiello and Arthur Redding, who also read early drafts, still resonate with me and have found their ways into the book. For the insights and continued support and guidance of seminar leader Brent Hayes Edwards, I am particularly grateful. Likewise, the participants and leaders Lara Langer Cohen and Jordan Alexander Stein of the American Antiquarian Society's summer seminar "Early African American Print Culture," and Paul Erikson have added to the book in immeasurable ways. A recent reunion of some of us at the Center for the History of Print and Digital Culture's conference "African American Expression in Print and

Digital Culture" at the University of Wisconsin, Madison, helped me rethink a few ideas during the book's final stage of revision.

I would like to thank the archivists at the Baldwin Room of the Toronto Public Library, the Archives of Ontario, the Missouri State Historical Society and Newspaper Library, the Calloway County Courthouse, the American Antiquarian Society, and the Library of Congress for sharing their collections and their knowledge. Chapter 4 is a revised and updated version of "Interracial Sexual Abuse and Legal Subjectivity in Antebellum Law and Literature," originally published in *American Literature* 8.81, 65–92 (© 2009, Duke University Press, all rights reserved, reprinted by permission of the publisher). I thank especially Priscilla Wald and the editors and anonymous readers for their insights and suggestions at the article stage.

My longtime friends and colleagues from the Association for the Study of Law, Culture, and the Humanities have contributed to my thinking in incalculable ways, particularly Steven Winter, David Caudill, and the late Penny Pether whose razor-sharp insights and sense of humor I miss deeply. I'm thankful to Paul Finkelman for his work, our conversations, and friendship. I also met my close friend and colleague Cheryl Suzack through this association—there are no words for the depth of my gratitude for her unwavering friendship and support.

I would like to express my thanks to the members of the Celia Project for stretching my thinking about Celia's case from their work, our annual meetings, and our correspondence: Martha S. Jones, Hannah Rosen, Adrienne Davis, Ariela Gross, Crystal Feimster, Arlene R. Keizer, Alison Gorsuch, and Brandi Hughes. This project is a tremendously gratifying collaboration in many ways, and I can think of no other group of intellectuals with whom I could spend one day in intense meetings and writing sessions and the next wandering through a rural Missouri cow field, slightly concerned about the presence of chiggers and snakes and moved by the life of this remarkable woman.

I'd also like to thank the Five College Atlantic Studies Seminar, particularly Laura Doyle and Britt Rusert, for the invitation to copresent my work to the seminar and for their useful insights about the book. This brings me to the place I have called home now for the past few years.

At Smith College I have found a home: physically, professionally, intellectually, and personally. I am grateful to my colleagues across the disciplines, particularly in English (my home department), American Studies (the program with which I am affiliated), the book studies and archives concentrations (on whose boards I serve), and in Africana Studies and the Study of Women and Gender. I'd like to thank especially Richard Millington, Michael Thurston, Michael Gorra, Dawn Fulton, and Daphne Lamothe for being such generous and careful readers and for their friendship and great humor. I'm also thankful for the wisdom, collegiality, and friendship of Nancy Bradbury, Floyd Cheung, Craig Davis, Dean Flower, the late Luc Gilleman, Ambreen Hai, Jefferson Hunter, Gillian Kendall, Naomi Miller, William Oram, Douglas Patey, Cornelia Pearsall, Eric Reeves, Sharon Seelig, Nalini Bhushan, Rick Fantasia, Alexandra Keller, Christen Mucher, Kevin Quashie, Laura Rauscher, Kevin Rozario, Marilyn Schuster, Frazer Ward, Steve Waksman, Louis Wilson, and Susan Van Dyne. I'd like to thank Lester Tome, Elizabeth Klarich, and Randall Griffey for their great friendship, conversations, and camaraderie. The students at Smith continue to inspire and challenge. I would particularly like to thank former students and research assistants Kendra Poppy, Allison Pilatsky, and Precious Musa, along with Madeline Zehnder and Ingrid Brioso-Rieumont for their work and conversations about Black American literature.

I'm grateful to everyone at the University Press of Florida, especially Stephanye Hunter and Sian Hunter. Sian's reputation as a terrific editor is matched only by my experience with her. Thank you to Gordon Hutner for introducing us and for his interest in and support for my work. I'd also like to thank the anonymous readers and Erica Ball, whose careful and brilliant insights were a pleasure to work with and helped me see how to make the book stronger.

To my good friends and family who have supported this book in ways they may never realize, a hearty thank you for your love, patience, and time: Ian Gogolek, Mary Jo Smith, Don MacGregor, Paul Brown, Yonas Ghebreyesus, Kathy Pickard, Mark and Lisa Mitchell, Brent Wilde, Raji Soni, Ralph Callebert, Natasha Barykina, Vince Barbee, Keith Bridger, James Sommerville, Brad Smith, Lesley Grant, Gerardo Alicea, Amy Campbell, Caroline Christie, Walter Colby, Liz Elder, Colin Hoffmeister, Jennifer and Gary Kmetz, Robin Longo, Chet Mitchell, Kelly Tyler, Mike Wall, Donna Webster, Emily Wojcik-Thurston, Josh Jones, Martin Kerry, Steve and Karen Stone, Sharon and Chris George, Carl and Pat Thomas, Gord and Marilyn Fair, Liz and John Baker, Jim and Gloria Ross, the entire Gray clan (Charlie, Linda, Bob, Mary, Duane, Nancy, Colleen, David Lynch, and

Jennifer and Grant MacDonnell), Henry and Colleen Piotrowski, Helena and Sam Trabulsi, Derek, Barbara, and Louise Hodson, Sarah and Neil Hallett, Rachel and Chris Dobson, and Dianne and Michael Melitzer. I want to thank my parents, David and Edith Gray, who taught me not only how to read but also how to love to read and encouraged me through everything I've ever wanted to do (except chemistry): this book is for you.

Finally, to my best friend and partner in everything, Ken Ross, thank you for helping me see this project through in every way. Similar to the way you materialized from the imaginary friend Kenny I had as a kid, I hope this is the first of many projects we'll imagine and realize together. And, of course, these acknowledgments would be incomplete without a thank-you and a scratch to our Grimsby, whose constant companionship and sense of humor puts a smile on my face every day.

Introduction

Human, Person, Self: Blackness and Well-Being

This book studies rhetorics of health and well-being in black literary projects of self-making.[1] The opening epigraphs on page vii demonstrate how the concern for slave/black well-being was a focus for both pro- and antislavery argument. One side argues that in slavery "the Negro . . . multiplies in increased physical well-being," and the other side contends that abolition is "essential to the well-being [of society] as a whole." Featured in these quotations are influential nineteenth-century thinkers from the medical and legal professions. In the final epigraph, black intellectual Martin R. Delany dismisses both disciplines. He argues, "Law has as much to do with the hideous monster, slavery, as medicine or any other respectable business." This book demonstrates the various forms through which a selection of black intellectuals, narrators, and novelists—from the fugitive slave to the free black elite—converse with, employ, and rework medical and legal discourses as they articulate their own senses of what it means to be healthy and well.

Black Well-Being examines the rhetorics through which both sides of the slavery debates through justifications for or rejections of slavery promoted black health and society's overall welfare. These debates reached their most heated fever by the mid-nineteenth century. As the disputes coincided with the rise in medical and legal professionalism, theorists from both disciplines weighed in as experts, often vehemently. Britain had ended slavery in the colonies and entered into a process of gradual emancipation, and the United States became increasingly divided over the issue. The republic's future and individual and communal ways of life and economies, et cetera, were at stake. Blacks in general in America at the time faced the harshest restrictions on their freedoms. Influential black and white thinkers weighed and hotly disputed the implications of emigration and colonization. The era also saw the largest wave to date of black migration to colonial Canada where, in their new home, communities of fugitive slaves and free blacks gathered, published newspapers, and debated issues of education, temperance, abolition, and gender rights. Medical writers placed under intense scrutiny Black Americans' physical bodies, susceptibility or immunity to certain diseases, as well as their intellectual and moral capabilities. Legislators enacted new and revised previous slave statutes and codes to endorse unprecedented strictness, consequently severely limiting even free black mobility and personal safety, in the North as well as the South.

In such an intense and complex political context, *Black Well-Being* traces and analyzes six black thinkers' preoccupation with health and the body in projects of literary self-making in the United States, colonial Canada, England, and the Caribbean. The book conducts close readings of emigration polemics by free black intellectuals Mary Ann Shadd and Martin Robison Delany, both published in 1852, as well as three women's slave narratives by Mary Prince and two lesser-known narrators, Sophia Pooley and Lavina Wormeny. These narratives traverse geographic locations as wide-ranging as the West Indies, England, colonial Canada, and the United States. This book resists a United States–centered approach to reading black literature, even as it acknowledges the substantial body of work that came out of U.S. slavery, emigration, and criminal convictions. *Black Americans* here typically describes black authors/orators in the Americas more broadly, emphasizing the transcolonial and transnational context of the black literature studied here. The chapter that does have a U.S.-based focus on health and legal personhood compares the documents generated by the 1855 murder trial of a slave woman, Celia, convicted of killing her owner, alongside Harriet Jacobs's famous canonical narrative, *Incidents in the Life of a Slave Girl*. The conclusion of this book focuses on fictive imaginings of black rebellion outside the United States by two prominent black authors and activists who in their time were better known for public speaking, autobiographical writing, and journalism: Frederick Douglass and Martin Delany.

Taken together, these texts' attention to health and physicality reveal a striking range of approaches to understanding black selfhood. The book conceives selfhood as one's sense of consciousness and embodiment and an individual's definitions of and relations with what constitutes the outside world. It reads these authors' rhetorics of health and well-being as articulations of their individual senses of self. The book understands health and well-being as connected categories, the former more directly concerned with positive physical and mental experiences, which may derive from a healthful diet, exercise, and relations with others, and the latter an extension of these resources to an overall sense of happiness, energy, and fulfillment.[2] This selection of authors/orators—some well known, some less well known, some formerly enslaved, some free, some of enormous public influence, working in a variety of literary forms and genres—all emphasize black health as a central concern in the projects of articulating their senses of self and of advocating their political theories in the service of black community formation toward the mid-nineteenth century. Furthermore, apart from Martin Delany, who briefly attended medical school, these figures were neither trained doctors or lawyers nor considered authorities on these subjects.

Despite the number of black physician-authors available for study (such as James McCune Smith and Mary Seacole, to name two) or the body of work available about African/African American healing practices, this book is more interested in the ways in which the black thinkers featured here centralize well-being in their works and converse with broader medico-legal discourses about black health from outside the professionalizing realms of medicine, science, and law or explicitly African traditions, which claimed to have a stake in black well-being. Likely one would expect discourses of health and well-being to feature prominently in works by black physician-authors of the mid-nineteenth century, but the centrality of these concepts in works by nonphysicians reveals that health is a central register for these lay writers as well. Whether propagandistic, phenomenological, or self-defensive, to name a few deployments of discourses of health, these works reveal the multiple functions that rhetorics of black health and well-being perform in literary projects of self-definition. Revisiting canonical works through this lens, paying close attention to the literary qualities of works that have not yet found their way into the Black American canon, and demonstrating the literary value of relatively understudied black literature, this book aims to offer close readings that account for the diverse understandings of the black self that emerged from the fraught political, medical, and legal context of the early to mid-nineteenth-century Black Atlantic.

The book focuses on the period between the publication of Mary Prince's *History* in 1831 and Martin Delany's *Blake*, its final serial installment appearing in 1862. This relatively narrow window of Black American literary production coincides with the passage of the British Slavery Abolition Act of 1833, the U.S. Fugitive Slave Act of 1850, and the anticipation and onset of the U.S. Civil War, fraught years whose legislation sent ripple effects throughout both Old and New Worlds. This selection of literature appearing during these intervening years demonstrates how a focus on health and well-being crafts compelling, if at times competing, black senses of self that the dominant cultures in Britain, the United States, colonial Canada, and the Caribbean overlooked or undermined regardless of their varied racial politics.

Personhood, Humanness, Selfhood

In the first half of the nineteenth century, discourses of medicine and law were the most important definers of personhood, a condition crucial to the acquisition of legal rights. Despite our current popular tendency to interchange or conflate the terms *human* and *person*, antebellum American medicine and law understood them as distinct, if overlapping designations. It is also commonly assumed that slaves were considered subhuman and that they were chattel. But neither of those assumptions is technically accurate. In the antebellum era, all persons were humans, but not all humans enjoyed the same rights and protection as persons. Literary critics Jeannine DeLombard and Saidiya Hartman as well as legal historians Paul Finkelman and Ariela Gross have done excellent work demonstrating the political stakes of the legal designation "person" for black people in the nineteenth-century United States. A human might enjoy legal protection of life and limb (as would a person) but he or she might not necessarily enjoy the right to own property or vote. Beyond distinctions of human and person, the law allowed that a slave was at once human, person, *and* property. James Madison (as "Publius" and with Alexander Hamilton and John Jay) articulated the designation of mixed character in *The Federalist* of 1788. "Publius" explained that "In being protected . . . in his life and in his limbs, against the violence of all others . . . and in being punishable himself for all violence committed against others—the slave is . . . regarded by the law . . . as a moral person, not as a mere article of property" (300–301). But this did not mean that slaves were regarded wholly as moral persons. The fact that they were also article[s] of property complicated their legal designation as moral persons. Furthermore, they and all blacks were excluded from U.S. citizenship.

A few years following the publication of *The Federalist*, the U.S. 1790 Naturalization Act stipulated, "That any alien, being a free white person, who shall have resided within the limits and under the jurisdiction of the United States for the term of two years, may be admitted to become a citizen thereof." As literary critic Siobhan Sommerville notes, the Act "reinforced the assumption that slaves were not potential citizens—whether by birthright or naturalization: slave status removed an individual from being recognized as a potential participant in a contractual or consensual relationship with the state (except as property). Slaves, along with the larger category of people not considered 'white,' were thus constructed as 'unnaturalizable'" (667). In effect, the Act anticipated the potential for black political participation in the nation and endeavored to prevent it. Indeed, blacks in the United States could not acquire citizenship until the passage of the Fourteenth Amendment in 1868. The logic of this exclusionary Naturalization Act resurfaced in the intervening years before the Civil War through legislation that further restricted black civic participation and had tremendous influence on black patterns of migration both within the United States and beyond. Furthermore, as literary critic Priscilla Wald points out, "the slave remained within United States culture as a visible symbol of legal nonpersonhood: neither *potential* citizen nor alien" (*Constituting* 43). Coincidentally, in colonial Canada, Britain's Imperial Act of 1790 allowed loyalists to bring slaves with them into Upper Canada. By 1793 slavery was technically prohibited in the province, but the law was not enforced. Even the 1833 British Imperial Act, which banned the sale, importation, or trade of new slaves, did not free those already enslaved in the colonies. U.S. and British Imperial law on the migration patterns and rights of black people in the United States, Britain, colonial Canada, and parts of the Caribbean influenced and determined their access to legal protection and civic personhood.

As persons, slaves enjoyed neither the same legal rights as white male property owners, white male nonproperty owners, male servants, and white women, nor as free black property owners, black nonproperty owners, or black servants. As the book will demonstrate, enslaved women were even more vulnerable in their status as persons and property, particularly in situations of sexual coercion. Despite the dismal implications of slaves' legal personhood, it is important to bear in mind the often overlooked or understated reality that this period regarded black people, enslaved or otherwise, as human—though as we'll see, even that designation created legal contradictions. Making this distinction allows for a more accurate interrogation of legal personhood and a fuller understanding of the lengths to which medical and legal discourses and practices had to go to ensure white supremacy. The understood fact of slave humanity across national and colonial borders emphasizes how the paternalistic rhetoric that tried to underscore slave humanity in defense of the institution of slavery also differentiated grades of humanity to justify the violation of what we now think of as human rights. This study seeks to comprehend how these black authors and orators defined themselves in print in an era that was utterly preoccupied with categorizing them and hypothesizing about the relative value of their humanity and their (in)capacity for civil participation.

Proslavery medical writers were in agreement that Black Americans—whom they termed *Negroes* and considered distinct from African peoples (that is, living in Africa)—were human, but they were careful not to refer to them as persons. The middle of the nineteenth century witnessed the rise of American theories of polygenesis, which argued, controversially contra Genesis, that man was not descended from a single pair. These theorists included medical doctors, naturalists, and ethnographers, to name a few. They agreed that "Negroes" constituted a type, species, or race of man, but that they "[stood] at the lowest point in the scale of human beings" (Nott, *Essay on the Natural History* 17). Even tacitly proslavery monogenists, such as Doctor of Divinity John Bachman, who argued in defense of the single pair theory still acknowledged black inferiority: "a lower grade of intellect would not exclude the negro from the species to which we belong" (212). Either way it seems inclusion in the human family from one or more original sources did not prevent the relegation of "Negroes" to the lowest rung of humanity. "Both sides . . . accepted the premise of black inferiority" (Thomas and Sillen 4). In short, being human did little to garner rights; personhood was the legal category that determined access to rights through civic standing.

Indeed, the term *person* was weighed down in general. Americanist literary critic Jeannine DeLombard usefully details the stages of specification that *person* underwent in antebellum U.S. law. It is worth quoting in full her reading of the two editions of John Bouvier's *Law Dictionary: Adapted to the Constitution and Laws of the United States of America and of the Several States of the American Union* (1839 and 1856): "The first edition's entry for 'person' opens by distinguishing 'natural persona,' such as 'men, women, and children,' from an 'artificial person,' namely, 'a corporation.' The entry goes on to divide natural persons first by gender (with women having only limited civil capacity), and then by condition, into 'free persons and slaves.' Because they belong to a master, enslaved natural persons 'are sometimes ranked not with persons but with things.' Seeking to avoid such confusing redundancy, the entry in the revised 1856 edition clarifies that 'in law, man and person are not exactly synonymous terms.' Whereas 'any human being is a man, whether he be a member of society or not, whatever may be the rank he holds, or whatever may be his age, sex, &c.,' legally 'a person is a man considered according to the rank he holds in society, with all the rights to which the place he holds entitles him, and the duties which it imposes.' All men may have been created equal, but not all were recognized as persons" (*In the Shadow* 6). DeLombard's navigation through Bouvier's two editions' definition of *person* distinguishes the importance of rank embedded in the word's legal meaning and the various grades of hierarchy it encompasses.

Even more confusing and thus emphasizing a similar contradiction in need of clarification (or justification) was English law's consideration of slave humanity and personhood. Literary critic V.C.D. Mtubani details the ways in which the influential Navigation Acts prompted an appeal to the Solicitor-General in 1677 who "declared, unequivocally, that 'negroes ought to be esteemed goods and commodities within the Acts of Trade and Navigation'" (71). But the "commodities" designation was not without contradiction from another important act. Mtubani's survey of "see-sawing" legal rulings on slave rights between 1677 and 1825 demonstrates that "The conflict between the Habeas Corpus Act and the Navigation Acts or between the English common law and the Navigation Acts could not really be solved until Parliament decided which one had to take precedence. Since Parliament itself, in the Navigation Acts, considered Blacks to be property and commodities, it would be difficult to apply the Habeas Corpus Act to them, although they were implicitly covered by it. Even when Blacks were recognized as human beings, no steps were taken to enforce such recognition" (74). In contrast to English legal confusion over the issue of slave status, it seems the United States' distinction of human and person and the privileging of civic standing provided a way to acknowledge slaves' humanity but deny whatever slender human rights they may have had. Perhaps paradoxically, the heavy lifting required of the dominant culture to explain and protect mechanisms of white supremacy reify critical race theory's central tenet that racism is normal. Its institutional and cultural embeddedness makes the task of explaining it and justifying it seem unusual and arduous.

Such limiting and confused explanations of black humanity and personhood perhaps emphasize an added and urgent impetus for contemporary Black American thinkers to assert their own examples of self-definition, embodied, dynamic, and undetermined by the structures and values of the dominant culture. The work of the authors and orators featured here challenge not only Bouvier's rubric and English law's incoherence, for example, but also reveal their phenomenological discord with Western notions of the individual. Italian philosopher Roberto Esposito has traced Christian and Roman (religious and legal) formulations "that separate the category of person from the living being on which it is also grafted. The person doesn't coincide with the body in which it inheres, just as the mask is never completely one with the actor's face." He continues to delineate the "layered spheres" of the individual that determine equality from the eighteenth century on, "one capable of reason and will and therefore fully human and the other reduced to biology, practically assimilated to the animal. While the first, called the person, is considered to be the center of juridical imputation, the second, coinciding with the body, constitutes on the one hand the required layer and on the other hand a piece of property akin to an internal slave" (*Dispositif* 25). Introducing race, particularly blackness, into the question of humanness, literary and cultural critic Alexander Weheliye argues, "If racialization is understood not as a biological or cultural descriptor but as a conglomerate of sociopolitical relations that discipline humanity into full humans, not-quite-humans, and nonhumans, then blackness designates a changing system of unequal power structures that apportion and delimit which humans can lay claim to full human status and which humans cannot" (3). Given the constraints of such schema particularly on those who were actual slaves, former slaves, or capable of being enslaved in the New World, mid-nineteenth-century black literary negotiations of this person/body split, degrees of humanity, and contemplation of selfhood are political and philosophical and radically promising. From Mary Prince's critique of the sovereign self to Martin Delany's depiction of healthy sexuality, for example, these authors and orators offer a range of exciting epistemologies for understanding the self.

Theories of selfhood from philosophers like Paul Ricoeur (1992) and Margrit Shildrick (2002), resonating from Levinas, are especially helpful in delineating the false and illusory, not to mention treacherous, valorization of autonomy and the Enlightenment ideal of an independent, enclosed self as distinct from others. This ideal dominated nineteenth-century America and relegated black people to the bottom of the human spectrum. Ricoeur argues that "the burdensome character of existence and of the task of having-to-be expresses what is most crucial in the paradox of an otherness constitutive of the self and in this way reveals for the first time the full force of the expression 'oneself as another'" (327). For Ricoeur here, it is the other that constitutes the self. This constitutive sense of other, and therefore self, offers one way Black Americans may have called into question nineteenth-century medical and legal attempts to distinguish permanent types/races and therefore to imagine and legislate that one is naturally and permanently inferior to another. Nevertheless, the autonomous ideal self and therefore community for writers like Mary Ann Shadd and Martin Delany became central to their conception and promotion of emigration and by extension black individual and political health.

One startling, if persistent, example of the sort of biopolitical logic confronting Black American thinkers in the mid-nineteenth century comes from well-known, highly respected, and tremendously influential southern physician Josiah Nott, who rebutted the suggestion that "Negroes should be gradually educated and emancipated . . . and thus be absorbed and become a part of our flesh and bone, and a part of our civilization." In *An Essay on the Natural History of History*, he refuted the argument, writing, "A great aim of philanthropy should be, to keep the ruling Races of the world as pure and wise as possible, for it is only through them that the others can be made prosperous and happy" (19). The alluring discourses of purity neither surprisingly nor uniquely influenced proslavery physician writers and legal theorists but some black antislavery thinkers as well, such as Martin

Delany. Arguments like Nott's promoting the reification of boundaries demarcating self and other—in his context black and white—individually and communally, and in the service of maintaining the integrity of "flesh and bone" as the first defense of civilization, found articulation in slave codes. These codes forbidding, for example, the education of slaves were attempts at preserving arbitrary distinctions, which proslavery ideologues needed in order to maintain white supremacy. Some black thinkers, such as Mary Prince, for example, challenged assertions of the pure, complete, enclosed self—black or white.

Reading Mary Prince's *History*, we may assume that her sense of the permeability of self may be more in line with what Shildrick outlines as contradictory responses to others. Shildrick extends some of Ricoeur's ideas using the image of the monster to demonstrate the porous character of putative borders between notions of self and other, and to undermine their hierarchical ordering that privileges self and sameness over other and difference. She states, "Given that the western logos is structured according to an infinite series of binaries that ground all knowledge in the play of sameness and difference, it is only by making such distinctions, by having a clear sense of self and other, that it is possible to mark out the parameters of self-identity. If we know what we are by what we are not, then the other, in its apparent separation and distinction, serves a positive function of securing the boundaries of the self. And yet time and again the monstrous cannot be confined to the place of the other; it is not simply alien, but arouses always the contradictory responses of denial *and* recognition, disgust *and* empathy, exclusion *and* identification" (17). Shildrick draws out the self/other binary to expose the consistent collapse of those boundaries whenever we try to erect or maintain them. Recently, literary critic Monique Allewaert has employed the term *parahuman* to "challenge the hierarchical organization of life-forms that was common to colonial anthropological and natural histories . . . [putting] animals, parahumans, and humans in horizontal relation (that is to say, *para* or beside each other) without conflating them . . . [to demonstrate that] the parahuman in the eighteenth and nineteenth centuries reveals a perversion of the category of the human that was effected by diasporic Africans' performance of their parahumanity" (86). Such a perversion of the category "human" is something Prince's *History* interrogates rigorously in its narrating of pain. Curiosity about differences between races during the Enlightenment era and attempts to categorize sameness and difference produced the illusion of a pure, secure white identity, which actually required continual defense against threats to it, threats which Prince's *History*, for example, instantiate repeatedly. Institutions like medicine and law provided potential means of interrogating and securing sovereign, autonomous, and permanent distinctions between self and other, individually and communally, according to concerns of race, gender, class, sexuality, and ability.[3]

Useful for this study and highly influential in the field in general (indeed, almost to the point of fatigue) has been the work of theorist Giorgio Agamben. In *Homo Sacer* (1998), the philosopher does not directly address African slavery, but his theorizations of the state of exception, bare life, and the refugee usefully frame potential nineteenth-century American questions of self. He distinguishes modern from classical democracy through the former's preoccupation with vindicating and liberating the *zoe*—the bare or naked life without rights—and, there, paradoxically or ironically replacing subjection with freedom and happiness. Modern democracies constitute themselves by excluding people from access to democratic rights, but Agamben asserts that this exclusion is simultaneously an inclusion. This state of being both outside and inside is that of the slave or, in Agamben's terms, the refugee. By extension, terms such as Wald's "legal nonperson" and others like "non-alien" and "citizen-alien," which have been deployed to explain a simultaneous inclusion and exclusion, do similar work.[4] How or when, in particular, is the slave also the refugee? How must democratic politics reconcile these states that it both does and does not recognize? What is at stake when abolitionists, such as Benjamin Drew, editor of *The Refugee; or, The Narratives of the Fugitive Slaves in Canada*, explicitly identify former slaves as refugees? Furthermore, did slaves self-identify as refugees? Nicole Waligora-Davis, for example, argues that "when African Americans self-identify as 'refugees' or 'stateless persons' they intentionally elicit the aporetic tension belying their contradictory civil status: *the citizen who is not*" and thereby "testify to the effectiveness of state attempts to dislocate them" (xv). Waligora-Davis refers to post-Katrina New Orleans, but does the category of the refugee hold a similar significance when citizenship in the home nation was not an option?[5]

These questions suggest the heteronomous nature of democracy that seeks definition through exclusion and therefore relies on that which it excludes and, in turn, includes it. The subject position of the excluded|included then takes on another dimension of fragmentation or doubling or both. If black well-being does not require wholeness or autonomy, perhaps concepts beyond the limits of the individual self do not either. From such indistinct and destabilizing positions, these black nineteenth-century literary figurations articulate politics of selfhood through considerations of physical condition. Their work prompts us to reassess our own investments in fantasies of sovereignty, security, and autonomy.

There is, of course, not one mid-nineteenth-century theory of black selfhood. Nevertheless, one common element to the authors/orators' senses of self is its rootedness in the body. Whether the black thinkers here seem to espouse a sense of self that comes into being through narrative construction, the articulation of ethics and ethical responsibility, or notions of intersubjectivity (black and/or white), to name a few theories of selfhood, the development of which philosopher Dan Zahavi usefully traces and interrogates in modern philosophy, these thinkers' senses of self are predominantly embodied. Philosopher Charles Taylor argues, "It is assumed that something we call consciousness or self-consciousness could be clearly distinguished from its embodiment . . . that our self-awareness is somehow detachable from its embodiment. . . . The perfectly detachable consciousness is an illusion. . . . The stance of detachment generates the picture of ourselves as pure independent consciousness, which underpins and justifies this stance and is the basis of the radical promise of self-control and -remaking it holds out" (172–173). The black thinkers featured in this study understood very well the embodied nature of consciousness. They explore these embodied senses of self through their various engagements with and challenges to the external institutional forces that supported such notions of detached consciousness and therefore attempted to measure and rank black body parts as racially distinctive and indicative of character and to calculate blacks' intellectual and moral capacities in order to determine (that is, restrict) their legal rights. The value of close readings of selected texts in this context illuminates telling contradictions, rhetorical, structural, and formal subtleties and complexities and the nuances of interdisciplinary arguments within and between the works studied, more so than a broader literary historical survey could manage.

This book analyzes conflicting, oftentimes messy articulations of black selfhood. From the classical healthy mind-in-body ideal to the disabled physique, their portrayals of black physicality offer a striking range of strategic approaches to creating a nineteenth-century politics of well-being opposed to as well as independent of medically and legally informed systems of subjugation. These authors' wide-ranging analyses of black well-being expose the instability of national and colonial social and geopolitical constructs and the mythologies that support them, such as American exceptionalism, the civilizing enterprise of imperial Britain, and colonial Canada's role as a safe haven from American racism and injustice. Their considerations of well-being, a fundamental, desirable aspect of selfhood, demonstrate the broad and complex scope of their early to mid-nineteenth-century black political philosophy. Their varied articulations, I hope, will bolster the need for an urgent reassessment of our twenty-first-century approaches to biopolitics, health, law, literature, personhood, and humanness toward the development of theories and models of ethical practice that truly account for the contextually discursive composition of the self.

Black Well-Being

Black Well-Being commences with a brief history of medico-political theory that contributed to systems of black subjugation, focusing in particular on the ideas of early to mid-nineteenth-century race scientists and legal theorists. This overview travels from Europe to the United States, colonial Canada, and the Caribbean to chart the development and circulation of prominent ideas about blackness and health that emerged from this transcolonial and transnational context. Thinkers appearing in this chapter include influential white intellectuals of the Enlightenment from disciplines such as politics, philosophy, religion, medicine, and what would become anthropology as they grappled with and debated issues of political rights, human life, capacities for personhood, and "Negro" disease. Some prominent figures whose work the chapter interrogates most closely include mid-nineteenth-century medical doctors such as craniologist Samuel George Morton, phrenologist George Combe, and ethnologists/polygenesists Josiah C. Nott and J. Aitken Meigs, physician Samuel A. Cartwright, and naturalist John Bachman, as well as jurist and senator William Harper, legal theorist Thomas R. R. Cobb, and professor and college president Thomas Roderick Dew. The chapter lays out the complex medical, scientific, professional, and political context and influential white thinkers with which/whom the nineteenth-century black literature featured in the subsequent chapters engaged.

Emerging in this context and engaging explicitly with its racism are two polemics urging black exodus from the United States. The writers' ideals of black health and political independence are commensurate. *A Plea for Emigration; or, Notes on Canada West* by Mary Ann Shadd and *The Condition, Elevation, Emigration, and Destiny of the Colored People of the United States* by Martin Robison Delany appeared in the United States in 1852. They are fascinating texts as much for their argument as for their formal aspects, and to this day, unfortunately, they remain understudied. Literary critic Eric Gardner rightly and influentially encourages the field of Black American literary studies to explore the rich variety of black publications in the period beyond the printed book.[6] Although Shadd and Delany were first of all newspaper people and despite my deep scholarly interest in early Black American cultures of print, my focus in the chapter is on their books. They have received less attention than they merit, particularly from literary critics. There is still much more to discover about *Plea* and *Condition* by reading them closely together both for their literary qualities, specifically their rhetorics of health, and for their political philosophy. Emulating more the conventions of the almanac than those of wildly popular early-to mid-nineteenth-century narratives authored by British émigrés to Canada, Shadd and Delany urge black evacuation through a claim for black health and well-being, vivifying the crucial relation they see between corporeal and political ideals. Each advocates the connection between a healthy black body and black political independence, irreconcilable with U.S. residency. Their quest for and designation of healthful places of settlement draw from classical Greek characterizations, which idealize *hygia* or "a condition of completeness and contentment" (Tountas 186). Such an ideal forms the primary vehicle for their propaganda.

Recent scholarship has begun to theorize elements of classicism in eighteenth- and nineteenth-century black-authored texts. *Black Well-Being* introduces health into these emerging discussions. Tracey Walters (*African American Literature and the Classicist Tradition* 2007), Patrice Rankine (*Ulysses in Black: Ralph Ellison, Classicism, and African American Literature* 2006), William Cook and James Tatum (*African American Writers and the Classical Tradition* 2010), and Eric Ashley Hairston (*The Ebony Column: Classics, Civilization, and the African American Reclamation of the West* 2013) interrogate the influences and deployments of the classical tradition on and in African American literature from the eighteenth century on. The controversy surrounding such investigations ranges from disputed claims about the African origins of ancient Greece, to the place of Black American literature in a larger classically influenced eighteenth- and nineteenth-century American literary tradition, to what Hairston vehemently describes as "the phobia apparent in far too much scholarship that to embrace the West is to deracinate, fragment, or decimate blackness—to somehow disrupt the very molecular structure of cultural identity and the black experience" (xv).

In recognizing appeals to classical virtues in Shadd's and Delany's emigration propaganda as well as classical literary elements in Douglass's and Delany's fiction, *Black Well-Being*'s objective is less to engage in the ongoing controversial debates about classicism and Black American literature than to demonstrate the way these authors, free and/or fugitive and elite—all with at least some classical education behind them—draw on ancient ideals about health and well-being to promote emigration from the United States, critique white supremacist ideology (somewhat ironically perhaps, as these same classical ideals have been used precisely in the promotion of such racist ideology), and craft an ideal black selfhood. This book's introduction of black theories of health and well-being drawn from classical thought signals a new contribution to the undertheorized subject of classicism in Black American literature.

Close attention to Shadd's stylistic strategies reveals not only her independent persona with seemingly little interest in such models of domestic economy, but also her deftness at the art of persuasion as she exhorts black men and women to seek alternative models outside the United States. Carla Peterson acknowledges that Shadd is unusual in that she was one of the few women who advocated emigration. She argues, "While never directly confronting the socially conservative ideology of a Negro nationality, black women refused by and large to endorse emigration, preferring instead to conceptualize home and community within North America and to reconfigure, as [Maria] Stewart had, the dominant culture's model of domestic economy to suit their particular purposes" (*Doers* 112). There is no doubt that Shadd's is a work of propaganda, whose primary concern is the need for a healthful place of settlement. Rhetorical analysis of *Plea* in conjunction with *Condition* demonstrates the deeply shared political ideals of the two authors, regardless of gender differences. Their sense of the healthy body as commensurable with a healthy political state is rooted, at times problematically, in antiquity. Their mutual appreciation for each other's ideas published in letters to the black press also reveals a more equal gender dynamic between the two thinkers, which, as Jane Rhodes has probably best demonstrated, was certainly not common between Shadd and her male contemporaries.[7] That sense of gender equality between Shadd and Delany specifically is often overlooked today.

In light of the passage of the Fugitive Slave Law, which severely threatened the safety of free blacks everywhere in the United States, and the growing influence of the American Colonization Society (ACS), which advocated black removal from the United States and relocation in Africa, Shadd's and Delany's models propagandized—rhetorically, conceptually, and materially—the potential of the classical healthy mind in a healthy body. Their quests for an ideal black self question U.S. law's restrictive understanding of the category of the person and examine colonial as well as independent places where they might exercise the right to political participation and autonomy. Like most of their contemporaries, Shadd and Delany were enraged by the American Colonization Society and flatly rejected white schemes for blacks' "return" to Africa. Rather, they evaluated resettlement locations in colonial Canada and Central America largely on the basis of their health advantages, which by extension would benefit settlers politically. Their search for political agency and outright autonomy emphasizes what they saw as the relation between physical and mental health and self-governance.

Writing primarily for a free or fugitive black northern audience, Shadd and Delany, at times, converse directly with and challenge proslavery medical theory. Their work, like that of many of their contemporaries, does not escape the tendency to cohere methodologically and theoretically with the works of such white supremacist physician-authors as Josiah Clark Nott and Samuel Adolphus Cartwright—if toward starkly different ends. These works underscore their varied and conflicted approaches to black political philosophy. Despite the initial coherence of Shadd's and Delany's concerns and philosophies and their respect for each other as writers and intellectuals, these emigrationists disagreed fundamentally with each other on issues of geopolitics. Their reasons had to do with attitudes toward the British monarchy, fear of American annexation, and a practically militant sense of duty to forestall the expansion of U.S. slavery. Though their ideals were in many ways as problematic as they were impractical, these writers conceptually, rhetorically, and structurally centralize healthy black physicality—ultimately unrealizable in the mid-nineteenth-century United States. The authors' correlation of blacks' ability to improve their health with their capacity for political participation—if not ultimate independence—articulates a core U.S. democratic crisis, which more than a century and a half later remains unresolved.[8]

In stark contrast to the idealistic promotion of emigration and the ideal of the healthy self examined in chapter 2, the book turns from idealism to reality through the genre most prominently associated with mid-nineteenth-century Black American literature and which abolitionist Theodore Parker argued contained "All the original romance of America" (qtd. in Wald, *Constituting* 79). Building on scholarship that complicates this notion of the quintessentially American nature of the genre, chapter 3 reads three women's slave narratives that demonstrate how epistemologies of health and tensions between colony and nation on the issue of black wellbeing frustrate projects of national definition and nation-building. The central role of this genre in black intellectual and literary history has been the site of well-traveled—some even say, worn out—scholarly ground, but this book contends that rhetorics of health offer a new potential for the genre's continued and deepening complex relevance. At focus are slave narratives of three formerly enslaved women in seldom-compared geopolitical and literary contexts. The narratives are, most famously, Mary Prince's (1831), Sophia Pooley's (1856), and Lavina Wormeny's (1861). These women's rhetorics of health articulate notions of selfhood that challenge contemporary medical and legal definitions of humanness and personhood and produce radically promising alternatives to such categories and to the overall valorization of autonomy.

These women's works illuminate the confrontation of national and colonial politics. Prince was enslaved in the West Indies and published her narrative in England, Pooley was enslaved in colonial Canada and published in the United States, and Wormeny was enslaved in the United States and published in colonial Canada. This triangle of enslavement and narrative production emphasizes the circulation of power and print among empire, nation, and colony and highlights not only the various dominant and oppressive powers at work but the history of intellectual resistance as particularized through matters of health and well-being as well. By asking how these interrelated literary and geopolitical circuits affected these women's health and well-being, chapter 3 demonstrates the strikingly complex and radically different sense of self each conveys in contrast to the findings of white authenticators' physical examinations of them. Perhaps the contrast between white and black notions of selfhood is not surprising when we consider context, power differentials, and personal history, but close readings reveal the remarkable ways in which these women's articulations of ill health, pain, and debility preempt and undermine ideas of the white authenticators who were trying to help them. The chapter also underscores differences between these enslaved women's notions of health and selfhood and those of the free elite thinkers from chapter 2 and of the free/fugitive elite thinkers of the final chapter.

A critical disability studies lens that sees value in vulnerability and the instability of the body is useful for looking at this particular historical context. In a period when nearly every institutional authority had a vested interest in fragmenting slave subjectivity—some literally dissecting slave bodies—these women, rather than adhere to the desire for wholeness, show us the impossibility of such a notion of self. In doing so, they expose this not only as a fiction of selfhood but of national and proto-national sovereignty as well. They disrupt distinctions between human and nonhuman and demonstrate the danger of the ideal of the whole, pure, autonomous self not only for the black and enslaved but for the white and free, too. It's not so much that they're doing white people a favor by pointing out these dangerous discourses, but rather their attention to them becomes the focus of a particular critique of white ideology that hasn't been fully addressed yet. The women's portrayals of health and self also speak to a broader nineteenth-century preoccupation with clearly demarcated ideas about selfhood and sovereignty in the project of established and emergent national politics. As colonial Canada, for example, defined itself in contradistinction to the United States (politically, medically, legally, and morally), the narratives of fugitive slaves also served as proto-nationalistic articulations. These women's stories reveal the interdependent or heteronymous nature of political identities, specifically black identities, even as they seek greater political independence.

If the improvement of black well-being in the antebellum United States was as inaccessible as the emigrationists suggested yet many people of African descent remained, what was their recourse? The book proceeds from injury, illness, and disability to interrogate how the prevention of harm within the United States functions as a mode of conceptualizing selfhood in the context of slave sexual coercion and abuse. Women slaves' sexual vulnerability exposed them to a particular kind of harm, and few had recorded their experiences of it. Two stories on the subject of slave sexuality, *State of Missouri v. Celia* (1855) and *Incidents in the Life of a Slave Girl* (1861), involved criminal responses to years of abuse. The word *stories* here to describe one literary and one legal narrative evokes Wald's assertion that the human is grounded in stories, not biology ("American Studies" 186). Central to this inquiry is the status of women slaves' sexual and psychological health and legal personhood in the context of sexual abuse.

As previously outlined, James Madison's articulation of slaves' "mixed character" in *The Federalist* of 1788 laid the groundwork in detailing slaves' status as both property and person. Identifying the ways in which slaves could be thought of as merely property, alongside the "irrational" beings, Madison also delineated the reasons why those in bondage were simultaneously considered persons—protected from injury as well as criminally liable. Abolitionist William Lloyd Garrison, in his introduction to Frederick Douglass's *Narrative*, discounts the first part of Madison's explanation of slave personhood (protection from injury) on the basis of the inadmissibility of slave testimony against whites, arguing that "there is no legal protection in fact, whatever there may be in form, for the slave population" (xii). Furthermore, a slaveholder's legal recourse to sue for damages if his property was injured offered no protection for the slave who suffered at the hands of his or her owner. One cannot trespass on one's own property. In instances of sexual abuse, this gap in protection from injury carried an even more horrific significance.

This chapter builds on the vast amount of exceptional scholarship *Incidents* has generated, particularly regarding discourses of sentimentalism and seduction,[9] and it reads the narrative through the lens of crime and women's sexual and psychological health. Literary analysis of newspaper coverage and the trial summary of Celia's case in comparison with Jacobs's narrative demonstrates the relation between mid-nineteenth-century popular cultural understandings of female crime and sexual abuse, which draws on available discourses of sentimentalism and seduction as interpretive strategies but ultimately reveals black women's inability to access them fully in either law or popular print. It also demonstrates the lengths proslavery factions would go to protect their right to govern enslaved women's sexual health and the dire extents to which enslaved women themselves would go to protect their sexual and psychological well-being.

Celia's story, which took me to a Missouri archive of court documents and newspaper coverage, and Jacobs's published account "written by herself" reveal that even though the women knew they would be held criminally responsible as persons, they broke the law to prevent further sexual abuse by their owners. I suggest there is something perhaps inherently human in such a gesture for which the law did not account in its preoccupation with the category of the person. One woman suffered state-sanctioned execution; the other escaped and published her story. Protection from harm in these instances prompted, if not required, illegal acts that ironically for both and tragically for one confirmed her legal personhood—though they did very little to garner for them any rights as humans. Furthermore, their actions freed them from situations of sexual abuse but resulted in increased ill health and in Celia's instance the death of her unborn child and her own execution. Perhaps here more than anywhere else in this book, the limits of the category of person are obvious and bleak.[10]

Possibly in a move toward a more optimistic or at least less depressing conclusion, the book shifts focus from women's nonfiction to men's fiction, from women's actual pained bodies to men's imagined revolt and heroism. Following Celia's and Jacobs's sexual exploitation and central to these imaginings of heroic rebellion/revolution is a healthy, vigorous black sexuality. The stories this chapter features are in part male revenge fantasies envisioning the raining down of black vengeance for the atrocities that white slaveholders committed, particularly against enslaved women, and articulations of black valor very much using elements of classical heroism as a category of critique. The authors enact a taking back of stolen freedom and revisit their previous ideas about emigration. Frederick Douglass in "The Heroic Slave" (1853) and Martin R. Delany in *Blake* (1859, 1861–62) imagine political independence through organized violence. In both works, revolution rejects abolitionism, emigration, and the desperate recourse to individual crime. Whereas Celia and Jacobs suffered sexual abuse and turned to criminal acts to protect their health and well-being and test the limits of the law's understanding of them as persons and indeed women, the protagonists here craft a black selfhood beyond the legally and medically inscribed parameters of the person. They depict ideals of masculine independence or the Greek *areté* (virtue, human excellence) through armed revolts. They insert the black hero into a broader American literary interest in classicism to critique and dramatize the overthrow of white supremacy and the acquisition of black political autonomy, vital to which is the concept and practice of a healthy and robust sexuality.

The heroes' armed revolts, or their imaginings about them, are very much about eliminating black men's dependence on white owners and achieving a free, married status through which they can care for dependents of their own. Recall the passage from Harper's *Memoir* noted in the epigraph about slaveholders' responsibility for slaves' well-being "in every way." Douglass's and Delany's heroes here reject the status of "wards and dependents" of white men and rather envision well-being through an important aspect of selfhood denied to slaves: freedom of sexual expression. Scholars of black masculinity and marriage have recently offered excellent readings, particularly of *Blake*, but most see women's roles in the works as secondary and conforming to dominant cultural notions of gender.[11] This chapter's comparative analysis of these two texts reads the authors' navigations of gender issues slightly differently.

The argument about the centrality of women in these works represents a departure from previous scholarship critical of Douglass and Delany for having relegated women to the sidelines of these tales of masculine rebellion. Rather, the fictive works centralize health and healthy, vigorous sexuality—particularly in marriage—as crucial to the revolutionary's desire for freedom and, even deeper, to his desires as a human being. Such an ideal self draws together the notions of completeness and contentment we see outlined in the promotion of emigration. Douglass and Delany present an ideal black male self that foments political revolution in order to claim domestic rights and the right to sexual expression. The healthy sexuality in *Blake*, for example, is analogous to a healthy political order. Whereas Celia and Jacobs interrogate the limits of the person for women of the period and demonstrate the centrality of sexual choice in imagining selfhood, here Douglass and Delany imagine and indeed fantasize about the possibilities of reclaiming from the control of white oppressors a black masculine self, sexual, intellectual, and moral. Their protagonists' desire for their partners and their movements to various Caribbean locations signify both the authors' imagined violent responses to white oppression as well as the longing for loving and tender intimate partnerships.

Through these two works, the authors also contribute to previously published depictions of black revolutionaries, notably Nat Turner, whose account of the Virginia rebellion appears in Thomas Ruffin Gray's recorded "Confessions of Nat Turner" (1831) and the fictional Dred of Harriet Beecher Stowe's eponymous novel (1856) and emphasize the familial to critique the separation of families so horrifically central to the institution of New World African slavery. On an artistic note, by turning to the novella/novel form, Douglass and Delany demonstrate their literary expansion into this mode of creative expression during the time of rising interest in the American novel and in the period of the American Renaissance. They craft and insert a healthy, sexual black hero into the classical tradition to dramatize the possibility of black political autonomy.

Transcolonial African Diasporas

The black thinkers in this book frustrate categories of Enlightenment philosophy, medicine, and law and formulate new ways of thinking about interactions between individuals in the project of Black American self-making. Place is central to their work. As the authors question the definitions of colony, nation, empire, and republic, I've attempted to emphasize the complex importance of place—geopolitical specificity—to considerations of slavery and race within the United States and beyond. To this end, I develop the concept of *transcolonial diasporas* to investigate African diasporic concerns in slave narratives of Canada and parts of the Caribbean before they became nations. I suggest qualifying *diaspora* with a term that has the potential to situate it methodologically and historically. The prefix and root of *transcolonial* gesture to the movements and fluidity that characterize *diaspora* as well as to diasporic histories, particularly of colonization. The term also conjures up histories of violence. Brent Hayes Edwards argues, for example, that "in appropriating a term so closely associated with Jewish thought, we are forced to think not in terms of some closed or autonomous system of African dispersal but explicitly in terms of a complex past of forced migrations and racialization" (12–13). Recently Weheliye addresses the comparative method of diaspora, cautioning that "the empirical existence of national boundaries, or linguistic differences that often help define the national ones, become the ultimate indicators of differentiation and are in danger of entering the discursive record as transcendental truths, rather than as structures and institutions that have served repeatedly to relegate black subjects to the status of western modernity's nonhuman other" (31). Attentive to both the history of violence that such comparative methods emphasize and the danger they pose in overlooking the national structural and institutional processes of self-definition that rely on black difference, read otherness, *transcolonial* does not replace *diaspora* but rather conjoins the terms in certain methodological approaches in order to theorize particular historical contexts. *Transcolonial* offers a more distinct and ideally more critical potential for considering interrelated identity concerns in and among geopolitical locations *before* they became nations—a distinction worth keeping in mind as it emphasizes the complicated importance of carefully crafted individual identities in the creation and definition of national cultures.

Transcolonial signals the permeability of self and other within and among these interconnected concepts, which are vital to diaspora studies. The concept centers on the colony and underscores its historical, cultural, and ideological role in considerations of the spatial, temporal, and social movements of colonized peoples during slavery when the colony was instrumental to their salvaging of humanity and quest for rights attending citizenship through personhood. As the authors and orators featured here articulate new states of being or becoming, they remind us of the infiniteness of such a task, as we in our own time continually rethink what it means to be human and a person and how to determine the rights that attend such conditions.

At the middle of these interconnected concerns is race. It has become difficult to articulate and define "race" particularly around questions of biological and cultural understandings of the concept. Scientific fields such as genetics and epigenetics often find themselves at odds with various humanities and social sciences approaches to critical race theory and feminist science studies, as they attempt to find ways of articulating and accounting for human variation. Though epigenetics may trace transgenerational or heritable genetic conditions back to particular histories of environmental exposure, for example, feminist science studies (for one) cautions of the dangerous potential to pathologize groups of people who may have descended from and might share these histories of exposure, thereby perpetuating or re-inscribing the injustices that epigeneticists claim caused the condition in the first place.

Additionally, the scientifically supported notion of race as socially rather than biologically constructed often conflicts with individual realities. The tension lies in avoiding biologically deterministic arguments while accounting for embodied and experienced difference. This book contributes to a conceptualization of race that takes this tension into account, recognizing that even though race is not rooted in biology, the social construction of race locates racial difference in the body. Now, when the United States is grappling with a seeming epidemic of white police killings of unarmed black people, one only twelve years old, the reality of racism and its shaping of opportunities and protections for the people who experience it is particularly vivid. The project of theorizing race requires interdisciplinary examination of specific historical and political directives regarding scientific and cultural notions of it. Along with the sciences and social sciences, the humanities must continue to contribute meaningfully to debates about race and human variation and, particularly through the study of literature, art, music, and dance, look for important new insights into the ways people historically have understood and currently understand and experience both.

The book conceives race as a combination of perceptions that result from the interrelations of material and conceptual genetic and geographic commonalities and differences among and between peoples, their socially inherited and produced constructs about themselves and others, and their individually and collectively imagined qualities. The project of imagining and defining race works toward the acquisition of ethical and meaningful languages to discuss it that emphasize linguistic, disciplinary, and cultural differences. The ability to understand such languages of difference is an ethical goal, which I hope will find in the term *race* a productive, meaningful, and sensitive value in thinking about the nineteenth century as well as our own time.

Why Now? Black Well-Being and the Legacies of New World Slavery

This inquiry coincides with a general North American popular preoccupation with health and healing. Therapeutic rhetoric permeates popular culture from the unprecedented volume of and interest in medical information available in the popular media to the widely televised fascination with physical healing (Dr. Oz), racial healing (Oprah), psychological healing (Dr. Phil), celebrity rehabilitation, the tracing of DNA genealogy (from Henry Louis Gates Jr. and Oprah to Thomas Jefferson's mixed-race descendents), and medical tourism. The nineteenth-century works analyzed here I hope prompt us to reconsider our own physicality and embodied sense of self in relation to our political systems and medicine and law and ask if our present, dominant cultural and legal conception of what it means to be a person is ethical or even functional.

Sadly, the history of New World slavery is incomplete. Despite oftenheralded examples of black success, most notably and most lauded of these being Barack Obama's ascendency to the U.S. presidency and the fantasy of a postracial world, the legacies of race-based enslavement continue to inflict harm. North America and the Caribbean remain sites of institutional and personal racial injustice and violence. Statistics reveal stark disparities between black and overall populations in North American legal, medical, and social contexts. For example, the U.S. Department of Justice report on prison and jail inmates indicates that in 2006 black men represented 41 percent of the more than 2 million men in custody (Sabol 9). Medical historian Harriet A. Washington notes that African Americans' life expectancy "is as much as six years less than that of whites" (3). African American women, along with Hispanic women, represent less than 25 percent of all women in the United States, but for AIDS cases among women they comprise more than 79 percent (NIAID 2006). Similarly, Health Canada reports that black people represent only 2 percent of the Canadian population, but by 2003 they accounted for 20 percent of all AIDS cases ("Healthy Diverse"). The Black Women's Health Project estimates that 15 percent of African Canadians in Nova Scotia have not completed a high school education, and the unemployment rate for Black Nova Scotians more than doubles the province's rate. Blacks' health and social condition in the United States and Canada remain in a worse state than that of whites despite changes in legislation following the period that this book studies. As recently as December 2011, Alison Crawford of the CBC *News* reported the impending federal prison ombudsman inquiry into a "52% spike in the proportion of black offenders filling [Canadian] federal jails over the last ten years." Tracing such disparities back to a time of overt oppression reveals ways that the power differentials have merely shifted. As legal scholar Michelle Alexander succinctly explains, "We have not ended racial caste in America; we have merely redesigned it" (2). The stark realities that disadvantage Black Americans remain. Further investigation into the continuing import of slavery on North American conceptions of race, rights, health, and citizenship is necessary if we are to work toward more equitable and just societies.

History tells us only part of the story. As literary critic Jonathan Elmer explains, "Precisely because of its solicitation of ambiguity, literature can register ideological and historical contradictions with greater sensitivity and nuance than other discourses" (7). The writers and orators studied in this book certainly register historical contradictions in the manner Elmer describes and during a period when such incongruities may have been bleakest and carried particularly tragic consequences. The literature in this book not only teaches us much about physicality, humanity, person, and self in the early to mid-nineteenth century but about the state and power of those concepts in our own time as well.

→ 1 ←

The Ruled and Regulated Self

Medicine and Race Science in the Black New World

In the early to mid-nineteenth century, medicine and law became instrumental in the debates about slavery. These professions' theorists and practitioners became authorities on how best to ensure the health and welfare of American society as a whole and of the societies particular to their individual geographic, political, and economic locales. In many instances, their participation in slavery debates contributed substantially to the continued and indeed increased rule and regulation of black people. Regardless of which side of the debate these thinkers supported, their putative goal was black well-being, which they believed in turn would benefit everyone.

Monogenism and Polygenism

In the eighteenth century the aboriginals and the Africans in the colonies were of great interest to Europeans. Their physical responses to climate and disease became classificatory criteria, and perceptions about superior African health, particularly in tropical climates, justified enslavement and racial categorization. As Enlightenment thinkers tried to establish what religion had previously explained, the idea of a natural order still prevailed. For example, race historian Bruce Dain notes, "When Jefferson and other major white intellectuals of the American Enlightenment recognized natural complexity, . . . they tended to throw up their hands and retreat to confident statements about the natural truths that presumably could be perfectly grasped by man" (9). Despite the persistence of a belief in nature's hierarchical order, eighteenth-century British and European scientists were fairly uniform in their rejection of the medieval "great chain of being" (the hierarchical ordering of living things which positioned man at the top) and in their acceptance of monogenism. As historian Nancy Stepan points out, "In the most important debate on man before the nineteenth century, namely, the debate on the origin and status of the Indian in the New World, almost every writer assumed the monogenist view that the Indian was a man like other men, with a rational soul, and therefore on principle not to be enslaved or treated like a beast of burden." She adds, "Though Christian faith was not strong enough to prevent the *de facto* enslavement of the Indian in the Americas, *de jure* the Indian was one with the European" (2). Africans, on the other hand, were contemptible in European thought even earlier than the sixteenth century as a result of white reactions to encounters with Africans in Africa. Comparisons that writers like physician Charles White drew between Africans and apes (*An Account of the Regular Gradations in Man*, 1799) supported observations that Europeans made in Africa, and these views relegated Negroes to the bottom of the chain of humans. Observing physical characteristics of the Negro including the angle of the jaw, bones of the nose, eye sockets, and bones of the skull and the leg, White concluded, "In all these points it differed from the European, and approached the ape" (43). This is one of many such observations White made. Others included observations about blacks' sexual organs, specifically larger penises and smaller testes, differing from the European and approximating the ape (61).

Nevertheless, the figures associated with the founding of anthropology rejected the "chain" and its use for racialist purposes. Swedish botanist Carl von Linné, or Linnaeus as he was known, French naturalist Georges-Louis Leclerc, also known as Comte de Buffon, and German anatomist Johann Friedrich Blumenbach all supported monogenism, an outgrowth of Jewish and Christian theology, which dominated the eighteenth century. Blumenbach, in particular, added many characteristics to the list that separated humans from animals and emphasized similarities between the races of humans. These included erect posture, a flat broad pelvis, and two hands. However, by the century's end, particularly in the United States, doubts about monogenism arose. Scientists and intellectuals began to subscribe to the view that races were separated to such an extent—physically, intellectually, and morally—that they might constitute different biological species. Building on the work of craniologist Samuel George Morton, to whose work the outgrowth of the American School of Ethnology is attributed, key proponents of polygenesis in the United States include Swiss biologist and physician Louis Agassiz, American surgeon Josiah Nott, and Egyptologist George Gliddon.

British science was slower to accept the shifts in thought that were occurring on the continent. Physician and slavery opponent James Cowles Prichard's *Researches into the Physical History of Man* (1813) firmly supported the monogenist view and dedicated his work to Blumenbach. His conclusions that races merely constituted varieties of a single species prevailed in British race theory into the 1840s. Prichard, like Blumenbach, emphasized the similarities between the races: "I have endeavoured to show, that no remarkable instance of variety in organization exists among human races to which a parallel may not be found in many of the inferior tribes; and in the second place, that all human races coincide in regard to many particulars in which tribes of animals, when specifically distinct, are always found to differ" (vol. 2, 1). Therefore, according to Prichard, there are clear distinctions between human and animal, and all humans are of the same species. Prichard flatly denied that people of African descent were an intermediary link between human and ape and attributed this view to Linnaeus's early general association of man and ape.

In the New World, the polygenist argument became an appealing buttress for slavery. Jamaican resident Edward Long in his *History of Jamaica* (1774) argued that blacks' mental and moral inferiority was such that they constituted a species distinct from Europeans: "The measure of the several orders and varieties of those Blacks may be as compleat as that of any race of mortals; filling up space, or degree, beyond which they are not destined to pass; and discriminating them from the rest of men, not in *kind*, but in *species*" (vol. 2, 375). Nevertheless, attitudes in the early part of the nineteenth century were not uniform, and some forms of monogenism persisted. Although Thomas Jefferson's influential and controversial *Notes on the State of Virginia* (1781) promoted the notion of black inferiority, both mental and physical, his language is ambiguous on the issue of polygenism. For example, he argues, "I advance it therefore as a suspicion only, that the blacks, whether originally a distinct race, or made distinct by time and circumstance, are inferior to the whites in the endowments of both body and mind" (270). By contrast, Jefferson was specific in his estimation of American Indians as being modeled in mind as "*Homo sapiens europaeus*" (12).

Samuel Stanhope Smith, Presbyterian minister and president of the College of New Jersey (now Princeton University), disagreed with Jefferson on blacks' intellectual and artistic capabilities even as he agreed that they were inferior to whites. Nevertheless, he also rejected polygenism. His *Essay on the Causes of the Variety of Complexion and Figure in the Human Species* (1810) espoused a monogenist view that accounted for diversity within the species, one that extended to moral and mental abilities. Referring to Jefferson's *Notes* wherein the author dismisses blacks' ability to produce original creative works, Smith argues, "These remarks upon the genius of the African negro appear to me to have so little foundation in true philosophy that few observations will be necessary to refute them" (267). He goes on to argue that "climate, the mode of living, or the state of society, or even accidental causes in early life, contribute to vary the shape of that bony case which encompasses the brain" (268). Smith concludes, "I am inclined, however, to ascribe the apparent dullness of the negro principally to the wretched state of his existence first in his original country, where he is at once a poor and abject savage, and subjected to an atrocious despotism and afterwards in those regions to which he is transported to finish his days in slavery and toil" (268). For Smith, genius required freedom. In the 1810 edition of this essay, he appended remarks in reply to White's strictures on the first edition. Smith critiqued White's ideas, arguing that "establishing a criterion of a distinct species, of that large enumeration of properties wherein he supposes the African to differ from the Europeans" is "either founded in error and misinformation, or . . . easily explained by the known operation of the powers of nature" (287). Despite Jefferson's ambiguity and Smith's relative optimism, the imperialist project would yield much starker opinions on race and species. Indeed racism and racial science would merge, particularly in mid-nineteenth-century America, and would have a significant impact on the nation's perceptions of health and its practice of medicine.

Rule and Regulation

The phrase "rule and regulation" carried particular resonance in the early to mid-nineteenth century because it was the time of the ascendency of statistics, catalogued bodily measurements, and the introduction of the concept of the "normal" as a standard. "Rule" bore the dual connotation of measurement and domination. American craniologist Dr. Samuel George Morton was measuring crania of different races, German phrenologists

Franz Josef Gall and Johann Gaspar Spurzheim and Scottish phrenologist George Combe were developing systems of measuring and comparing portions of the brain, and American surgeon and ethnologist Dr. Josiah Nott was separating the human race into "permanent" types. All of their work was either intended or interpreted to distinguish intellectual and moral capacities of the people they studied. Most were in agreement that the brain was the seat of the mind, and there was tremendous interest in the meaning of differently featured faces and proportional skulls. The skull and face were potentially revealing containers of the brain/mind. Medical men sought the art to find the mind's construction in the face. From the "idiot" to the criminal to the genius, many believed that by looking at, feeling, and measuring heads they could practice precisely that art. The impact of racial features, skull size, and brain development on these sciences featured prominently in medical and phrenological writings.

Of these medical men, craniologist Samuel George Morton is probably most famously accredited with spawning the science that most influenced racist thought, and indeed he believed that blacks were "the lowest grade of humanity" (*Crania Americana* 7), but as historian Ann Fabian has recently argued, it was more the way his work was taken up by proslavery physician-authors after his death that reared into adulthood the progeny of his thinking that became known as scientific racism. Fabian explains, "There would have been less harm in [his] intellectual work if in the decade after Morton's death slavery's defenders had not turned his observations from descriptions of differences in the shape, size, and form of skulls in humans and animals into social commentary on the differences among men" (10).

One of the most prominent thinkers to rework Morton's observations into a racist schema was Josiah Clark Nott. His biographer, Reginald Horsman, describes him as "an impassioned racist who firmly believed in the integrity of what he was doing" and argues that "he both influenced and was influenced by some of the best minds of his time throughout the United States and Europe. To the end of his life, when all he had defended had collapsed, he still believed that he had devoted himself to the passionate pursuit of scientific truth" (3). Nott's book *Types of Mankind* was enormously popular in the 1850s, and he published many other books and lectures. He is a vivid example of a highly intellectual and influential mid-nineteenth-century professional whose prejudices and politics clouded his work. Influenced by the work of Morton, Nott's ideas coincided with those of prominent Swiss scientist Agassiz, who promoted polygenetic theories in the United States. Nott worked as a surgeon, wrote extensively about ethnology, promoted the need for southern medical schools, and in 1860 founded the Medical College of Alabama. He is regarded as one of the main figures associated with mid-nineteenth-century American polygenesis and southern medical distinctiveness. He was well traveled both nationally and internationally and had an exceptional medical mind, but as Horsman duly notes, "When Nott wrote on race, he abandoned the scientific tolerance and good sense that usually pervaded his medical writings" (91). Nott's writings along with those of other proslavery physicians, naturalists, phrenologists, polygenists, and monogenists, in the minds of their authors scientifically substantiated long-held stereotypes about various races' intellectual and moral characters and capacities, and in many instances the law served to enforce these divisions between races, types, and species of mankind. His influence was substantial, and his legacy serves as a sad reminder of the intellectual pitfalls and tangible tragedies that can emerge from the entangled web of politics, prejudice, science, and the fiction of professional objectivity.

With so much at stake in defining people racially, the law adopted a schema of racial markers derived from the medical community to determine to whom the slave statutes would apply. For example, legal historian Thomas D. Morris points out that prominent nineteenth-century proslavery legal theorist Thomas R. R. Cobb argued that "the black color alone does not constitute the negro, nor does the fact of a residence and origin in Africa. . . . : the negro race is marked by a black complexion, crisped or woolly hair, compressed cranium, and a flat nose. The projection of the lower parts of the face and the thick lips evidently approximate it to the monkey tribe" (qtd. in Morris 22). Cobb's description is anatomical, noting complexion, hair texture, cranial characteristics, and facial features. It strongly echoes and condenses contemporary medical descriptions of black people. First, Morton detailed "a black complexion, and black, woolly hair; the eyes are large and prominent, the nose broad and flat, the lips thick, and the mouth wide: the head is long and narrow, the forehead low, the cheek-bones prominent, the jaws projecting, and the chin small" (6–7). Building on Morton's description, and still predating Cobb's, Nott, in his second lecture on the "Natural History of the Caucasian and Negro Races," explained, "The head of the Negro is smaller by a full tenth—the forehead is narrower and more receding, in consequence of which the anterior or intellectual portion of the brain is defective.—The upper jaw is broader and more projecting—the under jaw inclines out, and is deficient in chin; the lips are larger and correspond with the bony structure; the teeth point obliquely forward and resemble in shape those of Carnivorous animals; the bones of the head are thicker, more dense and heavy, and the same fact exists with regard to the other bones of the skeleton" (23). Nott's rhetoric of defect and deficit are typical of the physician's predisposition to use difference to rank human types and to draw on Morton's work to hypothesize about intellectual capacity. He uses craniology, phrenology, and anatomy to make his observation, and his findings dovetail nicely with what A. Leon Higginbotham Jr. and Anne F. Jacobs identify as the first of ten "basic, underlying precepts" that permeated the law of slavery: "*Inferiority*: Presume, preserve, protect, and defend the ideal of the superiority of whites and the inferiority of blacks" (qtd. in Morris 9–10).

In Nott's same lecture he compares the Negro with the ape: "Now it will be seen from this hasty sketch, how many points of resemblance Anatomists have established between the Negro and Ape. It is seen in the head and face, the arms and hands, the compressed chest, the bones and muscles of the pelvis, the flat long thighs, the forward bend of the knee, in the leg, foot, and toes. In short, place beside each other average specimens of the Caucasian, Negro, and Ourang Outang, and you will perceive a regular and striking gradation—substitute for the Negro a Bushman or Hottentot from the Cape of Good Hope, and the contrast is still stronger" (24). Furthermore, Nott follows up on the anatomists' belief in such a connection in his later and most widely read work, *Types of Mankind*, which he dedicated to Morton and which sold 3,500 copies within six months of publication and went through ten editions by 1871. He quotes Harvard anatomist Dr. Jeffries Wyman, who claimed that "'it cannot be denied, however wide the separation, that the Negro and Orang do afford the points where man and the brute, when the totality of their organization is considered, most nearly approach each other'" (457). As for Cobb's description of hair as a racial characteristic, we find a rather extreme account of the hair that physicians understood as characteristic of the Negro in Lt. Col. Charles Hamilton Smith's *Natural History of the Human Species*. Smith qualifies his section heading "Woolly-Haired Tropical Type" by explaining, "By this denomination is understood, not wool, strictly speaking, but hair so highly frizzled as to appear like the wool of Iceland sheep, and in coarseness so rude, that the wool of a Negro head, struck with the knuckles, frequently cuts the skin to the bone" (223). One wonders at the force of a strike that could gash the knuckles to the extent described! That aside, though, these examples demonstrate considerable overlap in medical and legal discourse on the perceived markers of race, which determine whom the slave laws govern and whom they protect. Indeed, Cobb references Morton several times throughout his *Inquiry into the Law of Negro Slavery in the United States*, noting that as "impartial and scientific as he is acknowledged to be, Dr. Morton states that 'It makes little difference whether the mental inferiority of the negro, the Samoyede, or the Indian, is natural or acquired; for if they ever possessed equal intelligence with the Caucasian, they have lost it, and if they never had it, they had nothing to lose'" (31). Through physical comparisons to the features of monkeys or orangutans, descriptions of hair, and posited correlations between skull size and shape and brain capacity, the relation between the two disciplines' proslavery writers presented ideas about race that were as influential as they were controversial.

Beyond physical appearance, though, immunity was another distinguishing factor, which some physicians believed separated the races. Recent medical historians have considered disease and immunity as key factors promoting African slavery in the New World. For example, medical historian Kenneth Kiple has argued that in the Caribbean and the United States, African immunity to certain diseases tragically incurred for Africans a tremendous social cost. After attempting to enslave/enserf poor European emigrants who escaped their peonage, Europeans enslaved the aboriginal populations they invaded. By doing so, they infected their bondsmen and women with illnesses previously unknown to them. Aboriginal decline coincided with the importation of West Africans who were familiar with diseases from the Old World and as immune to them as white people, but who also brought with them tropical diseases unknown to both Native and European populations. Such migration further devastated the aboriginal communities of the New World and threatened the settlers/invaders with illness and death. While aboriginals and Europeans were dying of diseases like yellow fever, Africans seemed unaffected, and thus the demand for black labor increased.[1] Slaveholders, impressed by Africans' seeming physical endurance in the face of sicknesses that were devastating other populations, thought their prayers had been answered; they believed Africans would make better slaves than aboriginals because they were hardier.[2]

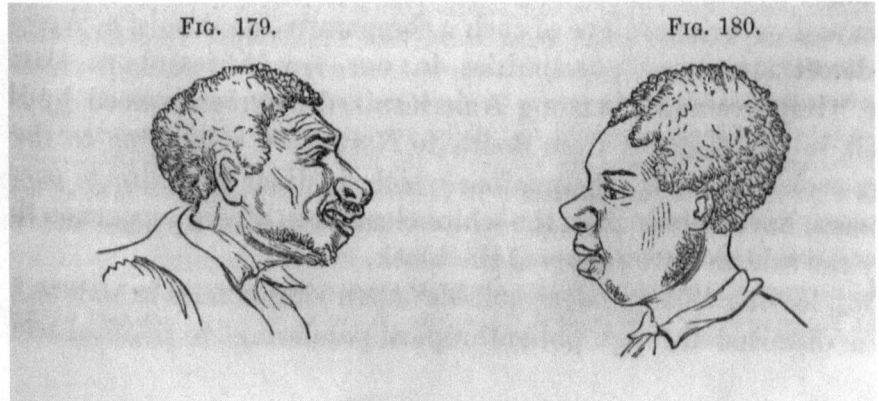

Figure 1. From Nott and Gliddon's *Types of Mankind*: "As a mnemonic, we here subjoin, sketched by a friend, the likenesses of two Negroes (Figs. 179, 180), who ply their avocations every day in the streets of Mobile; where anybody could in a single morning collect a hundred others quite as strongly marked. Fig. 179 (whose portrait was caught when, chuckling with delight, he was 'shelling out corn' to a favorite hog) may be considered caricatured, although one need not travel far to procure, in daguerreotype, features fully as animal; but Fig. 180 is a fair average sample of ordinary field-Negroes in the United States" (259–60).

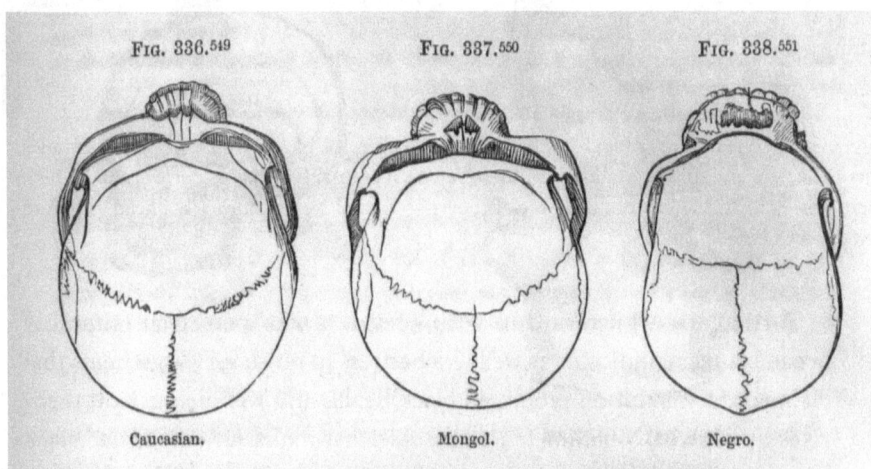

Figure 2. From *Types of Mankind*: "Although I do not believe in the intellectual equality of races, and can find no ground in natural or in human history for such popular credence, I belong not to those who are disposed to degrade any type of humanity to the level of brute-creation. Nevertheless, a man must be blind not to be struck by similitudes between some of the lower races of mankind, viewed as connecting links in the animal kingdom; nor can it be rationally affirmed, that the Orang-Outan and Chimpanzee are more widely separated from certain African and Oceanic Negroes than are the latter from the Teutonic or Pelagic types" (457).

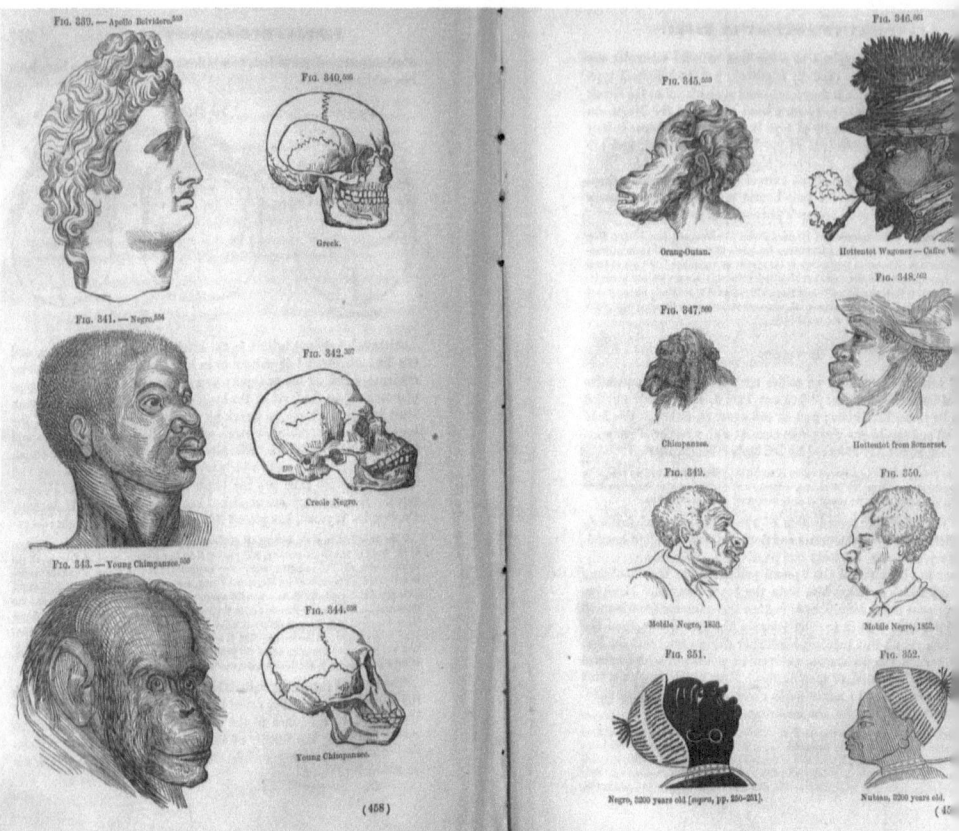

Figure 3. From *Types of Mankind*: "It will doubtless be objected by some that extreme examples are here selected; and this is candidly admitted; yet, each animal type has a centre around which it fluctuates—and such a head as the Greek is never seen on a Negro, nor such a head as that of the Negro on a Greek" (460).

Particularly with regard to yellow fever, blacks' perceived immunity became a racial indicator as well as a buttress to proslavery arguments that claimed the institution promoted black health and well-being. Nott theorizes in his work on climate and disease that a quarter amount of black blood would protect people from yellow fever. He argues, "The mulattoes brought from Maryland to Virginia to Mobile or New Orleans, suffer infinitely less from the diseases of these localities, than do the pure whites of the same States. In fact, the smallest admixture of negro blood, as in the Quarteroon or Quinteroon, is a great, though not absolute, protection against yellow fever. . . . I hazard nothing in the assertion, that one-

Figure 4. "Tableau to accompany Prof. Agassiz's 'Sketch,'—Nott and Gliddon's *Types of Mankind*, 1854." Pertaining to the "Negro," Agassiz's sketch reads, "I am prepared to show that the differences existing between the races of men are of the same kind as the differences observed between the different families, genera, and species of monkeys or other animals; and that these different species of animals differ in the same degree one from the other as the races of men—nay, the differences between distinct races are often greater than those distinguishing species of animals one from the other. The chimpanzee and gorilla do not differ more one from the other than the Mandingo and the Guinea Negro: they together do not differ more from the orang than the Malay or white man differs from the Negro" (lxxiv–lxxv).

fourth negro blood is a more perfect protection against yellow fever, than is vaccine against small-pox" (*Indigenous* 368). Four years prior to the publication of this essay, Nott had lost four children and a brother-in-law to yellow fever in less than one week. Part of his argument about "mulatto" and Negro immunity seems to support his claims that the climate of the southern United States is optimal for black people to the extent that they are even immune to diseases affecting, indeed killing, white southerners. He explains, "The condition [of slaves], both moral and physical, has been steadily improving, in the United States; and is now much better than that of slaves half a century ago, either here or in the West Indies" (387). Here he begins to make the claim for slave well-being in the southern United States and describes their condition as having improved there, the area offering a better location for black health than the West Indies.

It is noteworthy that in this essay Nott neglects to refer to the yellow fever controversy surrounding the 1793 Philadelphia epidemic that saw black nurses, who because they were presumed to be immune had stayed to help the sick, accused of misappropriating funds. Some of the nurses died of the disease, and a scathing rebuttal to Matthew Carey's accusations in his *Short Account of the Malignant Fever, 1793* appeared in Absalom Jones and Richard Allen's *Narrative of the Proceedings of the Black People, during the Late Awful Calamity in Philadelphia, in the Year 1793*. Nott references Carey indirectly in an excerpt he quotes from J. B. De Bow's census regarding the importation of slaves. In fact, the January 1855 issue of *De Bow's Review*, which contains the original and references the famous publisher "Mr. Carey, of Pennsylvania" also applauds the late printer in a section on American publishers (140) appearing much later in the same issue than the piece on the "African Slave Trade" (16). It is highly likely that Nott would have been familiar with Jones and Allen's pamphlet and chose to ignore it along with all other evidence of black susceptibility to the disease. Such a stark disregard for the fact that black people contract and die from yellow fever reveals the extent to which the perception of black immunity prevailed despite much evidence to the contrary. Such race-based medical theories, far from promoting black well-being, instead cost black lives.

But Nott was interested in advocating not only that the southern climate promoted black health but also that the northern states had a detrimental effect on black well-being: "We have positive data for the mortality of the free negroes in Northern States, where the climate, as well as social condition, is unfavorable to this class; and the ratio is from one death in twenty, to one in thirty annually, of the entire number. In Boston, the most northern point, the mortality is highest; and rather less in New York and Philadelphia. I can procure no statistics from Canada, where the blacks must suffer terribly from that climate" (388). His correlation of northern geography and black mortality invites readers to see a relationship between black freedom and death. Furthermore, he does not seem to have tried to find the data on Canada. His rival, monogenist and Doctor of Divinity John Bachman agrees with Nott that "the blacks of the North are the most degraded of their population" (209) but that "The African . . . has become constitutionally assimilated to the temperature of every State in our Union, and we are informed that large settlements of this race now exist in Upper Canada" (272–73). Mary Ann Shadd and Martin Delany had also published their emigration writings detailing settlement in colonial Canada, Shadd even promoting the colony as a healthy place; however, it is not likely that Nott would have been familiar with their works, for newspaper correspondence indicates that even among the black communities in pre-Confederation Canada and the United States, there was concern that not enough had been done to publicize those authors' publications. I'll say more about this in the next chapter. Nonetheless, these examples demonstrate the ways in which physician arguments about black health and well-being align with proslavery ideology—even in the face of scientific evidence to the contrary and whether the writers even agree in theory. From physical appearance to immunity and longevity, these thinkers produce medical and scientific justifications for southern slavery on the purported basis of promoting black health, whether they agree that blacks are a separate species of man or not.

Black Health and "Negro Diseases"

By midcentury, the United States had already enacted the Fugitive Slave Act, which allowed for the suspension of *habeas corpus* as well as the capture of escapees in free states and their return to slave states and to their owners. Furthermore, the law decreed that bystanders were to assist in catching slaves: "All good citizens are hereby commanded to aid and assist in the prompt and efficient execution of this law, whenever their services may be required." In another section, the law allows slave catchers "to use such reasonable force and restraint as may be necessary, under the circumstances of the case, to take and remove such fugitive person back to the State or Territory whence he or she may have escaped as aforesaid. In no trial or hearing under this act shall the testimony of such alleged fugitive be admitted in evidence; and the certificates in this and the first [fourth] section mentioned, shall be conclusive of the right of the person or persons in whose favor granted, to remove such fugitive to the State or Territory from which he escaped, and shall prevent all molestation of such person or persons by any process issued by any court, judge, magistrate, or other person whomsoever." In short, the law extended the rights of owners and overseers to retrieve fugitives, forbade fugitives a jury trial or the right to testify, and protected slave catchers from state or court intervention, whether a free or slave state. The contention among free blacks was that the law threatened them to the extent that they could be mistakenly or deliberately captured and enslaved on the premise that they were fugitives.[3] After 1850, there was no place in the United States that could fully and legally protect black people from enslavement. Colonial Canada, where slavery had been abolished in 1834, quickly became, then, a potential refuge and the subject of emigration debates in public meetings and in print.

As the rise of racial science in the United States coincided with the passage of the Fugitive Slave Law, the subject of Negro diseases garnered much interest in the South. Blacks' apparent immunity to certain diseases functioned socially to promote and maintain their enslavement. By midcentury, even racial scientists who focused on black pathologies still posited certain characteristics of fortitude among blacks in the New World, such as an increased tolerance for pain and the ability to endure remarkably strenuous working conditions. Even acknowledging slaves' physical pain, southern jurist and senator William Harper went so far as to argue that slaves had unique responses to whipping. He argues, "Such punishment would be degrading to a freeman, who had the thoughts and aspirations of a freeman. In general it is not degrading to a Slave, nor is it felt to be so" (100). Cobb in his *Inquiry into the Law of Negro Slavery* also asserts, "The negro is not malicious. His disposition is to forgive injuries, and to forget the past. His gratitude is sometimes enduring, and his fidelity often remarkable. His passions and affections are seldom very strong, and are never very lasting. The dance will allay his most poignant grief, and a few days blot out the memory of his most bitter bereavement. His natural affection is not strong, and consequently he is cruel to his own offspring, and suffers little by separation from them" (30). In support of his arguments, he references English surgeon and president of the Royal College of Surgeons of London William Lawrence's *Lectures on Physiology*. Such medically supported legal discourse provided convenient theories for slaveholders, to be sure. Similarly convenient was the pathologization of slave "vice." Legal historian Ariela Gross comments, "Buyers realized that if a slave's vice was a 'habit' akin to a disease, she was reduced to a status closer to animal than if her vice were a purposeful one. . . . Complete malleability and immutable 'addiction' to vice both negate the idea that a slave behaved a certain way out of the conscious choice of a rational mind or the yearnings of a human soul" ("Pandora" 304). The medicalization of vice increased around midcentury as well, coinciding with the prevalence of polygenesis and interest in Negro diseases. Pathologization of habit and vice coincided, too, with slaveholder arguments advocating that, in general, "because slavery kept [slaves] from vices such as alcohol and tobacco, blacks were protected from 'the attacks of many diseases to which [they] would otherwise be subject, and moderate the violence and frequency of others to which [they are] constantly liable'" (Weiner and Hough 31).

The study of black diseases in the South was in keeping with the empirical method prevalent in the larger American context; it was also a means of professional advancement—as southern doctors argued, the population and environment demanded it. However, among certain established physician-authors, black illness necessitated increased regulation of enslaved bodies. Whereas black health was one justification for enslavement in the United States, by the middle of the nineteenth century black illness was also used as a justification for increased regulation of Black Americans. While physician Henry Patterson was rejoicing that "the Negro thrives under the shadow of his white master . . . and multiplies in increased physical well-being" ("Memoir of Samuel George Morton" in Nott and Gliddon's *Types* xxxii) and law professor Thomas Roderick Dew was lauding that a "merrier being does not exist on the face of the globe than the negro slave of the United States" (66), diseases like drapetomania (running away) and dysesthesia Ethiopia (rascality) were emerging.

It is important to note, however, that the medical interest in black diseases was not always geared to the perpetuation of white racial dominance. There is significant evidence to suggest that there were differences in infection rates and that certain diseases were particular to certain groups of people in specific locations; many physicians were genuinely interested in determining why and how best to respond. Scholars are now learning that some of the determinations of nineteenth-century doctors find support in later medical knowledge to which the early physicians did not yet have access. Though examples of overtly racist uses of medical knowledge and practice certainly exist, the rise of southern American medical sectionalism was not completely politically motivated as some scholars have implied, and such separatist impulses were not restricted to the United States. Wherever there were Old World physicians practicing in the New World, treatments that worked in one location often did not have the same effectiveness in the other. Environmentalism prevailed to varying extents throughout the medical history of the eighteenth and nineteenth centuries, so different climates could naturally be assumed to affect populations differently. Furthermore, the classification of peoples in different geographical areas as well as the categorization of their diseases was a long-standing interest of doctors.

In colonial Canada, most early physicians were British educated, a fact of which the establishment in the colony was particularly proud. In keeping with a long-standing colonial Canadian tradition of defining itself against its geographic neighbor, the United States, the medical profession of British North America was no different. Literary scholar John Pengwyrne Matthews has usefully articulated the colonial tendency in Canada to import British institutions as wholly as possible. Colonial Canadian doctors prided themselves on passing medical licensing laws in 1788, prior to their counterparts in the American South. Nineteenth-century physician Daniel McNeil Parker, among others, targeted the United States as a source for the influx of quacks into colonial Canada. He wrote of "one who had obtained a diploma from a western United States manufactory, whose portals had never been darkened by his presence, but who, on remitting $100 or $150 with a commendatory letter signed by several of his neighbours, received from the authorities of the so-called medical school the document asked for—a diploma" (Canniff Papers, OA).[4]

Anti-American sentiments certainly existed among the early Canadian medical community who regarded U.S. physicians as professionally inferior and politically dangerous, but such sentiments were not uniform across the profession specifically or across the colony in general. In fact, one of the reasons Martin Delany was reluctant to promote British North America as anything more than a temporary refuge for African Americans was his perception of the colony's Americanism. In one example, he criticizes the "extravagant" nature of the "laudatories heaped upon the Americans, within the hearing of the writer, while traveling the provinces the last fall, by one of the Canadian officiaries, in comparing their superior intelligence to what he termed the 'stupid aristocracy'" (*Condition* 191).[5] Furthermore, it was also his fear that such Americanism would lead to the republic's annexation of colonial Canada and, therefore, the widespread enactment of racist legislation across the continent.

With regard to race and medicine, the *British American Journal* provides insight into the medical intrigue in the South's interest in "Negro diseases." The primary interest regarding race and disease in nineteenth-century British North America focused on the colony's indigenous population, understandably as it outnumbered other "raced" groups at the time, including Africans, despite the colony's former practice of slaveholding. The other primary interest in terms of disease classification among ethnicities concentrated on immigrant diseases, notably those of white European immigrants.

Nevertheless, the prestigious journal corresponded with the most influential medical journal in the southern United States at the time, the *New Orleans Medical and Surgical Journal*, and reprinted some of its articles on the subject. In one instance, after the *BAJ* published a survey of "Negro diseases" by prominent U.S. physician Daniel Drake, a complementary study by Montreal doctor William Winder appeared. Medical historians Marli F. Weiner and Mazie Hough refer to Drake as a "pioneering medical geographer" who disagreed with theories claiming black healthiness in the New World (71). Winder acknowledged Drake's work in his introduction: "There having appeared in a former number of this Journal, a paper on the diseases of the slaves of the Southern States, it occurred to me, that something of the same kind on those of the Aborigines of this continent might prove worthy of attention" (255).

Unlike Drake's report, which focuses wholly on descriptions of diseases, Winder's *BAJ* article includes examples of aboriginal remedies for the afflictions he details, and he applauds their general effectiveness. Medical historian Todd Savitt notes that in the southern United States, there was a dual medical system of white and African remedies, the former mistrustful of the latter.[6] Though the Montreal doctor's report differs from Drake's in this respect, it reveals that there was some measure of U.S. medical influence on colonial Canadian medicine, even if it did not apply to the same population. Drake's work inspired that study and another report on immigrant sickness that he encouraged colonial Canadian physicians to conduct, data from which he drew some ideas for his own comprehensive *Systematic Treatise . . . on the Principal Diseases of the Interior Valley of North America* (1850). The correspondence between the two papers and the physicians represented therein also expose a two-way traffic of medical knowledge extending between the Deep South and the northern colony on issues of race and ethnicity.[7] Furthermore, they speak to the role of medicine in projects of proto-nationalism and cultural definition.

Apart from such instances, however, there seems to have been relatively little interest in the relationship between medicine and race with regard to people of African descent in British North America when compared with the United States, and indeed there is very little historical work done on the subject to date—despite the colony's slaveholding history. One reason might be the relatively small population of slaves in colonial Canada compared with other New World locations. Also, when compared with the United States, the rise of racial science as a biological study occurred after the abolition of slavery in the British colonies. The colonial Canadian reluctance to ally with American medical practice may explain the relative dearth of medical writing on blacks in pre-Confederation Canada. Furthermore, by the time U.S. southern medical sectionalism was really under way, the colony north of the 49th was already being regarded as a potential haven from the evils of the "peculiar institution," a point of pride among many British North Americans, regardless of the racism many of them still harbored against black people. Nineteenth-century physician and medical historian William Canniff, for example, argued, "There can be no greater indication of a truly civilized people than a successful attempt to emancipate those in bondage. In this respect Upper Canada was very far in advance of the United States, and even of England herself" (*History* 569). Given the political rhetoric of civilization Canniff employs to underscore the backwardness of medicine in the American South combined with differential black populations in colonial Canada and the United States, perhaps it is not surprising that writings on diseases particular to black people do not appear with the same frequency in the colony as they did in the United States.

In 1852—and I emphasize this year as coinciding with Shadd's and Delany's emigration works—prominent southern physician Samuel Adolphus Cartwright's paper "Slavery in the Light of Ethnology" appeared in the *New Orleans Medical and Surgical Journal*. The article followed one published in the same journal the previous year in which he coined the term "drapetomania," the pathological designation of a slave's desire to flee his owner. Cartwright's work on drapetomania was the product of his "Report on the Diseases and Physical Peculiarities of the Negro Race," a paper he was asked to deliver as chairman of the Louisiana State Medical Convention committee. "Slavery in the Light of Ethnology" further pursues topics of pathology and peculiarity to conclude, "The framers of [the U.S.] Constitution were aware of these [physiological] facts, and built the Constitution upon the basis of natural distinctions or physical differences in the two races composing the American population" (697). With this fundamental legislative document in mind, Cartwright continues to develop what he terms "the philosophy of the Negro constitution" (697), using juridical rhetoric to do so.[8]

Educated at the University of Pennsylvania, Cartwright began practicing medicine in Natchez, Mississippi, in 1822 and moved to New Orleans in 1848, where, as medical historian John Duffy explains, "sporadic efforts were made to require licensing of physicians, but quacks flourished in spite of all efforts" (5). The lack of such laws contributed to the defensiveness of licensed southern physicians like Nott and Cartwright who demanded southern medical distinctiveness at a time when they relied on northern schools for training. In the years leading up to the Civil War, efforts to secure a separate southern system stemmed from a general trend toward empiricism in which *place* became an exceedingly important factor in the diagnosis and treatment of disease. Further, medical historian John Harley Warner has shown that such efforts were actually part of a larger endeavor in America to carve out its own system separate from European centers of medical knowledge. Warner notes that though such a movement was typified by the country as a whole, it was exaggerated in the South where, he explains, "Physicians shared with other southerners a sensitivity to charges brought against their region of economic and political inferiority, immorality, and social backwardness" ("Reform" 208).

Cartwright, writing at a time of such scientific and political defensiveness, was one of the most strident advocates for southern medical distinctiveness and wrote on the subject for the prominent *New Orleans Medical and Surgical Journal.* He believed southern physicians ought to look to the ancient Greeks, not contemporary Europeans, for medical models because of the similarity between Greek and southern American climates and because of Hippocrates' reliance on observation over recognized medical wisdom.[9] Among writing southern physicians, however, Cartwright was somewhat unusual in that he regularly mixed medicine and politics and used several southern journals as forums not only to advocate southern distinctiveness but also to justify southern politics through scientific argument.

In the 1852 article in question, Cartwright posited that the "two races, the Anglo-Saxon and the negro, have antipodal constitutions" (705), a "fact" that "no human laws or governmental changes can ever obliterate" (697). Central to Cartwright's notion that the framers of the U.S. Constitution supported these "great truths of natural history" is his conclusion—"proved" by spirometrical observation and blacks' "want of muscular and mental activity"—that "Negroes consume less oxygen than the white race" (698). His invocation of the U.S. Constitution to differentiate between blacks' and whites' physiological constitutions rhetorically substantiates his scientific claim. He proposes a medical cure for blacks' weak pulmonary apparatuses, arguing that "whipping the lungs to increased action by the application of blisters over the origin of the respiratory nerves, a remedy so inexpedient . . . in most of the maladies of the white man, has a magic charm about it in the treatment of those of the negro" (704). Cartwright's punishing rhetoric, however, develops into a theory of the relationship between slaves' labor and their contentedness. He argues that "the white man, from the physiological laws governing his economy, *can not labor and live:* but the negro thrives, luxuriates and enjoys existence more than any laboring peasantry to be found on the continent of Europe" (705). Cartwright's conflation of politics and physiological law provides the scientific ground on which he attempts to build his justification for southern slave law, especially in Louisiana.

Whereas eighteenth-century physicians attributed environmental factors like climate and cleanliness to Negro diseases, by the 1830s such notions gave way to "assumptions of racial predisposition to various illnesses" (Kiple, *Dimension* 177). Despite such belief in black and white anatomical differences, Savitt and later Washington point out how the medical community in the United States used Black Americans in research and experimentation, neither of which was limited to the South. Savitt does, however, demonstrate the *predominant* use of blacks in the Old South for such medical purposes. He argues, "Blacks were considered more available and more accessible in that white-dominated society: they were rendered physically visible by their skin color but were legally invisible because of their slave status" (78). Furthermore, the nineteenth-century empiricist orientation in American medicine, in general, provided a context in which physicians in the South felt justified in claiming their geographical area as their exclusive medical territory and subject of expertise because the environment and population were unique to it. The South had the nation's largest black population, and their diseases were distinctive; thus their physicians demanded recognition of their medical system as separate.

The medical claims of black distinctiveness on the one hand and the use of black bodies for research and experimentation on the other hand is paradoxical and similarly contradictory as the logic of the law that understood slaves as human, person, and property. Particularly in the example of J. Marion Sims, who used black women for gynecological experiments that were then used to treat white women, the contradiction is striking. The number of contradictions and the amount of contrary evidence that professionals had to overlook as they actively constructed race in the service of white supremacist ideology demonstrates the remarkable lengths to which some of the period's professionals would go to secure/maintain their political dominance. As historian Patrick Rael posits, "In contrast to Latin American slave societies, which could envision degrees of legal semifreedom, the colonies (and later states) of British mainland North America predicated their very identities on the stark contrast between freedom and slavery. Resulting regional differences over matters as weighty as the definition of freedom, citizenship, and slavery introduced legal and logical inconsistencies that the antebellum generation contained with only the greatest difficulty, and which eventually precipitated civil war" (26). We can add here to Rael's assessment of legal and logical contradictions medical and scientific inconsistencies as well. A certain degree of provincialism also informed southern physicians' approach. Warner argues that the American medical establishment in general suffered from a sense of marginality and inferiority as it occupied a place geographically and intellectually peripheral to Europe. We can recall colonial Canadian pride on this point as well. The South, in turn, felt an exaggerated degree of such general American defensiveness.

Even if not defensive about southern medicine, Nott was politically strategic in his appeals for southern medical schools. As Horsman points out, "Even in suggesting that southern students had a reason for studying at southern schools," Nott "kept to medical not racial reasons" (231). His argument focused on study with professors who knew the climate and diseases best. In Nott's 1851 essay on natural history and slavery, he also expresses southern anxiety about the North: "A deep feeling of distrust towards the North now pervades the whole South—and the most confiding must admit, that doubt and uncertainty enshroud the future" (25). He laments, "The physicians in the United States, as in England, are, with few exceptions, wholly ignorant of the physical history of mankind and are unqualified for expressing an opinion on a fact so simple as this" (*Biblical History* 42). Nott is referring to assumptions made about blacks' intellectual capacity. He argues, "Their highest civilization is attained in the state of slavery, and when left to themselves, after a certain advance, as in St. Domingo, a retrograde movement is inevitable" (42–43). Whereas Nott valorizes knowledge about what he understood to be the physical history of mankind, his opponent Bachman writes that polygenists "were not in possession of such materials as would furnish them with the means of disproving [monogenist] doctrine." He continues, "In our medical schools indeed—in the present stage of these inquiries—such teachings in a lecture room are not only uncalled for, but are impolitic, unwise, and fraught with unmixed evil" (216). He further counters Nott's lamentation by arguing, "Among our physicians not one in a thousand has devoted himself to any branch of natural science, nor can we conceive that this, although desirable, is positively essential to his profession" (218). As these debates raged, it is not surprising that Nott left the subject of race out of his appeals for southern medical schools, even though his lectures and medical writings emphasized at every turn the inferiority of black people as a separate type or species of mankind and that they suffered diseases differently than did whites. The difficulty of maintaining distinctions between medicine and race science in this context is obvious: theory and practice as well as academic and legislative politics collide, rendering each less discrete.[10]

Cartwright was one of the most prominent and controversial figures of this growing interest in "Negro diseases." Whereas Nott studied existing diseases' effects on black people (malaria, yellow fever, cholera, typhoid fever, smallpox, and plague) and ran an infirmary for blacks for many years,[11]

Cartwright invented new diseases particular to black people. Nott does reference Cartwright's work, but infrequently. Kiple notes that it is difficult to discern Cartwright's influence on his profession. Though he was criticized in 1851 for his theory that blacks and whites had different blood and for his criticism of northern medical schools, Kiple points out that as the Civil War drew near, there was more support for his theories and for the idea that specialists in black medicine were probably necessary (*Dimension* 181). Gross argues that it was more his support for polygenesis that put him at odds with religious southerners, but that—as noted earlier—of far greater interest was the notion of particular diseases affecting blacks.[12] Furthermore, the approach of war and corresponding interest in black medicine coincided with the increasing threat of abolitionism, signaling a conflation of science and politics among some physicians.

Cartwright's theories unabashedly supported the white political domination of Black Americans. For example, in the service of paternalistic justifications for slavery, he blatantly promoted his theory that people of African descent had weaker lungs than white people and were therefore more susceptible to respiratory ailments.[13] It was, however, Cartwright's willingness to politicize his medical theories that drew criticism from his colleagues who relied on at least the perception of scientific objectivity, especially as medicine increasingly professionalized during the nineteenth century.

Regardless of Cartwright's support of southern medical and political causes, his peers challenged his theories. In response to the 1851 *New Orleans Medical and Surgical Journal* article, one critic argued, "To mingle medicine and politics is an unholy contamination of the former, which no wily argument can justify, no apology atone for. Make our medical journals *politico-medical* organs, and farewell to science! farewell to virtuous ambition!" (qtd. in Krieger 269). Cartwright's studies threatened what Gross describes as doctors' claims "to honor as professional men, whose judgment could be trusted because of their honorable detachment and superior knowledge" (*Double* 123). Social epidemiologist Nancy Krieger notes, however, that none of Cartwright's critics "attacked either [his] support for slavery or his fundamental belief in innate racial differences. Instead, by appealing to neutrality in the name of objectivity, they implicitly endorsed the view that only those who explicitly *state* their politics *have* politics—and thus gave free rein to the period's prevailing racism and other unspoken prevalent beliefs" (269). Thus the critics who denied the influence of politics on "good" medicine simply buried it. Cartwright's critics, by denying any legal and political influence on their own medicine, furthered the notion that scientific purity was possible. Ironically, the belief in that very possibility was precisely the principle Cartwright relied on to argue that science provided the undisputable, objective, and "natural" basis for slave legislation. Hence, in some medical circles, it was Cartwright's use of juridical discourse that devalued his medical findings, not the findings themselves. Furthermore, the door that Cartwright's scientific arguments may have opened to the study of environmental and social effects of enslavement on health, his political and racial biases—made apparent through his rhetoric—simultaneously closed as he emphasized "natural" physiological differences as justifications for his and the South's politics.

Whatever need there may have been for black medicine in the antebellum United States, tragically it often took shape as another disciplinary apparatus regulating people of African descent. Physicians like Patterson, Drake, Nott, and Cartwright looked to classical rather than modern European medicine and preferred observation to recognized medical knowledge. They built on the work of Samuel Morton and extended medical arguments to justify enslavement and buttress, if not to influence, slave law. They advocated the implementation of treatments that would regulate the body's functions, that is, food and oxygen consumption, sleeping habits, et cetera. They supported ideas that the southern climate was the best for ensuring black health and well-being and claimed that slavery offered the best opportunity for blacks' "civilization." They reworked classical Greek ideals about health in the service of separating blacks from whites and distanced blacks as far as possible on the human spectrum from the ideal type of mankind. Nott probably put it most succinctly: "Such a head as the Greek is never seen on a Negro, nor such a head as that of the Negro on a Greek" (*Types* 460; see fig. 3). In a different vein and countering the restrictions on Black Americans that this kind of health care informed, Mary Ann Shadd and Martin Robison Delany also found substance in classical Greek approaches to health. They, however, saw in the ancients' ideals a way toward black political self-mastery.

→ 2 ←

Ancient Ideals and the Healthy Self

Mary Ann Shadd's *Plea for Emigration* and Martin Robison Delany's *Condition, Elevation, Emigration, and Destiny*

> She is a superior woman; and it is useless to deny it . . . however much we may differ with her on the subject of emigration. She obtained the floor . . . and succeeded in making one of the most convincing and telling speeches in favor of Canadian emigration I ever heard. . . . She at first had ten minutes granted her as had the other members. At their expiration, ten more were granted, and by this time came the hour of adjournment; but so interested was the House, that it granted additional time to her to finish . . . and the house was crowded and breathless in its attention to her masterly exposition of our present condition, and the advantages Canada opens to colored men of enterprise. Herein consisted the charm and potency of her speech.
>
> ETHIOP, *FREDERICK DOUGLASS' PAPER*, NOVEMBER 9, 1855

> New York is at present honored with several gentlemen of color, who are candidates for the higher professions, both of Medicine and Divinity. Among them are Peck, Gibbs, Delany, McDonough, and others "too numerous to mention." It is said that most of them intend to make the field of their future operations beyond the boundaries of this country.
>
> OBSERVER, *FREDERICK DOUGLASS' PAPER*, APRIL 1, 1852

Leading up to the middle of the century, when proslavery medical doctors and race scientists vehemently promoted black inferiority and legislators incorporated such hypotheses into the making and revising of slave codes, two Black Americans, a man and a woman, sat down to pen substantial works advocating black emigration from the United States, advice they would follow themselves. Both works were published in 1852. They pay particular attention to colonial Canada and come to divergent conclusions, though both authors would settle in the colony for extended periods. In 1852, Henry Clay, the "Great Compromiser" and co-founder of the American Colonization Society, died. It was also the year of Harriet Beecher Stowe's *Uncle Tom's Cabin*, Samuel A. Cartwright's "Slavery in the Light of Ethnology," William Harper's reprinted "Memoir on Slavery" in *The Pro-Slavery Argument as Maintained by the Most Distinguished Writers of the Southern States*, and Susanna Moodie's *Roughing It in the Bush*. American print culture in general indicated the racially charged environment of the nation, and colonial Canadian print (produced in the colony and published in Britain) prominently featured stories of emigration and life in the "Backwoods" or "Bush."[1]

By midcentury, several slave narratives by fugitives in colonial Canada had been published, reaching popular audiences also in Britain and the United States. Josiah Henson's was famously and debatably associated with Stowe's character, Uncle Tom. As the previous chapter demonstrates, racial science was gaining momentum in the United States with the growing interest in ethnology, polygenesis, and racially specific diseases, creating a cultural climate in which "by the 1850s," race historian Bruce Dain explains, "the great American issues of the day [were] race and slavery" (197). Shadd and Delany published at the nexus of these dominant North American concerns. Their works offer not only settlement locations outside U.S. political governance but suggestions for self-becoming outside American race theory as well. A comparative literary analysis of these two relatively understudied works, published the same year, reveals the centrality of health to their promotion of emigration and of the ancient world to their conceptions of selfhood.

The complex debates about monogenism and polygenism, adaptability, environmentalism, and biology continued as Shadd and Delany in North America articulated their pursuit of black political authority. Josiah Nott was extending Samuel George Morton's craniological findings from the late 1830s into arguments about separate species and permanent black inferiority by the mid-1840s. Ten years after Nott's "Two Lectures on the Natural History of the Caucasian and Negro Races," and two years after Shadd's *Plea* and Delany's *Condition*, Nott's work with George Gliddon would culminate in the nearly 800-page volume *Types of Mankind*, which became wildly popular in the United States, much more widely read and distributed than Morton's work, to whom the volume was dedicated. Shadd and Delany advocated emigration at the height of the convergence of these theories, the passage of the Fugitive Slave Act, and intense debates about African colonization. Maurice Wallace argues that Delany's *Condition* was the "first significant political analysis of its kind" (70). I want to place Shadd's *Plea* in the same arena. As noted in the introduction, Shadd was also unique in that most black women refrained from promoting emigration, let alone published sustained work on the subject. Jane Rhodes explains how members of the black male establishment in Canada West "were equally disturbed by Mary Ann's independence and her refusal to be submissive to [them]. Mary Ann committed the ultimate act of defiance when she took it upon herself to write and publish a pamphlet on black emigration to disseminate her ideas to an audience beyond Windsor" (43). The controversies of the medical and scientific communities, the Fugitive Slave Act, debates within black communities, and gendered power struggles crossed geopolitical borders and provided the context for Shadd's and Delany's comprehensive considerations of this sensitive subject.

In contrast (and perhaps in response) to justificatory medical and scientific discourses about Africans' superior health and therefore suitability for enslavement in the colonies, and writing primarily for a free or fugitive Northern black audience, Shadd and Delany focus on the promotion of African Americans' good health in order to advocate their emigration from the slaveholding United States. In keeping with most of their contemporaries, they also hotly reject colonization schemes. Shadd's and Delany's reiterations of the classical Greek ideal of social organization based on the correlation between individual and state health also harken back more recently, as Bernd Herzogenrath notes, to colonial American models for community building in which the body represented societal cohesion. Herzogenrath cites representations of the body|politic ranging from John Winthrop's corporeal metaphors (particularly his use of ligaments and connective tissue), to Thomas Hobbes's *Leviathan* and the snake iconography of Benjamin Franklin's Fugio coin of 1787 to illustrate early American ideas about bodily and political unity (and disunity in the instance of Franklin's snake). But Shadd's and Delany's re-articulations of individual and state

Figure 5. Canada West, 1852 map from the author's personal collection. J & F Tallis, London, Edinburgh, and Dublin.

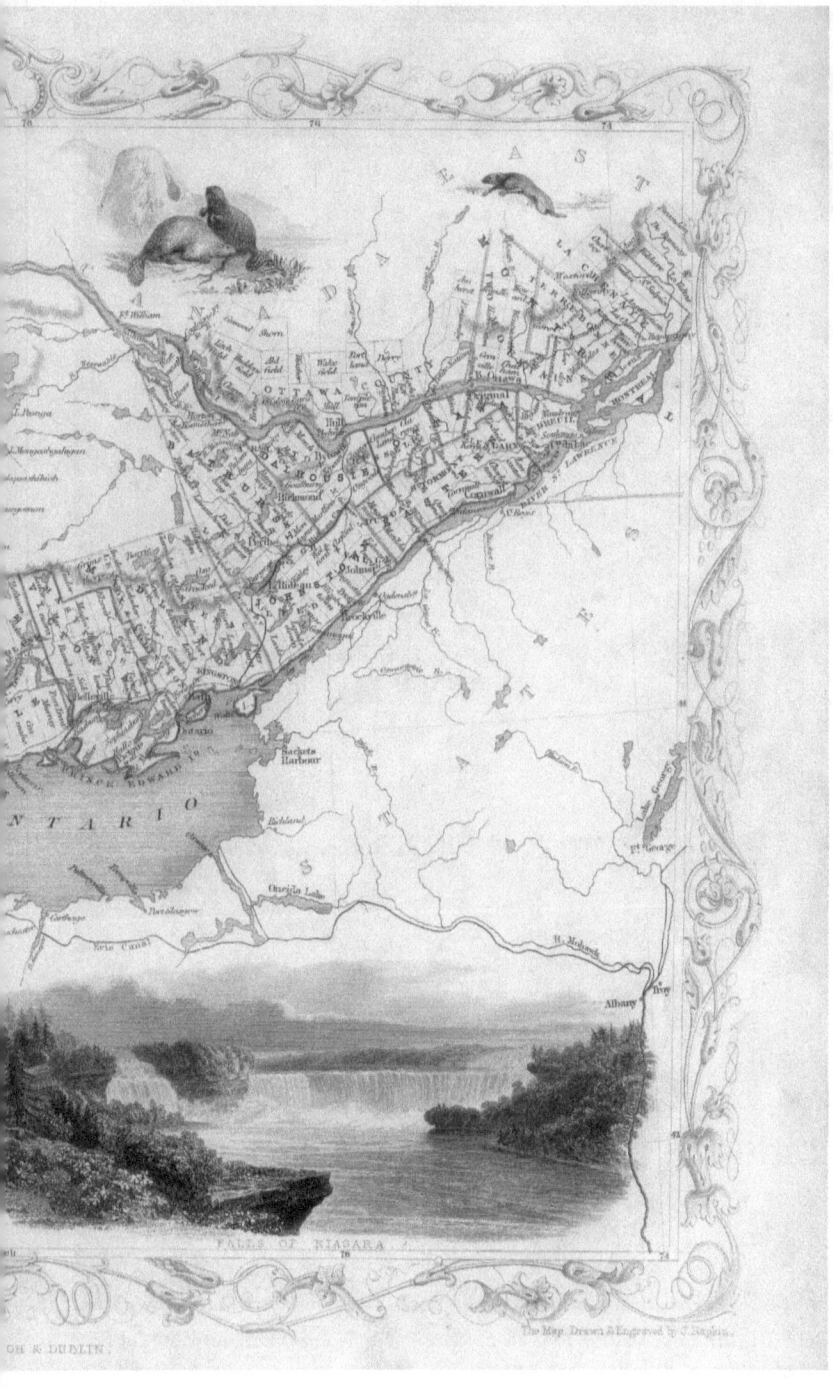

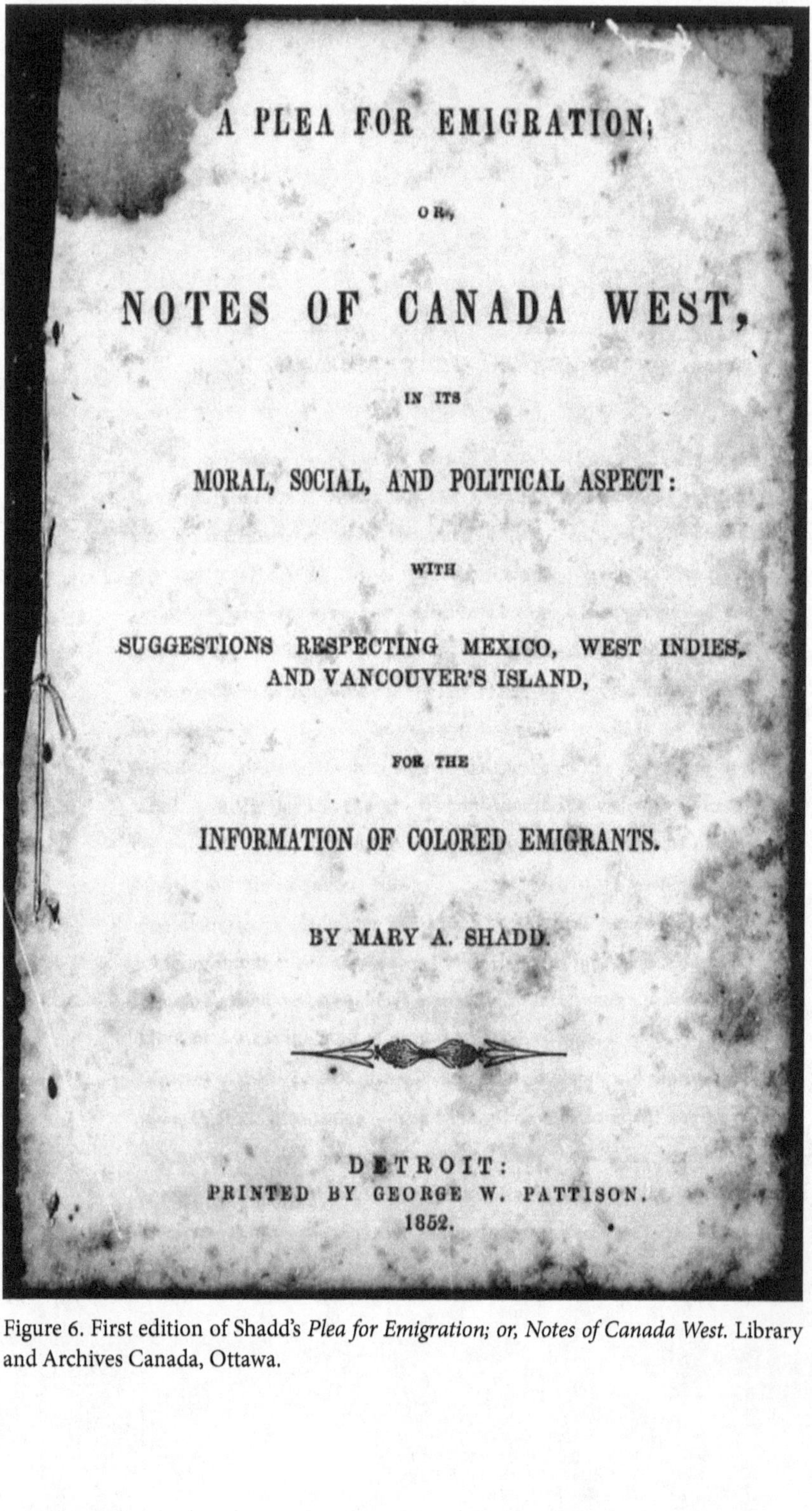

A PLEA FOR EMIGRATION;

OR,

NOTES OF CANADA WEST,

IN ITS

MORAL, SOCIAL, AND POLITICAL ASPECT:

WITH

SUGGESTIONS RESPECTING MEXICO, WEST INDIES, AND VANCOUVER'S ISLAND,

FOR THE

INFORMATION OF COLORED EMIGRANTS.

BY MARY A. SHADD.

DETROIT:
PRINTED BY GEORGE W. PATTISON.
1852.

Figure 6. First edition of Shadd's *Plea for Emigration; or, Notes of Canada West*. Library and Archives Canada, Ottawa.

health make a particularly Black American statement about the pursuit of wholeness and autonomy in that they are figured remedies to the U.S. national maladies that are slavery and racial injustice. Such rehabilitative discourse frames their calls for emigration and promotion of political participation—and further, for Delany, a justification for independent black political rule premised on black physical superiority. Delany's endorsement of such physicality may be ironic in that it signified for racial scientists a criterion demarcating human species; however, it supported his logic that policy, not inferiority, was responsible for the oppressed condition of black people in America.[2]

My central contention is that the authors' valorization of health and promotion of political independence through a reworking of classical ideals function propagandistically and polemically to promote emigration. Their recourse to classical democratic ideals at best overlooks and at worst disparages the realities of those whom disability and illness would inevitably continue to affect after emigration but demonstrates the centrality of health to their conceptions of black selfhood. Critique of socially produced suffering contains a different emphasis than do analyses of the political motivations underlying the ideology of disease, for, in the latter, belief in biological predispositions to certain illnesses is the focus of proslavery argumentation promoting control of the enslaved population and enabling social environments of suffering.

Shadd's and Delany's theoretical engagements with their historical and scientific contexts are daring, if at times incongruous. The authors theorize the possibility and endorse the achievement of a complete—fulfilled—black sense of self at a time when legal, medical, governmental, and economic institutions functioned, at times in conjunction, to divide and subjugate it. The authors refuse to privilege mind or body or to de-emphasize black physicality for propagandistic purposes, despite whites' routine hyper-corporealization/sexualization of blacks. Rather, they underscore the health of the black body that is at once physical, intellectual, emotional, and moral. Somewhat ironically perhaps they promote a Platonist completeness that slavery, itself defended by Plato, prohibits. Their rehabilitative and restorative rhetorics of physicality—though at times elitist, ableist, and even racist—reject white-controlled channels of abolition, emancipation, and colonization and instead demand black political autonomy through emigration. In short, they demonstrate the perceived necessity of an alternative rehabilitative discourse in the project of rejecting oppressive medically informed restorative theories and rhetorics.

Mary Ann Shadd was founder, editor, and correspondent for the second black newspaper in colonial Canada, the *Provincial Freeman* (1853–57). She later became a Civil War recruiter and graduate of Howard University Law School. Emulating other colonial almanacs of the time, Shadd's *Plea for Emigration; or, Notes of Canada West* (1852) also depicts exodus as the only option for Black Americans, free or enslaved, with health forming a key consideration in her suggested settlement locations. She designates Canada West as a most healthful place for relocation. Furthermore, she relates black well-being to the acquisition of citizenship, impossible in the United States even for free blacks born there, and calls for blacks' almost militaristic duty to forestall the expansion of U.S. slavery.

Shadd was a free black woman from Wilmington, Delaware, who became one of the most influential Black Americans in colonial Canada; she was also one of the most controversial black figures in British North America. The eldest daughter of abolitionist lecturer Abraham Shadd and Harriet Parnell, Mary Ann was educated at boarding school in West Chester, Pennsylvania. Upon graduation, she returned to Wilmington where no public education was available to people of African descent and opened a school for black children. Shadd also taught in various cities in Pennsylvania, New Jersey, and New York before immigrating to Canada West around the time of the government's enactment of the Fugitive Slave Law. There she established a racially integrated school that received support from the American Missionary Association. Her advocacy of racial integration and criticism of the Refugee Home Society in Canada West put her at odds with other prominent members of the black community there, whose priorities were to support fugitives—in Shadd's mind at free blacks' expense—and who advocated racial segregation. To this end and in response to an attack in the first black abolitionist newspaper in colonial Canada, *The Voice of the Fugitive*, Shadd and prominent black abolitionist and intellectual Samuel Ringgold Ward founded a rival publication, the *Provincial Freeman*. Shadd supported integration and education. Her politics set her apart from other black leaders in Canada West as controversial and somewhat elitist. A single black woman and public figure, Shadd often garnered as much criticism as she did respect from her male contemporaries. As a writer, she was enormously influential, particularly through her editorship of the *Provincial Freeman*, but *Plea* marks her singularly most direct, extensive contribution to nineteenth-century letters and black political theory.

Martin Delany also foregrounds health in his polemical *Condition, Elevation, Emigration, and Destiny of the Colored People of the United States*, figuring well-being in terms of a particularly gendered notion of racial uplift—the development of black manhood—as well as concentration on commercial production and the acquisition of citizenship rights. Born in West Virginia of a slave father and free mother, Delany had free status—enslavement and freedom following the condition of the mother. He was educated in Pittsburgh and trained in medicine by a white doctor. Delany practiced as a bleeder, leecher, and cupper in 1836. He was admitted to Harvard Medical College and then dismissed because his colleagues deemed "'the admission of blacks to the medical Lectures highly detrimental to the interests, and welfare, of the Institution of which [they were] members, calculated alike to lower its reputation in this and other parts of the country, to lessen the value of a diploma from it, and to diminish the number of its students'" (qtd. in Ullman 115–16). Defiant, Delany practiced medicine in the United States and colonial Canada, where he began writing his novel, *Blake; or, The Huts of America* (1859, 1861–62), a fictive exploration of revolutionary promise, which I discuss in chapter 5. He lectured on comparative anatomy, published a program for cholera prevention in the colony, became leader of an expedition to Africa, and then served as a major in the U.S. Army. Delany in this study appropriates a sort of intermediary position between the book's professional physician-writers and its lay authors and orators whose cultural concerns are health and well-being. His work theorizes race and politics more explicitly and in greater depth than Shadd's *Plea*, and his assertion of black physical superiority frames his call for black self-rule. For Delany, black selfhood is synonymous with black manhood.

Delany has recently enjoyed somewhat a resurgence in academic interest—even though his *Condition* still garners less critical attention than his other works—but Shadd remains of interest mostly as a historical figure (woman, editor, army recruiter, law student, with a collection of "firsts" or "notables" attending her name and actions) than a writer or thinker whose works themselves merit close study.[3] Delany, however, didn't see it that way. He was an early promoter of Shadd's talent. In an 1849 letter to the *North*

Star, he commended Shadd's pamphlet, *Hints to the Colored People of the North* and noted that "Miss Shadd is an excellent girl, and will henceforth give her whole attention to writing" (January 16th). I like to recall Delany's early recognition of Shadd's literary talent and dedication in hope that after more than a century and a half, literary scholars will study her writings in earnest, extending the work of historians and pay attention to her as an author and intellectual whose literature deserves acknowledgment for its contributions to black literary history as well as American literary history more broadly. As recently as July 2013, cultural communication scholar Carolyn Calloway-Thomas highlights Shadd's empirical rhetoric as an example of the "first influential North American Black female to use a quantitative approach fortified by moral philosophy as a central argument, which functioned as an organizing principle" (241). Despite Calloway-Thomas's emphasis on Shadd's contribution to a tradition of Black American firsts, she does, unlike many Shadd scholars, pay close attention to her writing style. I read this as signaling a turn in scholarly interest in this literary and historical figure. Shadd still appears neither in the most recent edition of the *Norton Anthology of African American Literature* nor the 2014 Wiley Blackwell *Anthology*, and though her inclusion in the 2012 edition of *The Dictionary of Early American Philosophers* suggests her prominence as a thinker, the entry itself reveals very little about her actual contribution to early American philosophical thought.[4]

For various reasons, notably her stance on emigration as well as her status as a single black (not to mention determined) woman for much of her writing and editing career, Shadd met with resistance from the free black intelligentsia. In our time, perhaps her interest in Canada seems tangential to scholarship on African American literature and questions of canonicity. It's difficult to say, though I suspect the field's turn to cultures of print and the expansion of digital accessibility will contribute to an increased interest in Shadd as a journalist. In her time, a significant factor obscuring her earlier work seems to be its neglect by Frederick Douglass. Neither *Plea* nor Delany's *Condition* enjoyed Douglass's promotion, and this still seems a major stumbling block to Shadd's acceptance as an author and not just a historical figure.

Referring to the silence surrounding *Condition*'s publication, Robert Levine has usefully traced Delany and Douglass's journalistic fisticuffs as they appeared in the pages of *Frederick Douglass' Paper*. It began with

Delany's criticism of Douglass in July 1852 for not even offering notice of *Condition*'s publication: "This work, a copy of which I sent you in May, on its issue, has never been noticed in the columns of your paper.... You could have given it a circulating notice, by saying such a book had been written by me, (saying anything else about or against it you pleased), and let those who read it pass their own opinions also. But you heaped upon it a cold and deathly silence" (July 23). In April of the following year, Douglass chastised Delany for his harsh words directed at Stowe and then criticized *Condition* for "leav[ing] us just where it finds us, without chart or compass, and in more doubt and perplexity than before we read it" (April 1). Levine surmises that "it may well have been that the main reason he chose not to review *Condition* was because, faced with the two principal (and politically opposed) antislavery works of spring 1852, he decided to invest his cultural capital and prestige in promoting the book he believed had the greatest possibility of improving the condition of blacks in the United States: *Uncle Tom's Cabin*" (71). Levine's suggestion seems most probable and heightens the importance of the publishing context for both Delany and Shadd as their works vied for attention in the year during which appeared a condemnation of slavery that would become in its time, apart from the Bible, the best-selling book.

There is another aspect of Douglass and Delany's debate that does not appear in (or really apply to) Levine's study of the two men, but it sheds more light on Douglass's potential effect on the reception of Shadd's work and about the hotly contested climate during which these debates took place and these writings appeared. In a subsequent letter to the *Provincial Freeman* in 1856, Delany attacks Douglass's initial silence on Shadd's work as well as his more recent lauding of her talents. Summarizing Douglass, Delany begins, "Miss Mary Ann Shadd (now Mrs. Cary), is made the special subject of compliment, with traits of talents and literary acquirements, which places her without an equal among the colored ladies of the United States." Then comes his critique: "Is this a recent discovery? Are the talents and acquired ability of Miss Shadd just beginning to develop themselves that this great keen eyed expositor of our 'awakened mental abilities' has just discovered them? Is Miss Shadd of to-day any more deserving of a complimentary notice than Miss Shadd of a few years ago whom *Frederick Douglass* never deigned to notice but to disparage?"[5] Delany concludes the letter with an even more sarcastic swipe at Douglass when he argues, "The

Freeman in fact, has a much larger circulation among the colored people than *Frederick Douglass' Paper*. But we had quite forgotten our position and must beg to thank the Editor . . . for arresting the names of a few Emigrationists from the obscurity to which they were consigned, and showing to the public at large, that they might possibly possess some talents, and thereby merit his notice. For this we are very thankful, and bow uncovered with obsequious reverence!" (July 12, 1856). Whatever Delany's personal feelings about Douglass may have been at this point, the letters demonstrate the complex politics that played out in these influential newspapers about the best future course for Black Americans and the fraught historical and literary moment during which Shadd and Delany's emigration polemics appeared as well as the lasting feud that followed their publication and frustrated reception.[6]

Beyond Douglass's actual or presumed effect on Shadd's and Delany's popular print reception at midcentury, the two authors' at times elitist and conservative stances on issues of class, I suspect, also contribute to their works' having fallen somewhat to the margins of black literary and historical studies. Likewise, extending past the authors' own time, their advocacy of emigration positions them somewhat at odds with subsequent scholarly and literary traditions of the recovery/reclamation of African American literary texts and emphasis on the desire for black U.S. citizenship.

In the scholarship that does interrogate their complication of black political ideals, an overlooked aspect of Shadd's and Delany's entries into midcentury emigration debates is their concentration on health and well-being as the critical frame through which they reject colonization and promote black exodus from the United States—another potentially exclusionary standpoint. Nevertheless, their classical Greek corporeal analogies for the healthy state provide the lens through which their rhetorics of physicality articulate a complex and unique negotiation and rejection of nineteenth-century racism that racial and medical science informed. I mean "rhetorics of physicality" to denote the rhetorical principles informing the theoretical study and depiction of corporeal physicality. Shadd's and Delany's rhetorics of physical health in depicting the pursuit of political self-mastery, for example, run counter to those of Nott, Cartwright, and others who argue that the "negro's" constitution fails to master itself and therefore requires enslavement. By revisiting ancient ideals about health and democratic civil order, the authors critique proponents of white supremacy and tackle the many limitations they tried to place on the black body and, by extension, Black Americans' sense of self, their physical, moral, and intellectual capabilities.[7]

In conflict with Morton, Nott, Cartwright, and other racial scientists and doctors, Shadd's and Delany's work presents the promise of a black condition based on a model of political autonomy very closely tied to health and well-being, one that rather than conceptualizing a mind/body dualism and privileging the former, instead understands them as producing subjecthood in concert. In doing so, their emphasis on health de-emphasizes the body's definition as property—in oneself or in another or as belonging to another. Furthermore, Shadd's and Delany's theories offer criteria for a black political philosophy that stresses the role of physical place and the importance of movement. Their works aspire—if troublingly—to a politics of healthy wholeness in order to attain a freedom and fulfillment that promises to repair the fragmented senses of self that the discourses of U.S. medicine and law produced. Their theory rejects colonization, tires of abolitionism, and refuses to wait for emancipation. It is a project to reclaim black rights that white people have stolen, even if it requires residency outside the United States—it does not anticipate or entertain whites' possible return of those rights through abolition and emancipation, particularly, as Marcus Wood outlines, under the auspices of the gift.[8]

Shadd and Delany wrote emigration propaganda from the standpoint of free black professionals in defiance of whites' regulation of black people in the New World at a time when race theory in general figured biology as a key racial determinant and when the United States, in particular, placed the most severe restrictions on black mobility. Not only was mobility curtailed, but the era saw the most active regulation—medical and legal—of enslaved blacks' labor, re/production, intellectual development, interpersonal relationships, and food and oxygen consumption as well. Disregarding such corporeal control, these authors develop a rhetorics of physicality that directly confronts proslavery and white supremacist theory on specific aspects of regulation—much of which mid-nineteenth-century Southern valorization of classical empirical ideals informed and justified—as they highlight health to promote black autonomy and articulate the promise of a free black self that is physically, morally, and intellectually capable of individual and collective self-mastery and self-governance outside the United States.

Before Shadd's immigration to Canada West and her subsequent newspaper career, her pamphlet *A Plea for Emigration; or, Notes of Canada West, in Its Moral, Social, and Political Aspect with Suggestions Respecting Mexico, West Indies and Vancouver's Island for the Information of Colored Emigrants* appeared in Detroit in 1852. The work claims to respond to the need for information about emigration options for both the free and fugitive black communities of the United States. Less polemical than Delany's *Condition*, Shadd's *Plea* spends little time arguing for emigration but rather presumes its necessity and therefore presents a source of intelligence on the subject. Peterson acknowledges that Shadd differed from Frances Watkins Harper, who "deemphasize[s] the African-American body and focus[es] instead on emotional response" (127). Furthermore, I argue, Shadd weaves considerations of health into nearly every aspect of her report advocating the improvement of Black Americans' condition. According to Shadd, the body that racist policies and their proponents tried to limit would find itself unrestricted and restored to a state of physical, mental, and moral health if it found the right environment. Furthermore, the ideal black body would realize a commensurate black politics.

The relationship between health and self-sufficiency|mastery in Shadd's *Plea* calls on readers to reject the limitations of U.S. black regulation, physical, intellectual, and political. She creates a picture of a "healthy" British province in contrast to the common trope of a pestilent Africa and in opposition to a proslavery United States that places all Black Americans at risk. By making one location healthy and pathologizing another, Shadd grafts black well-being and illness onto the healthy and diseased geopolitical spaces Black Americans occupy.[9] Conversing with proslavery discourse, she offers an alternative to black subjugation and demonstrates how to realize it through emigration, a movement from illness to health, from restriction and regulation to freedom and self-mastery. Alluding to political ideals of ancient Greece, Shadd challenges her readers to view the black self|citizen in ways that compete with principles of Enlightenment modernity, to identify a sense of self that is comprehensive and complex and extends beyond economies of property ownership.

Shadd articulates a discourse of fulfillment and wholeness evocative of the classical era that potentially closes the divides between mind and body that the Enlightenment opened up and proposes new, utopist definitions of black selfhood. By conceptualizing the possibility of good health as integral to freedom and a redefinition of personhood, she counters proslavery rehabilitative discourse with her own to suggest new ways that Black Americans might understand themselves politically. To this end, Shadd looks to the model of the monarchical head, which governs the body politic—even as she draws on classical figurations of individual and state health. Turning away from U.S. republican ideals, Shadd refuses to reproduce or recycle colonial American utopist political models, such as Winthrop's wherein, as Herzogenrath eloquently puts it, the body is figured as a system of parts "overcoding and subordinating the potential multiplicity into one body [and in which the body|politic] consists of a complex interplay of both hierarchical|democratic and hierarchical|totalitarian tendencies" (60). Rather, she promotes black émigrés' alignment with the British monarchy in Canada West, a figuration in which the crowned head governs and protects its parts.[10] In doing so, she participates in a broader antebellum black abolitionist and activist tradition of valorizing Britain as a paragon of freedom.[11]

The body|politic (or parts) for Shadd in this transcolonial African diasporic context would involve black individuals working toward the development of a communal ideal harkening to Plato, whose *Gorgias* "ties excellence and well-being to order, prefacing its observations of *arête* with a reminder that self-control and justice are accessible only to those whose *epithumiai* are rightly controlled" (Levin, "Eryximachus" 288). For Shadd, black emigration to the colony is a means, ultimately, of forming a community closely modeled on such an ancient political ideal. Shadd seeks a context wherein Black Americans can enjoy self-rule and justice under the aegis of benevolent state control, in this case the British Crown. Referring to colonial Canada where "[t]he climate is healthy, and [Black Americans] enjoy as good health as other settlers," Shadd notes that emigrants "may enjoy full 'privileges of British birth in the Province.'" She continues, "The general tone of society is healthy; vice is discountenanced, and infractions of the law promptly punished; and, added to this, there is an increasing anti-slavery sentiment, and a progressive system of religion" (89). We might note here, too, that her language engages at least implicitly with the "vices of character" we saw outlined in the previous chapter, particularly with regard to U.S. slaves and "Negro diseases." She writes of vice in a way that suggests that there is nothing particularly racial about vice, contrary to the contentions of slaveholding ideology.

As promising as her ideal may seem, Shadd's iteration of it shares some of the prohibitions Plato emphasized about health—physical and spiritual—and human worth. Philosopher Susan Levin's translation regarding Plato's *Republic* reads: "if a man afflicted with serious incurable physical ailments did not drown [while with the helmsman] this man is miserable for not dying and has received no benefit from him. But if a man has many incurable diseases in what is more valuable than his body, his soul, life for that man is not worth living, and he won't do him any favor if he rescues him from the sea or from prison or from anywhere else" (300). Levin goes on to explain that the greatest evil is corruption of soul. As does perhaps Levin's translation of Plato's ideas about health and human worth, Shadd's healthy ideal prompts one to wonder where her emphasis on individual and state health leaves those injured, ill, and disabled, who were numerous among both fugitive and free black populations, figures we will encounter in the next chapter. Shadd's *Plea* is propaganda. Her theory attempts to remove the integrity of individual personhood from economies of property ownership, where it had been located since the seventeenth century. Rather, her rhetorics present the possibility of locating subjecthood in a healthy self residing in a salubrious environment outside the United States and, at least at first, under the protective governance of Britain.

Shadd begins, "The people are in a strait. On the one hand, a pro-slavery administration, with its entire controllable force, is bearing upon them with fatal effect. On the other, the Colonization Society, in the garb of *Christianity* and *Philanthropy*, is seconding the efforts of the first named power, by bringing into the lists a vast social and immoral influence, thus making more effective the agencies employed" (43). The strait represents a dividing line on which Black Americans are "torn" between equally harmful options: to accept the proslavery administration of the United States, which had recently passed the Fugitive Slave Law, or ally themselves with the Colonization Society and depart for Africa. The image of the strait evokes 2 Samuel 24:14: "And David said unto Gad, I am in a great strait," referring to David's dilemma of choosing between three forms of punishment for his sin: famine, flight, or pestilence.

Here the government, Fugitive Slave Law, and American Colonization Society, respectively and figuratively, are sentences to starvation, exile, or disease. Shadd frames her argument as a remedy. Her religious (and medico-juridical) allusion favors the rehabilitative over retributive aspects of her analogy. Shadd adamantly advocates flight. Her portrayal of

Black Americans' political dilemma, which lands them in a strait, divided between two racist alternatives, might visually remind us of the multiple fragmentations nineteenth-century government, medicine, and law enacted upon Black Americans. In the scenario Shadd presents, both options prohibit satisfaction. The only choice is to reject the alternatives on either side of the divide and find what she proposes is the only other way to repair the broken self: immigrate to a healthy locale. Delany uses specific reference to brokenness in the appendix to his *Condition*: "We have been, by our oppressors, despoiled of our purity, and corrupted in our native characteristics, so that we have inherited their vices, and few of their virtues, leaving us in character, really a *broken people*" (221). Later, he refers to "Representatives of a Broken Nation" (224). This general discourse of brokenness, remedy, and rehabilitation explicitly details what Shadd more often implies.[12]

It is a given in *Plea* that Black Americans reject a proslavery government by moving from the United States; however, Shadd devotes a part of her "Introductory Remarks" to the rejection of colonization. There she begins to formulate her theory of health through rhetorics of physicality that critique the Colonization Society and Africa itself. Shadd remarks that "Tropical Africa, the land of promise of the colonizationists, teeming as she is with the breath of pestilence, a burning sun and fearful maladies, bids [the colonists] welcome; she feelingly invites to moral and physical death, under a voluntary escort of their most bitter enemies at home" (43). In her figuration, the promised land of the colonizationists is a place of sickness, pain, and death. The colonizationists (the "voluntary escort") are Black Americans' "most bitter enemies," leading them, in grim-reaper fashion, to their moral and physical death. The conflation of these deaths contradicts what Dain articulates as the Colonization Society's belief that "Blacks' return to Africa would slowly lift both Africa and America out of sin" (116). The characterization of the continent of Africa as diseased is a common trope among other black activists and authors of the period; Shadd employs it in the promotion of emigration to Canada West, which is by contrast a decidedly health*ful* place.

Shadd's interrelation of environment and health in Canada West reiterates her ideal healthy body|healthy politic. Her subsequent promotion of Canada West as the preferred alternative to colonization creates space in North America for the attainment of Black American political agency.

As historian Van Gosse points out, "From early on, African Americans in Canada voted, sat on juries, testified in courts, and fought in their own militia units under their own officers. Abroad, black Canadians were recognized as British subjects, with the privileges attached to that status. Nowhere in the United States could a black person reach this level of citizenship" (1012). Though Shadd's plan would require the acceptance of British rule, she splits the difference between remaining in the United States and "returning" to Africa. She proposes that by locating health and free political participation in Canada West, Black Americans can achieve a subjecthood that the previous two options preclude. Her theory depends on civilization rhetoric—perhaps tactically so, for she represents the United States and Africa as largely uncivilized as well as unhealthy—but within her support of British government, she articulates the potential for good health as a promising way to conceptualize Black American freedom and political action.[13]

Shadd maintains that in British America "the climate is healthy and temperate: epidemics are not of such frequency as in the United States, owing to a more equable temperature, and local diseases are unknown" (45). She emphasizes the centrality of health to her argument by comparing the healthfulness of Canada West (described above) and Canada East where "The land is of good quality, and vegetation is of rapid growth, but the general healthiness of the country is inferior to some of the other districts" (44–45). Within British America, Canada West offers the best settlement location because it is the most healthful of places. Shadd commences her argument from the Hippocratic premise that "An intelligent man understands that health is a person's most valuable possession" (Touniss 188). She continues: "In Canada West, the variation from a salubrious and eminently healthy climate is nowhere sufficient to cause the least solicitude: on the contrary, exempt from the steady and enfeebling warmth of southern latitudes, and the equally injurious characteristics of polar countries, it is highly conducive to mental and physical energy" (46).

Shadd rejects Africa, but her rhetorical structure seems also to converse (and rather directly so) here with Nott, who a year earlier argued that "the Negro Races['] . . . physical type is peculiar; their grade of intellect is greatly inferior; they are utterly wanting in *moral and physical energy*" (*Natural* 15, emphasis mine). Shadd counters Nott's assertion about energy. For Shadd, the temperate climate produces the temperate, energetic self. The environmental and therefore individual excesses of Africa, as Shadd depicts it, also correspond with the physical and spiritual self-indulgences Plato opposes. The climate that is "healthy and temperate" produces an "infrequency of violations of law" that is "unprecedented" *rather* than an "increase of vice, prejudice, improvidence, laziness, or a lack of energy" (45, 68). Self-control goes hand in hand with a commensurably moderate environment. Her theory is also reminiscent of Pythagorean doctrine in which "[h]ealth was a condition of perfect equilibrium, and the Pythagorean way of life meant preserving this equilibrium by practicing moderation and maintaining self-control and calmness" (Tountas 187). Her reiteration, even recitation, of contemporary "negro diseases" explicitly makes an environmentalist claim against Africa, but implicitly draws a parallel between Africa and the United States, too. Here Shadd is clear that she does not accept the racialized definitions of vice and deficiencies of character that Southern doctors promoted, but rather (along with other free black writers and reformers) sees blacks and whites as susceptible to the same vices.

Shadd's relation of climate to energy here does not rely on physiological distinctions between whites and blacks as, for example, Nott's, Drake's, and Cartwright's theories do, but she argues that the climate of Canada West will produce an enabling effect unknown in extremely cold or warm climes. Whereas physicians such as those listed above espoused the benefits of enslavement in the southern climate as producing an effect of increased energy, Shadd advocates the removal of blacks from the South altogether and uses similar environmental justifications about invigoration, in this instance, to promote the physical benefits of a colder climate. Cartwright, in particular, advocates adopting classical medical theories and practices based on a perceived similarity of Greek and southern U.S. climates, while Shadd draws on the ancients for their physiological as well as empirical|environmental medical arguments. Calloway-Thomas, for example, argues, "Inherent within [Shadd's] political geography are strong Aristotelian deliberative ideas, modes of reasoning, how to persuade, and skill-sets that were required for the ex-slaves to live well in civil society" (252). In Shadd's single-minded project to promote emigration, she shapes her propaganda to draw on classical Greek ideals and rhetoric to portray the possibility of a polis commensurate with an idealized black selfhood. She appropriates Greek philosophies of health and government as a mode of critique and persuasion.

Shadd's interest in "mental and physical energy" foregrounds the necessity of *both* for black success in a new location. She repairs rifts between mind and body, one of the many distinctions that slaveholders and proslavery theorists emphasize in order to maintain the institution and on which modern political economy in general relies, for example, the "vices of body" and "vices of character" that determined a slave's commercial and legal value. Shadd implicitly rejects Nott's 1851 assertion that, "If . . . the Negro Races stand at the lowest point in the scale of human beings, and we know of no moral or physical agencies which can redeem them from their degradation, it is clear that they are incapable of self-government, and that any attempt to improve their condition is warring against an immutable law of nature" (17). The combination of energies of which Shadd speaks provides the basis for black industriousness that will be essential to the personal and political agency that is the ultimate goal of emigration. Shadd argues, "I firmly believe that with an axe and a little energy, an independent position would result in a short period" (52). The climate promotes health, necessary for energy, which in turn garners the ideal of self-sufficiency—one might go so far as to say, self-mastery. Here Shadd draws together Plato's notion of the body's influence on the mind and Hippocrates's recognition of the relation between the physical, social, and political environments. For the ancient Greeks, as for Shadd, "an autonomous society means *ipso facto* autonomous persons. But, autonomous society or autonomous persons mean empowered society and empowered persons. Therefore, the notion of empowerment is not only related with *self-sufficiency* . . . but with the notion of autonomy as well" (Tountas 188–89). Shadd's depiction of the possibility of independence in Canada West also reiterates a broader call for black self-sufficiency in her promotion of emigration. As historian Erica Ball notes with regard to the importance of landownership, delegates to the 1848 National Black Convention urged that "young African American men who sought to live truly antislavery lives would need to prepare themselves to take up new forms of labor and embody the ideal of the self-made man" (46). This is precisely what many of Shadd's proposed émigrés would have to do. That her proposed location is still governed by a monarchy, and therefore not an example of the classical Greek ideal democracy, is not a problem for Shadd. She portrays the British monarchy as a protective rather than oppressive system, in stark contradistinction to the false democracy in the United States.

Shadd's argument allies with British North American propaganda against U.S. political policy. She promotes the notion that self-sufficiency is possible through relocation to the proper place and argues that in Canada West, "There is every inducement to buy [property]" and that there is "no lack of employment at fair prices, and no complexional or other qualification in existence" (59). Her reference to a lack of "complexional qualification" conjures the physical limitations the United States placed on blacks, lacking both citizenship and the right to own property. She anticipates W.E.B. Du Bois's "color line" (1903) and underscores the skin as the barrier, which contains the physical self but also that bars it from attaining political rights. In advocating immigration to Canada West, she rhetorically removes such restrictions from the black physique and encourages the realization of a healthy self that encompasses the body as an interrelated site of physical, mental, emotional, and moral functions.

Shadd sets out "the advantage of a residence in a country in which chattel slavery is not tolerated, and prejudice of *colour* has no existence whatever—the adaptation of that country, by climate, soil, and political character, to their physical and political necessities; and the superiority of a residence there over their present position at *home*" (60). In doing so, she weaves the evolutionary rhetoric of adaptation and superiority to craft a sense of self with animal, social, and political needs. This self is intimately related to and shares a mutually influential relationship with its environment and challenges the United States' economics of property ownership as tied to citizenship and race. Shadd argues that in the province "[t]he climate is healthy . . . [and black people] enjoy the 'privileges of British birth'" where there is an "aristocracy of birth not skin, as with Americans" (88–89). For Shadd, health combined with the possibility of citizenship provides a way for Black Americans to acquire subjecthood free from the United States' racially inflected/motivated articulations of possessive individualism.[14]

She argues that in the province, where "slavery is not tolerated [and] skin colour means nothing," the "native good sense of the fugitives, backed by proper schools, will eventually develop the real character of their operations and sacrifices. . . . The refugees express a strong desire for intellectual culture, and persons often begin their education at a time of life when many in other countries think they are too old" (60–63). Shadd's recourse to a sense of innate black character recalls some of the essentialist rhetoric of her proslavery contemporaries even as she valorizes the meaninglessness of skin color. More specifically, she pinpoints any meaning that skin color might hold as particularly related to man-made (use of "man" deliberate here) political constructions. Advocating the cultivation of an inherent quality through education also evokes the ancient ideal of eventual self-mastery, which those same proslavery contemporaries thought was impossible for black people to attain, hence the paternalistic argument for the institution.[15] Reaching toward a Greek ideal, Shadd rather advocates the possibility for black achievement of a classical political model founded on an integrated sense of the embodied black self as active and energetic, physically and intellectually. She reiterates the 1847 Convention declaration that "'man is a compound being, a being of mind, soul and body,'" the "tripartite model [that] . . . undergirded nearly every analysis of African American's plight" (Rael 127).

Thus the lack of racially motivated legislation in Canada West, beyond removing physical restrictions that American policy asserts on the enslaved, provides opportunity for black intellectual development. Though Shadd emphasizes what she sees as the unimportance of race in Canada West,[16] she does seem to appreciate the distinctions that class and status create, also in keeping with the Platonic sense that "[a] stable and orderly society . . . must rest on class divisions" (Bay 38). She does not criticize Canada West's "aristocracy of birth" but rather privileges it in opposition to American racism. Shadd sees greater freedom under monarchy than under republicanism, thus identifying her project not only with Canada (a state rejecting republicanism) but rather with the global superpower of the time: Great Britain.[17] She argues, "There would not be as in Africa, Mexico, or South America, hostile tribes to annoy the settler, or destroy at will towns and villages with their inhabitants: the strong arm of British power would summarily punish depredations made, of whatever character, and the emigrants would naturally assume the responsibility of British freemen" (99). Shadd sees the power of Great Britain not only to protect emigrants from harm but also to curb the spread of slavery. "More territory has been given up to slavery, the Fugitive Law has passed, and a concert of measures, seriously affecting their personal liberty, have been entered into by several of the Free States. So subtle, unseen and effective have been their movements, that, were it not that we remember there is a Great Britain, we would be overwhelmed, powerless, from the force of such successive shocks" (100).

Shadd conflates her ideal of the healthy body in a healthy state as autonomous *and* protected by a benevolent monarchy.

Whereas for Shadd, rehabilitative discourse seeks to cure political inequities, for Delany, recovery from illness and restoration to health means to remedy the "corruption of blood." For him it is a physiological degradation of Black Americans (the result of racist politics) that needs fixing. As does Shadd, Martin Delany develops a rhetorics of physicality and health in his emigration polemic appearing in the same year. Delany, however, advocates a radical politics of black autonomy that rejects Canada West as a permanent solution to the injurious political climate of the United States. At best, according to Delany, the colony might function as a temporary refuge for fugitive and free blacks *en route* to a better locale. He rejects the promise of abolition, seeming to understand the potential of emancipation as the two thefts that Marcus Wood outlines: first, the theft of black freedom and, second, of the possibility of black revolution. As the last chapter of the book will demonstrate, Delany later seems to fantasize about, perhaps even promote the fomenting of revolution via his novel *Blake*—emigration failing to secure the politics he desires. Levine explains, "In *Blake*, Delany somewhat differently attempts to resolve the problem of imperialism inherent in Blake's building of a black nation by connecting the revolutionary hero to the region through his personal history and black body. In doing so, Delany more explicitly brings to the center of the novel the problem of conjoining race and nation that had interested him since the 1852 publication of *Condition*" (203). I think this "problem of conjoining race and nation" succinctly sums up the cause of the sense of restlessness we get in *Condition*, which perhaps prompted criticism that the work did not offer a thorough enough program for improvement. But it is through that uneasy relation between race, the body, and nation that Delany interrogates the critical or analytical value of health and well-being. Whereas for Shadd health is a means of acquiring independence, for Delany it is an assertion of black racial superiority that necessitates more than the privileges of citizenship; it demands self-rule.

As Shadd does in her *Plea*, Delany asserts himself as an intellectual and a professional in *The Condition, Elevation, Emigration, and Destiny of the Colored People of the United States*. He argues, "A moral and mental, is as obnoxious as a physical servitude, and not to be tolerated; as the one may, eventually, lead to the other" (38). Similar to Shadd, Delany espouses the interconnectedness of one's moral, mental, and physical condition and promotes an ideal individual and political condition reminiscent of the ancients. In fact, near the beginning of the book he makes particular reference to Greek political theory in his comparative history of slavery: "In past ages there were many such classes, as the Israelites in Egypt, the Gladiators in Rome, and similar classes in Greece" (41). He longs for the ideals of classical Greek literature in his lament: "We have no reference to ancient times—we speak of modern things" (70). Delany also converses directly with nineteenth-century proslavery medical and legal theory and in particular with midcentury racial science.[18] Similar to Shadd's, his rehabilitative discourse frames his argument for emigration as a "remedy"—indeed the word appears at least five times in the volume in this precise context—for the "miserable position" blacks in America occupy (57). Furthermore, he characterizes the United States as particularly unhealthy in his descriptions and his rhetoric.

His purpose is to outline and advocate the opportunity for black people, "Broken People," to free themselves of U.S. regulation and to realize their potential for moral, intellectual, and physical well-being, which will result in their political independence. Robert Reid-Pharr explains that for Delany, "Black America can be actualized once she runs from herself, moves away from the very realities out of which she has been produced" (115). However, Delany's concept is uneasy and contradicts Shadd's theory that the protective governance of Great Britain will offer Black Americans the political agency they seek. Rather, Delany promotes black self-rule and proposes a politics that would later be recognized as Black Nationalism. He is much more extreme than Shadd in presenting the possibility of a triumphant black subjecthood—specifically male—and he is far more critical of colonial Canadian race relations.

He characterizes the political situation in the United States as pathological and that it is "*folly* to deny, *insanity* not to understand, *blindness* not to see" that "[w]hat the unfortunate classes are in Europe, such are [blacks] in the United States" (45, emphasis mine). His rhetoric of disability shifts to illness and suffering as he describes the situation which is "the result of an *unnatural* prejudice," even "Anti-Slavery men" refusing to "make common cause with [colored men] in *affliction*" (55, emphasis mine). He details the "colored men['s]" "*miserable* position in the community" as well as the "*injurious* character of the Colonization Society" (57–62, emphasis mine).

Delany structures his argument as a movement from the pathology of race relations in the United States toward the "remedy" of emigration. Health forms not only the content of his polemic, but its structure and rhetorical features as well. Similar to Shadd's work, *Condition*'s appeals to classical health and governance, and ideals of political autonomy function as modes of critique and persuasion.

Delany begins by reiterating what Spanish priest and historian Bartolomé de las Casas articulated in the early sixteenth century and what Delany's medical contemporaries and later Kiple and other medical historians have more recently rearticulated: that Africans were chosen as slaves because of their (perceived) ability to withstand certain hardships that the aboriginal population could not. He argues that it was not hatred that inspired the enslavement of black people, but rather that "the African race had long been known to Europeans, in all ages of the world's history, as a long-lived, hardy race, subject to the labor of various kinds, subsisting mainly by traffic, trade, and industry, and consequently being as foreign to the sympathies of the invaders of the continent as the Indians, they were selected, captured, brought here as a laboring class, and as a matter of policy held as such" (50). He refutes the "absurd idea" of African "natural inferiority" as the reason for enslavement and alludes to the relatively new nineteenth-century preoccupation with racial science to declare that the notion was only "recently adduced by the slaveholders and their abettors, in justification of the policy" (50). His conversation with medical history and contemporary race theory dispels some of the mythology of proslavery thought and frames his argument for the possibility of black physical and intellectual superiority and ultimate political autonomy.

Delany reiterates the correspondence between mind and body, familiar to his black Northern free or fugitive audience, and emphasizes exercise of physical and mental capacities to counter the restraints the oppressors of the slave system have placed on the development of black independence and asserts that slaves have internalized such restricted subjectivity and become "degraded." He not only recognizes the acceptance of racist attitudes but argues that they materialize as physiological facts from one generation to the next as well. Delany asserts, "The degradation of the slave parent has been entailed upon the child, induced by the subtle policy of the oppressor, in regular succession handed down from father to son—a system of regular submission and servitude, menialism and dependence, until it has become almost a physiological function of our system, an actual condition of our nature" (72). Thus racist social policy poisons the minds of the oppressed to the extent that they not only accept it but begin to "wear" it on the body as well. Later, Delany argues that the "offsprings of slaves and peasantry, have the general characteristics of their parents; and nothing but a different course of training and education, will change the character" (219). This is the pathological condition in the United States, transgenerationally infectious. Here Delany does not refer to such a condition rhetorically or metaphorically but discusses the actual physiological effect of slavery on the mind and body of the enslaved.

Delany also observes a conversely similar physiological *improvement* in Irish immigrants to the United States, analogous to his predictions about the effects of Black American emigration: "the instant they set their foot upon unrestricted soil; free to act and untrammeled to move; their physical condition undergoes a change, which in time becomes physiological, which is transmitted to the offspring, who when born under such circumstances, is a decidedly different being to what it would have been, had it been born under different circumstances" (219). Delany's analogy of Irish immigrants suggests the similar potential for Black Americans' mental and physiological improvement through emigration. In short, a free place is a healthful place. Before detailing and evaluating such healthful places, he establishes the premise that emigration is essential to black health and well-being. Arguing for a method of moving from a condition of degradation to one of health and self-sufficiency, he discounts religion as a remedy: "success in life . . . does not depend upon our religious character, but that the physical laws governing all earthly and temporary affairs, benefit equally the just and unjust. Any other doctrine than this, is *downright delusion*, unworthy of a free people, and only intended for slaves" (66, emphasis mine). To accept the logic of a pathological place is pathological in and of itself, as his reference to delusion implies.

Again emphasizing health as the frame of his argument, he asks the rhetorical question: "What then is the *remedy*, for our degradation and oppression?" (66, emphasis mine) and again later, "What we desire to learn now is, how to effect a *remedy*" (71, emphasis mine). His conclusion is that "Our elevation must be the result of *self-efforts*, and work of our *own hands*" (71, emphasis in original)—like Shadd, reiterating a broader value of self-sufficiency among black activists and reformers. Also similar to Shadd's appeal in *Plea*, Delany's harkens back to ancient Greek notions of self-sufficiency and independence (Protagoras) and, more particularly here with regard to Delany's argument, Socrates, "who distinguished ethics from religion and established the autonomy of the former" (Tountas 187). Such appeals to self-sufficiency became standard in Black American notions of elevation and were part of a broader American cultural ideal: "In the words of black authors, mind, morals, and the capacity to develop character merged in a vision of uplift that pervaded their thought. From cultural elites to writers in the expanding popular press, contemporary white thinkers issued remarkably similar statements" (Rael 129). Hence the cultural credence of Delany's and Shadd's appeals to a principle of self-sufficiency utterly at odds with life in an unhealthy place that deems them unfit for citizenship. This is where the appeal to a particularly classical ideal of the healthy body in a healthy state distinguishes their argument somewhat from broader notions of self-sufficiency within Black American communities and America in general.

By laying claim to and reworking ideals of antiquity that resurfaced in eighteenth- and nineteenth-century American social thought more broadly, Delany and Shadd create distinctly black utopic visions of self-governance and position themselves as potential commanders of their ideal polis. Delany and Shadd were seemingly comfortable with divisions of class. "In a dialogue with his disciple Glaucon on how to create a great republic, the great philosopher Socrates argues that the creation of an ideal society might require an 'audacious fiction.' A stable and orderly society, the philosopher maintains, must rest on class divisions" (Bay 38). Delany is explicit about social organization, arguing for the value of people of letters, as well as business- and craftsmen. In a sort of catalogue of elite black figures, Delany offers a host of men and women, Mary Ann Shadd among them, who demonstrate accomplishments academic, legal, literary, with classical education and languages. This class fits the rubric Socrates outlines: "So the citizens of the ideal republic will be divided by education and merit into three ranks: rulers, auxiliaries, and craftsmen. But the republic will prosper only if its citizens accept their ranks" (Bay 38). This final qualification about the acceptance of class divisions appears in a substantial footnote Delany includes as he discusses this first rank. In it he chastises those who attempt to exceed their rank as well as those who are of the first rank but don't use their talents in its service. The focus of his criticism is an early work of black ethnology by Robert Benjamin Lewis, *Light and Truth: Collected from the Bible and Ancient and Modern History, Containing the Universal History of the Colored and the Indian Race from the Creation of the World to the Present Time* (1836). Delany argues with reference to Lewis's book, "We much regret the fact, that there are but too many of our brethren, who undertake to dabble in literary matters, in the shape of newspaper and book-making, who are wholly unqualified for the important work. This, however, seems to be called forth by the palpable neglect, and indifference of those who have had the educational advantages, but neglected to make use of them" (fn 143).

Criticism of Lewis's book affords Delany opportunity to reinforce the rank divisions across black class lines while simultaneously excoriating the work of white ethnologist/Egyptologist George Gliddon (Nott's coauthor of *Types of Mankind*) "who makes all ancient black men, *white*," whereas Lewis "makes all ancient great white men, *black*—as Diogenes, Socrates, Themistocles, Pompey, Caesar, Cato, Cicero, Horace, Virgil, et cetera" (fn 143). In exposing the faults of Gliddon's and Lewis's methodology, Delany makes the case for the responsibility incumbent upon black men and women of letters, classically educated, who form that first rank or ruling class in an ideal society. At the same time, he makes the case for the value of the second and third ranks, the business- and craftsmen.

In fact, he argues that the tendency for black elites to have skipped over these secondary ranks and straight to the first has done the race a disservice. "What we most need then, is a good business practical Education; because, the Classical and Professional education of so many of our young men, before their parents are able to support them, and community ready to patronize them, only serves to lull their energy, and cripple their otherwise, praiseworthy efforts they would make in life" (208). Delany is quick to note that "he fully appreciates [a Classical and Professional education] having had some advantages himself" (208) but fears that Black Americans have "jumped too far; taking a leap from the deepest abyss to the highest summit; rising from the ridiculous to the sublime; without medium or intermission" (208). Delany's attentiveness to Socrates' "audacious fiction" offers a social structure from which Black Americans of various classes, backgrounds, and types of education might contribute to the ideal society he envisions. In determining a geographical location, the possibility for good health is a central contention for the fulfillment of his ideals of self-sufficiency and self-governance.

Delany discounts Liberia—the choice of the ACS—as "signally unhealthy, rendering it objectionable as a place of destination for the colored people of the United States" (185). Unlike Shadd, he only briefly and under only certain circumstances recommends settlement in Canada West, not because of its potential for healthy living, given its geography, but as an unhealthful place politically: "The climate being milder than that of the northern portions of New York, Ohio, Michigan, Indiana, Illinois, or any of the States bordering on the lakes, the soil is prolific in production of every description" (189). Beyond climate, he also praises its agriculture: "Grains, vegetables, fruits, and cattle, are of the very best kind; from a short tour by the writer, in that country in the fall, 1851, one year ago, he prefers Canada West to any part of North America, as a destination for the colored people" (189). His political objection to Canada West is his perceived certainty of the colony's susceptibility to American annexation. Canada West may provide temporary respite for fugitives, but it is not the location for his ideal society. In short, it may offer temporary comfort, but it is not the desired "remedy." "That country is the best, in which our manhood can be best developed; and that is Central and South America, and the West Indies—all belonging to this glorious Continent" (197–98). For Delany, manhood is selfhood, and the best places to develop that are Nicaragua and New Grenada, "the climate being healthy and highly favorable . . . opportunities for us to rise to the full stature of manhood . . . in these countries, colored men now fill the highest places in the country" (202). And, punctuating his point about the fulfillment of black selfhood and good health, he argues in the penultimate paragraph, "The black race may be found, inhabiting healthful improvement, every part of the globe where the white race reside; while there are parts of the globe where the black race reside, that the white race cannot live in health" (226). His implication that black people on the whole enjoy better health in a variety of geographic environments than do white people suggests the vital importance of choosing from a range of options a location that is geographically and politically conducive to "healthful improvement," especially as white supremacist policies are the main barrier to black political improvement—black well-being requires an environment wherein black selfhood/manhood can secure itself free from powerful white interference.

Delany certainly does not see a limit to blacks' capacity for improved condition and promotes the "perfectibility of intellect" notion to which "black elites and their allies gave great credence" (Rael 128). He warns his readers of the drastic effects of continued degradation. Without an outlet through which to exercise independence, Delany argues, the impulse to do so "degenerates" into a physiological condition of complacency in servitude. His use of the passive voice to characterize this unhealthy process serves as a warning to readers that they must exercise their physical and mental capacities if they are to achieve self-rule.

Highlighting the organizational role of power, Gregg Crane argues, "A wide variety of Northern and Southern intellectuals, authors, jurists, and politicians found in the very existence of slavery, war, class and racial domination ample proof that neither conscience nor consent but power actually structures and organizes law and society" (131). He identifies Delany as one of these intellectuals in whose writing power overshadows race as the focus of his politics as he adopts a "strategic positivism" to achieve his political goals. Crane writes, "Probably better than any white American, Martin Delany appreciated the degree to which power governed social and political association in nineteenth-century America despite pretensions to the contrary" (135). Delany's advocacy of black removal from white supremacist power of the United States and a perceived politically aligned Canada West altogether speaks to this. For Delany, Crane argues, "The failure of moral suasion to alter the nation's racist policy . . . made it clear that the only legal order capable of inscribing and protecting black Americans' rights would be grounded not in consent ('rights by sufferance') but in majority power" (140) because ethnic domination was the result of oppressors' self-interest and an imbalance of political and economic control (148). Shadd seems to an extent to share this understanding, and so deliberately calls on Black Americans to reject the United States in favor of the then-more-powerful British Empire. Her *Plea* is also an argument to garrison Canada West, Jamaica, and British Columbia against U.S. imperialist/slaveholding expansion. Furthermore she argues for the continued protection from slavery in Central and South America and the Caribbean: "The policy of the dominant party in the United States is to drive *free* coloured people out of the country, and to send them to Africa; and at the same time, to give the fullest guaranty to slaveholders, for the continuance of their system. To fulfill, to the letter, this latter, they make large calculations of a future interest in the West Indies, Honduras, and ultimately South America. They wish to consecrate to slavery and the slave power that portion of this continent; at the same time they deprecate the vicinity of freemen. To preserve those countries from the ravages of slavery should be the motive of their settlement by coloured men" (90). But Delany is neither satisfied with citizenship under a monarchy nor forestalling the expansion of slavery. He seeks a broader sense of self through black political autonomy.

Delany's work represents a call to dismantle the power structures on which racist thought sits comfortably. For Delany, racism is not the foundation of white political power; it is its beneficiary. In order for blacks to secure political autonomy, they must reject subjugation and the discourses, namely religion, medicine, and law that white supremacists use to support it. They must conceive themselves as embodying the promise of a politically relevant selfhood whose locus is in health and well-being apart from the U.S. government or colonizationist Africa.

These authors emphasize a connection between personal potential and physical fortitude and perceive the healthy black physique as free and unlimited in its capacity for individual development and self-betterment. They portray mobility and choice in exercising the ability to move freely, legally, and at will from one geographical location to another as a crucial component of autonomy that would allow black people in the New World to explore and fulfill their potential. Shadd's and Delany's ideological frames rework some of Plato's and Aristotle's notions of societal organization in their promotion of emigration, particularly these philosophers' "concepts of wholeness, unity, autonomy, [as well as] the *structure* of the state [as] . . . compared to the *anatomy* of the body" (Herzogenrath 2). Whereas Plato and Aristotle compare these notions to the body's anatomy, Shadd and Delany are specifically concerned with the black body's physiology, well-being, and centrality to community building. Referring to Aristotle's relation of freedom and well-being in his *Politics*, Foucault explains, "The individual's attitude toward himself, the way in which he ensured his own freedom with regard to himself, and the form of supremacy he maintained over himself were a contributing element to the well-being and good order of the city" (*Pleasure* 79). Shadd and Delany echo such a philosophy as they theorize and propagandize black individual and political independence.

The appeal for Black Americans of an autonomous condition of self-mastery in the context of antebellum U.S. race politics may seem obvious, but for Shadd and Delany its achievement was impossible within the confines of the slaveholding nation. Unlike many of their literary contemporaries, neither author had been enslaved, yet the Fugitive Slave Law rendered them vulnerable in new ways to slave laws while the colonizationists' alternative, for them as well as their primary readership, constituted another form of black regulation, degradation, and oppression. Asserting black political autonomy through the advocacy of emigration, Shadd and Delany rework the classical correlation between individual freedom and social order in their promotion of racial uplift and improved social condition. Among the practical goals they promote in their discourses of black betterment are access to education and realization of an ideal of self-reliance. Underpinning all practical and conceptual ideals is their philosophy of good health.

Although concepts of wholeness and autonomy have historically reproduced repressive and exclusionary orders—and Shadd's and Delany's writings in this respect certainly reassert such potentially problematic calculations in the context of black selfhood—here they also productively challenge the pathologization of the black body that informed much of the racism of their time. Each author depicts emigration's potential contribution to good health as vital to individual intellectual, political, and professional development as well as black social organization. Presenting themselves as among the professionals, intellectuals, and political leaders of their communities, Shadd and Delany converse with prevailing and emergent race and medical theories to identify and reject scientifically informed restrictions on the black physique and instead theorize its potential. Their public, printed entrance into emigration debates engages with proslavery and white supremacist theory and marks the centrality of health and well-being in the development of black political philosophy in the face of medical justification for the enslavement and oppression of people of African descent in North America.

Shadd's approaches succeeded to varying extents. Her advocacy of immigration to Canada certainly did not prevent further atrocities that resulted from the enactment of the Fugitive Slave Law (1850). Neither did the "privileges of British citizenship" secure for Black Americans in British North America a place free of racism. Nevertheless, as an activist, intellectual, and author, she helped build a substantial and politically influential black community in Canada West (now Ontario) that prospered to a greater extent than any other would in the area until well into the next century. And although Delany temporarily abandoned his emigrationist projects after the Civil War and turned his intellectual energies specifically toward a racially problematic ethnology, his *Condition* presented a bold argument that would evolve in later political writings and in his novel, all of which would garner for him a reputation as the father of Black Nationalism whose intellectual influence extends into our current time.

Shadd and Delany highlight health as a means of conversing with and rejecting contemporary race theory and establishing a nineteenth-century black politics of autonomy through a dynamic, comprehensive notion of the self. Their portrayals are reminiscent of classical ideals of self-mastery aspiring to a commensurable healthy, independent politic. They centralize the physique and white supremacist attempts to limit its potential. Insisting that blacks in the United States recognize access to well-being in securing individual, political, and professional autonomy through mobility, they pursue a model of healthy black selfhood through emigration, industry, intellect, and science. But as is the case in most political propaganda, their overtures and exhortations overlook reality as often as they are overshadowed by it. The theorization and pursuit of the ideal, healthy Black New World self in many ways grew out of the physical realities of the injured, ill, and disabled black self. Indeed the political and philosophical potential of such embodied notions of selfhood, in the accounts of formerly enslaved women to follow, it seems offer a more productive notion of what an ideal self might actually be.

→ 3 ←

The Self in Pain

Colonialism, Disability, and National Identity

MARY PRINCE, SOPHIA POOLEY, AND LAVINA WORMENY

The following nineteenth-century formerly enslaved women's narratives erode the demarcations of self and other on which modernity in general and modern slavery in particular relied, philosophically and practically. Dramatically different from Shadd's and Delany's later depictions of ideal healthy wholeness, these narratives of physical suffering and disability ultimately reveal a different sense of self, this time elusive and vulnerable not only for the enslaved but for enslavers as well. Through these depictions, the narrators also expose the complex ways in which empire, nation, and colony deploy race and health in their own projects of self-making and self-promotion. It is perhaps the tensions that these women reveal between white and black ideas about the interrelation of race and empire/nation/colony that so frustrated Martin Delany's imagining of self-governance in *Condition*. Rather than seek a sense of self that is whole and impervious, ultimately separate from white rule as Delany does, or protected midcentury by British law as Shadd does, the women featured here craft a sense of self that is amorphous, permeable, and vulnerable. It is a sense of self that is also a site of critique. Reading these accounts in conjunction with theories reimaging the physiological category of the human and the legal entity of the person opens up their texts to new ways of understanding the enslaved self and her physical and geopolitical environment, particularly through pain. This amorphous and oftentimes pained self, however, is also a site critical of the general nineteenth-century desire for individual and national security and autonomy. It prompts questions of the self as a category potentially beyond humanness, interrogates the implications of a body fused with labor and technology and the self as both product and producer. This chapter reads three nineteenth-century women's slave narratives produced in England and colonial Canada to focus on the narrators' varied depictions of physicality as means of critiquing colonial and (proto)national projects of self-definition and self-promotion.

Slave narratives can often be read as anthologies of physical and metaphorical scars presenting their narrators and other slaves as fragmented, materially and conceptually.[1] But such readings differ from these slave narrators' own characterizations of enslaved physicality, which is fluid rather than fragmented. The women slave narrators featured here undo demarcations ostensibly enclosing the self and contrast their editors' attempts at figuratively "carving up" and then repairing the black slave. The narrators offer a productive way for thinking more generally through the detrimental, impossible notion of the sovereign self that has shaped modern thought and, by extension, modern slavery.

Often slave narratives' white authentication represents an appropriation of black suffering. While it may seem intuitive that these mediators in an antislavery project would emphasize suffering, what happens in the narratives I present here is that they replicate the initial act of violence or even de-emphasize the experience, thereby reenacting another kind of violence by attempting to minimize slave suffering. White mediators here translate the pained, enslaved physique into a rhetorical system of popular antislavery tropes. In doing so, they further secure the self as *not* other. Even in service to an antislavery cause, their authenticating techniques undercut potentially more nuanced conceptions of self the narrators provide as well as reify the very distinctions on which the slave system relied: black and white, white and Indian, self and other.

Many scholars have addressed the prominent place the enslaved corporeal form occupies in slave literature. Critics such as Saidiya Hartman and Jenny Sharpe have underscored the limitations that white abolitionist ideology placed on black women's depictions of the body to ensure their complicity with the dominant society's religion- and gender-inflected moral standards. Hartman, for example, has identified how slave women's sexual abuse is read through a narrative of seduction that obscures exploitation, and Sharpe has argued that slave women have had to employ tactics of resistance and accommodation that reveal the limitations of antislavery discourse. Building on these ideas, however, I contend slave complicity functions problematically as the fugitive slaves are always already in a position of exclusion from the dominant society whose moral standards the narratives are meant to uphold. Furthermore, the women's uneasy physical and narrative entry into an already established England and emergent Canada reveals incongruities embedded in national projects of self-definition and construction. Ultimately, the narratives undermine the putatively solid demarcation between the dominant society and those it excludes, the lines drawn in the project of nation-building. Instead, these narrative depictions of physicality reveal a fluidity that wears away the boundary-making epistemological foundation on which modern slavery resided.

The narratives challenge social constructions of an England too pure to allow slavery and a colonial Canada that is morally and politically oppositional and therefore superior to the United States. Building on Hartman and Sharpe, I propose that the corporeal focus in black women's antislavery texts—though constrained by "cult of true womanhood" ideals and middle-class Christian editorial discretion—provides a space wherein the narrators develop an understanding of the enslaved body as a physical and analytical site, one performing functions that enable the author—to varying degrees—to critique white supremacist systems of rule and regulation and call into question the definition of such broad and disciplining categories as nation and colony, human and person. Most deeply, they question the sovereignty of the individual, the autonomous entity that defined modern freedom.

The narratives are by Mary Prince (1831), Sophia Pooley (1856), and Lavina Wormeny (1861). Of note first is the transcolonial African diasporic nature of literary production, which points to the heteronomy of modern slavery and abolition. As noted in the previous chapter, the amanuensis in England for West Indian Mary Prince's *History* was Susanna Strickland, later Moodie, a British subject who then immigrated to colonial Canada, her emigration narrative *Roughing It in the Bush* appearing in London in 1852.[2] Sophia Pooley gave her account of her enslavement to Benjamin Drew of the Boston Anti-Slavery Society. John P. Jewett & Co. subsequently published Pooley's piece as part of a collection titled *The Refugee: Narratives of Fugitive Slaves in Canada* (1856). This Boston publisher's titles included Harriet Beecher Stowe's *Uncle Tom's Cabin* (1852) as well as an expanded edition of Josiah Henson's narrative, which appeared in 1858 while he was living in colonial Canada. Finally, Lavina Wormeny escaped from slavery in Kentucky and told her story to black Montreal entrepreneur and landlord Thomas Cook; her narrative then appeared in the *Montreal Gazette* (1861). Thus the patterns of literary migrations here are reminiscent of the triangular routes of the slave trade and capture the force of the various individual, national, and colonial agendas involved in transcolonial African diasporic textual production. Although when compared with Prince's *History* the other two remain fairly obscure, they reveal much about the colony's involvement in and response to slavery in North America and about U.S. abolitionist interventions in colonial Canada. Furthermore, colonial Canadians defined Canada against the United States, and so could use slavery as a means of securing a proto-nationalism that articulated the colony as morally superior to the United States, which continued to enslave people long after British abolition and would eventually erupt into Civil War over it. They also had the support of the U.S. black activist and abolitionist community, who tended to celebrate Britain as a beacon of freedom.[3]

Two overall functions, however, of the American collection of Canadian slave narratives, *The Refugee*, are to support an American antislavery agenda and to promote the notion that blacks are capable colonists and that, in this case, a monarchy is superior to the U.S. republic. The title of Benjamin Drew's anthology in particular prompts me to ask how it might be useful to think about these women and their narratives through Giorgio Agamben's conception of the refugee: "a limit concept that radically calls into question the fundamental categories of the nation-state, from the birth-nation to the man-citizen link, and that thereby makes it possible to clear the way for a long-overdue renewal of categories in the service of a politics in which bare life is no longer separated and excepted, either in the state order or in the figure of human rights" (134). Extending from the work of Homi Bhabha and Shelley Wong's ideas about temporality authorizing the human and statelessness rendering one outside the developmental narrative, Nicole Waligora-Davis argues further that "to be a black refugee is to be excluded from modernity's narrative of the human" (xvi). Drawing on Agamben, she also allows that "the figure of the black refugee calls attention to the uses of freedom and citizenship as instruments of state alienation" (55). This revelatory figure that Waligora-Davis describes, who highlights the exclusion and oppression that freedom and citizenship discourses obscure, is how I think Prince, Pooley, and Wormeny—through forced transcolonial diasporic movements, national and colonial relocations, and their practices of critiquing these processes—reveal the critical potential of Agamben's refugee. Prince's, Pooley's, and Wormeny's narratives, through their rhetorics of physicality, assert a presence both representative of the detrimental individual and national effects of slavery and critical of national and colonial means of self-definition. They underscore anxieties about national or proto-national health and morality through which the formerly enslaved female physique, chronically ill and injured as well as strong and vital, becomes both revelatory and threatening. Indeed, contrary to antislavery rhetoric of the restorative effects of liberation, they demonstrate that ill-health follows them into freedom. Their discussions of disability offer a mode of understanding transcolonial African diasporic movements of fugitive slave women between colony and nation and expose disjunctures between colonial and national law, economics, medicine, and claims of national superiority. Ultimately, they demonstrate the conceptual and political vulnerability of systemic structures of oppression founded on boundaries that attempt to distinguish mind from body, human from person, self from other, nation from colony.

Becoming Prince

Mary Prince's accounts of her labors at several key transcolonial sites are most striking for their conception of the permeable relation between the enslaved and her work, particularly in the salt ponds of Turks Island.[4] Prince first articulates this notion when she depicts the product (salt) literally consuming her physically. Here the pained, leaky body of the enslaved extends beyond its physical enclosure (the skin) and into the products of its labor just as labor and its fruits penetrate that same boundary. Esposito has noted that in a Lockean model, "Just as work is an extension of the body, so is property an extension of work, a sort of prosthesis" (*Bíos* 128). Prince's status as a slave, of course, prevents her from owning property and therefore precludes property from becoming a prosthetic extension of her work; however, in her situation labor is an extension of her body *and vice versa*. This two-way traffic between body and labor signals the permeability of self and work that makes it difficult to tell where one ends and the other begins.

The narrative notes that Prince's owners attempted to regulate her taking of sleep (15, 21) and food (19, 25) as she nursed her owners' children and later worked in the salt ponds of Turks Island. The deprivation of sleep and food seem at first like physical, externally imposed processes that regulate the production of goods, but as the narrative progresses, we can see such processes take on a more internal imposition as the line between producer and the product becomes obscured. The descriptions of Prince's work for Mr. D—— in Turks Island begins: "Our feet and legs, from standing in the salt water for so many hours, soon became full of dreadful boils, which eat down in some cases to the very bone, afflicting the sufferers with great torment. We came home at twelve; ate our corn soup . . . went back to our employment . . . shoveled up the salt in large heaps, . . . washed the pickle from our limbs and cleaned the barrows" (19). The description of the boils that "eat" away the skin "to the very bone" provides an image of the salt ponds imitative of her ingestion of the "soup." As her flesh absorbs the salt in which she stands, there is a conflation of producer and product; the salt consumes her skin. Here we see an explicit example of what Gillian Einstein and Margrit Shildrick refer to as the postconventional body, quite in contrast to the white, able-bodied, masculine norm, "autonomous and self-owned" (293) or more recently Allewaert's parahuman, "an identificatory category that recalls yet is also beside and after the human and human rights" (110). Far from "autonomous and self-owned" and challenging the enclosed constitution of the valorized human, Prince's body in the salt mines demonstrates its penetrability, the porousness of its borders. The concepts of the postconventional and parahuman body offer a way of thinking about alternative senses of self, which Prince and the other women narrators of this chapter seem to craft, despite white medical authenticators' and editors' best attempts to describe them through discourses of the conventional or white, able-bodied, masculine norm.

Prince's description continues, "When we were ill, let our complaint be what it might, the only medicine given to us was a great bowl of hot salt water, with salt mixed with it, which made us very sick" (20–21). In this instance, the product she produces (salt) becomes a kind of cure-all, which is ingested and actually makes her ill. Thus the entanglement of salt as a product external to the physique of the slave who produces it, with its corrosive properties when applied to the skin, begins to invade the enslaved body and then later becomes totally internalized as an antidote (if poisonous) to any illness. Here the product is indistinguishable from the producer as it eats and is eaten. The distinction between internal and external is blurred. The body's physical experience of suffering and sickness fuses with the product of its labor to render the body and the product more than an extension of each other, as Esposito might explain it; they become one and the same. So first we see here in Prince's depictions of her suffering an image of the permeable, postconventional body that calls into question the veracity of the distinct, enclosed, whole human and highlights a particular vulnerability of the corporeal form in the context of colonial slavery.

Elizabeth Grosz's work is particularly useful in situating the human in a broader context, reimagining the limits of this category and opening up Prince's text to new interpretations of the self. She returns to Darwin and posits that evolutionary theory provides a way to understand humanity as fleeting, as part of a process of becoming (as opposed to, perhaps, being). In her estimation, the inventions of political and social organization "are forms of self-transformation and part of evolutionary becoming," which place "human accomplishments . . . as its most recent elaboration . . . that life has enabled" (24). Here Grosz extends the concept of the human very much in the way Einstein, Shildrick, and Allewaert do. She sees the human not as half of a binary category that positions the human and animal in opposition, relegating the latter as inferior and thus to be "got over" or "surpassed," but as part of a continuum of "becoming." Here the human is continually becoming, elaborating lines of life. She continues, "The human, when situated as one among many, is no longer in the position of speaking for and authorizing the analysis of the animal as other . . . and no longer takes on the right to name, to categorize, the rest of the world but is now forced . . . to become attuned to nature it was always part of but had only aimed to master and control" (24). What Grosz depicts is a much more amorphous concept of a constantly becoming entity that *becomes* in much the way the rest of nature does. In Grosz's reading of Darwin, the hierarchically ordered self/other (privileged human vs. animal/brute) binary breaks down. Prince's depictions of the body's fusion with the product of its labor make indistinguishable the borders demarcating the human from other substances. In later descriptions of others' pain, she blurs the distinctions between human and animal as well, as we'll see in a scene where she depicts maggots consuming a man's flesh, furthermore questioning the privileging of the classical, conventional, autonomous human being.

Prince's discourse about physical labor in the salt ponds is at once medically and conceptually critical of the system that threatens to corrode the very human bodies it depends upon for the production of its goods. The conflation of production and disability dramatizes Prince's argument that regulation of the enslaved body is actually debilitating. Such implications thereby potentially reinforce abolitionist arguments of the expendability of the enslaved to the enslavers. Prince's narrative itself is incongruous with antislavery contentions regarding such expendability—as Sharpe and others have argued—because her next owners, the Woods, refuse to release her despite the illnesses that limit her ability to work for them and the many opportunities they have to sell her. Instead, the narrative depicts slave labor's wearing down of the enslaved physique, which owners refuse to release even as the slave's material and productive capacities diminish. The reason has to do with the Woods' interpretation of slave character. The couple committed uneasily to an understanding of Prince as their property, absolutely, with which they might do as they please. Prince explains how on one occasion "he cursed and swore at me dreadfully, and said he would never sell my freedom" (33). Selling her because of illness or debility—never mind freeing her—would jeopardize the security of this arbitrary category, property, in which they have tried to fit her.

Dramatizing the permeability of the slave body to the product of Prince's labor and frustrating her owners' absolute categorization of her as human property, Prince shows us that slave subjectivity is materially as well as conceptually amorphous. Imagining distinctions between the categories of the human and the person reveals the production of social hierarchies. Esposito estimates, "On the one hand, person is the more general category since it encompasses the entire human species. On the other hand, it is the prism through which the human species is separated in the hierarchical division between types defined precisely by their constitutive difference" (*Dispositif* 22). More particularly with regard to race in the gradations of humanness, Alexander Weheliye argues that "the flesh epitomizes a central modern assemblage of racialization that highlights how bare life is not only a product of previously established distinctions but also, and more significantly, aids in the perpetuation of hierarchical categorizations along the lines of nationality, gender, religion, race, culture, sexuality, and so on" (43). In the early to mid-nineteenth century we can see this rubric wherein slaves are recognized as human, but they do not enjoy civil rights of legal persons, though they are considered persons in criminal legal contexts and implicitly protected by the *Habeas Corpus* Act (at least until its suspension in the United States). As distinct from the human, the "person" that underpins that act is, in Esposito's and Weheliye's formulations, the category that makes possible the hierarchical gradations of personhood and humanness in which political, legal, and social constructs invest. Prince is certainly understood as human even in the juridical understanding of her as property. As a person, she is also property. In both contexts, however, she is a human. Furthermore, even this distinction blurs later in England where she is legally free.

The logic behind Prince's argument that slave subjectivity is materially as well as conceptually amorphous leads me to question a medical anomaly that has long baffled historians and scientists. In the sugar colonies, it is reported that fertility rates among enslaved women were strikingly low when compared to those of the United States. In a contemporary study, Nott explains "that while blacks in the United States have increased *tenfold*, those of the British West Indies have decreased in the proportion of five to two" ("Acclimation" 387). In a much more recent study, Jenny Sharpe argues that such a phenomenon was long attributed to the exercise of enslaved women's knowledge of, and agency over, their own reproductive systems. She quotes sociologist Marietta Morrissey, who argues such thinking is "the product of a 'European and North American fascination with African women's reputed sexual and healing powers'" (xv). Historian Barbara Bush (1990) cites and discounts several other reasons for low fertility rates on smaller sugar plantations, such as inbreeding, dietary deficiencies, and disease (Karasch, 1987), malnutrition (Dancer, 1809), and epidemics (Craton, 1978). Prince's description of the salt ponds, though, points us to another theory that might open up the low fertility debates and widen this critique of conceptual distinctions of selfhood.

By showing how the "invasion" of salt into the interior of the enslaved body blurs the demarcation between producer and product, Prince's *History* prompts me to ask if the same process is possible with sugar. None of the theories noted—those that cite deficiency, malnutrition, and sexual habits as reasons for low fertility in the sugar colonies—has proposed that it may be the ingestion of the product, sugar, itself that shares the strongest correlation with diminished fertility rates. As the salt literally eats away the exterior of the enslaved body in Prince's narrative, so might the sugar in the colonies have invaded the interiors of enslaved women's bodies and limited their capacities to reproduce. As recently as the mid-1990s, fertility science posited a connection between metabolism and fertility proposing that a family history of diabetes may coincide with diminished fertility.[5] Correspondingly, high rates of diabetes found among "genetically similar African-origin populations within Cameroon and from Jamaica and Britain" have been related to genetics and environment and suggest a potential correlation between sugar production and glucose intolerance.[6] Thus the *History*'s consideration of the body's physical identification with the product it produces suggests to me a possible similar medical reason for low fertility rates in sugar-producing areas of the Caribbean during the eighteenth and nineteenth centuries. In each situation, the fusion of product and producer renders the latter unproductive or less productive, manually or maternally. Such merging of self and product here also implies a transgenerational effect so that the permeability of borders extends temporally and physically into future generations. Prince's physical experience in the salt ponds and the potential connection between sugar production and low fertility can help explain the ways in which enslaved women understood their own physicality. To what extent were enslaved women identified or did they identify themselves with medical conditions they purported to experience as a result of the work they performed in order to produce the products that held such a close bodily relationship to their own identities?

Another form of labor that Prince details in the narrative and that causes her considerable pain is washing clothes. Literary scholar Kathryn Temple has discussed the washing Prince did in England as "physically more difficult, more debilitating than salt mining on Turks Island" and acknowledges that "Washing was a pervasive problem in English culture: the English themselves devoted any number of popular songs and rhymes to the fact that they hated doing the laundry. . . . Thus it provided a powerful symbol for slavery, one that ensured immediate recognition and sympathy" (189–90). Debilitation from excessive work transfers from the colonies to the nation in Prince's discussions of the rheumatism from which she suffered while in the "servitude" of the Woods in England. Illness here characterizes transcolonial physical experience and functions as a trope of slavery carried onto free soil:

> The doctor had told my mistress long before I came from the West Indies, that I was a sickly body and the washing did not agree with me. But Mrs. Wood would not release me from the tub, so I was forced to do as I could. I grew worse, and could not stand to wash. I was then forced to sit down with the tub before me, and often through pain and weakness was reduced to kneel or to sit down on the floor to finish my task. When I complained to my mistress of this, she only got into a passion as usual, and said washing in hot water could not hurt any one;—that I was lazy and insolent, and wanted to be free of my work; but that she would make me do it. (32)

First, the West Indian doctor's identification of Prince's body as "sickly" professionally authenticates her condition. At this point in the narrative, the injuries Prince sustained in the salt mines have developed into a chronic illness that worsens in England as again her body becomes indistinguishable from the painful work it must perform. Elaine Scarry has argued that the body in pain begins to view itself as the agent of its suffering (53); however, the narrative consistently reminds the reader that the agent of Prince's pain is the unrelenting work of washing she is forced to do and connects her suffering physique to its labor—the extension of the sense of self as a category beyond the conventional concept of the enclosed human.

Contesting Testimonies

Despite Prince's fusing of the pained body with its work, editors' attempts to authenticate the narratives threaten to eclipse this fusion. The white-authored authenticating devices appended to or embedded in slave narratives, rather than reinforce the narrators' connection between body and labor, reify the separation between the woman and her work as well as the putative and hierarchical distinctions between self and other, white and black, free and fugitive even as they purport to argue for the former slave's admission to the world of the dominant society. As a result of proslavery tropes' often successful denigration of slave character as deceptive, lascivious, and slothful, antislavery advocates adopted methods of verification in which whites "testified" to the authenticity of published abolitionist material. In this context, medical and legal discourse integrates uneasily as the two emerging professions depend on each other practically and rhetorically. The writer's use of juridical discourse in antislavery literature metaphorically positions the reader as the jury in slavery's trial (DeLombard, *Slavery on Trial*). In keeping with such a model, slave narratives depended upon evidence of the abuses they claimed. Coinciding with the increased use of physician testimony in real courtrooms, the literature often appended testimony from medical doctors or other practitioners who authenticated narrators' claims of abuse. In the text, readers witness abuse as mediators document for them cruelties they see evident on the formerly enslaved body. In such narratives, the body becomes a text within a text wherein the abused and documented slave body supports the abolitionist meta-narrative of slavery as a moral, if not legal, crime.

The two disciplines of medicine and law, furthermore, become fungible in their authenticating roles. The narratives hint at the inescapable interrelatedness of the medical and legal in theory and practice. The appended and embedded medico-legal authentications provide a stark contrast to the narrators' own configurations of enslaved physicality and their own senses of self. The white-authored insertions support the conventional modern demarcations defining an enclosed, sovereign self whereas the narrators call such distinctions into question. Instead, they present a sense of self that is permeable, vulnerable, and interdependent for both black and white. Their figurations are perhaps less an ideal, and disability theorists would reject the value of this ideal anyway; rather, they offer productive and ethical modes of self-conceptualization that do not rely on fantasies of perfect health.

Regardless, it seems, of black women's ability to construct the self in ways that challenge dominant medical and legal notions of blackness, white authenticators attempted to read the marked body of the slave to explain what the slave herself was forbidden to tell in a court of law or to verify what the slave had told in her narrative. Literary scholar Janice Schroeder, with reference to West Indian colonial law and British parliamentary debates during the 1820s regarding flogging, argues, "Since a slave was not legally permitted to provide testimony on oath in a court of law against his or her master . . . the traces of punishment on the body of the slave were proposed to speak for her" (269). Schroeder posits that such an appropriation of the enslaved voice by her own body (and its subsequent use as antislavery propaganda) represents one in a list of external appropriations her voice underwent in the course of the production of slave narratives.

The list in each of my examples includes an antislavery editor, amanuensis, and contributors (often understood as medical or legal authorities—if laypeople) of appended materials. If Schroeder is right that the body was to speak for the enslaved, we can also read the category of "narrator" as having been subdivided into body and voice. The goal of antislavery propaganda was to present the body and voice acting as one, but abolitionists saw an imperative to provide visible "proof" that could verify the voice and, in doing so, figuratively anatomized the narrator into these two parts despite the antislavery insistence that the stories were "related by" or "from the lips of" the person they were "dividing." Referring to Pringle's wife's appended examination of Mary Prince's body, Schroeder continues, "Prince's scars become Mrs. Pringle's evidence since it is she who inspects Prince's body for the physical signs of the truth of her testimony and then appends her name to her statement or reading of Prince's body . . . [and] asserts a rhetorical measure of control over the scars she discovers and interprets for her audience" (270). Here the scar translates into textual evidence, medical, legal, and literary. In Prince's situation, it is not a doctor who supplies the medical examination appended to her narrative, yet the Pringles use juridically inflected medical testimony to support allegations of Prince's physical abuse, treatment to which she could not legally testify in court.

Not only does Mrs. Pringle's examination of Prince restage the violence enacted on the former slave, but the very use of Prince's body to provide proof also figuratively splits her by separating the body from the testifying voice that is supposed to authenticate the text. For example, Mrs. Pringle writes to a secretary of the "Birmingham Ladies' Society for Relief of Negro Slaves" that "the whole of the back part of [Prince's] body is distinctly scarred, and, as it were, *chequered*, with the vestiges of severe floggings" (64). As Mario Cesareo argues, Pringle fails conclusively to "testify about [her scars'] origins" and thereby "point[s] toward her suspect status" (116). She does, however, attempt to draw conclusions about them. Her first description is of Prince's back and, implicit in it, is Mrs. Pringle's privileged perspective, for she can see an area of Prince's body that would be most difficult for Prince to see. Pringle explains, "There are many large scars on other parts of her person, exhibiting an appearance as if the flesh had been deeply cut, or lacerated with *gashes*, by some instrument wielded by most unmerciful hands" (64). The image of the examination calls to mind the scenes of violence in which Prince stood, most likely stripped naked, with her back to her abuser. The scene replicates or restages the violence as Prince's naked body reveals what she cannot see when Prince and the examiners stand back to front, respectively. Therefore, the examiner not only appropriates Prince's body as a testament to human suffering but, to an extent, re-creates the scene for the reader, after Prince herself has recounted her sufferings in her own narrative. The appended examination imposed onto Prince's narrative becomes proof of pain. It also functions as a rhetorical severing of Prince's physique from her voice, which it then "sutures" back together.

This compendium of physical and metaphorical scars presents Prince as fragmented, materially and conceptually, in a way that differs from Prince's own characterization of enslaved physicality, which is fluid rather than fragmented. Historian Walter Johnson has demonstrated how in the slave market setting "the racialized meaning of [the slave] body, the color assigned to it, and the weight given to its various physical features in describing it depended upon the examiner rather than the examined" (157). Even in an antislavery context, Mrs. Pringle's and later Dr. Reddy's and Benjamin Drew's accounts reveal a stark contrast between what the white racialized gaze observes and what the slave narrator sees. The authenticator's interpretation of the enslaved self and the understanding of the examined self demonstrate two very different schemas of black selfhood. Prince's undoing of demarcations ostensibly enclosing the self—in contrast to Mrs. Pringle's "carving up" and repairing of the self—offers a productive way for thinking more generally through the detrimental, impossible notion of the sovereign self.

Sophia Pooley's narrative of slavery in colonial Canada also contains a verification of bodily injury resulting from abuse, which contraposes Pooley's image of enslaved physicality. Unlike Prince's *History*, in this narrative the authentication is interjected, not appended. The collection's editor, Benjamin Drew, provides the supplemental information. Pooley was the slave of Joseph Brant, an aboriginal leader in Upper Canada, and reported the abuses she suffered at the hands of his third wife: "She would tell me in Indian to do things, and then hit me with any thing that came to hand, because I did not understand her. I have a scar on my head from a wound she gave me with a hatchet; and this long scar over my eye is where she cut me with a knife. The skin dropped over my eye; a white woman bound it up" (194). Following the account of the violence and subsequent medical attention Pooley received, there appears a square-bracketed insertion into the narrative in which the editor states, "[The scars spoken of were quite perceptible, but the writer saw many worse looking cicatrices of wounds not inflicted by *Indian* savages, but by civilized (?) men]" (194). Here the editor penetrates the narration itself and, in an attempt to quantify and compare the abuses of aboriginal and white slaveholders, he authenticates the claim of abuse with a verification of physical evidence that actually contradicts the description Pooley gives of the wound's severity. He also manipulates tropes of Indian savagery and white civilization to underscore the brutality of white slave owners so that Pooley's narrative fits with the collection's antislavery ideology that would be pitched to a northern U.S. readership to stoke abolitionist argument against southern claims of slavery's gentility and black inferiority. Drew's collection implicitly asks: If slavery is gentle, why do blacks flee? If blacks are inferior, how is it they form flourishing communities under a supposedly oppressive monarchy?

As in Prince's example, the authentication in Pooley's narrative represents an appropriation of suffering; however, the mediator for the latter does not emphasize suffering or replicate the initial act of violence, but rather he de-emphasizes the experience and thereby reenacts a different kind of violence by attempting to minimize her suffering. He imposes a demarcation between white and aboriginal slaveholders with respect to their brutality whereas Pooley implies there is little general distinction among groups, only among individuals and without much regard for race. In both instances, white mediators convert the pained, enslaved physique into a rhetorical system of popular antislavery tropes, further securing the self as *not* other. Even in service to an antislavery cause, their authenticating techniques undermine the more nuanced conceptions of self that the narrators provide and reify the very distinctions between black and white, white and Indian, self and other, on which slavery relied.

Lavina Wormeny's narrative also includes an appended authentication of suffering and provides an example of medical evidence that, unlike the previous two examples, purports—at first—to have been furnished by someone outside the narrative's editorial purview and who is a medical doctor. Such an example presents a much more detailed and comprehensive account of Wormeny's physique and allows us to consider the role of the physician in antislavery promotion and to ask: Where did such layers of interpretation leave the original [?] body of the enslaved woman?

Each stage of narrative appropriation signifies a removal of the enslaved subject from herself to the point at which the body, very much alive during the examinations, becomes in description a kind of corpse. Reddy begins his report: "On making examination I found her body very much distorted, her spine curved towards the right side, and the ribs forced completely in the same direction, having a very bulged appearance" (165). Reddy's medical account can be read as reducing Wormeny's body to a collection of injuries. Furthermore, there is no mention of the pain Wormeny likely felt at the time of the examination as a result of repeated injury. He continues, "A V shaped piece has been slit out of each ear; there is a depression on the right parietal bone where it had been fractured and is now very tender to the touch" (165). Here the touch and its sensation of bone tenderness belong to the physician, not to the subject of the examination.[7] In this way, Wormeny is disembodied during the exam, as her senses are not part of the report, which includes details of broken teeth, a severed finger, branded skin, and scars to the head, back, ankles, and the soles of her feet. It is somewhat ironic that one purpose of the inclusion of the doctor's report was ostensibly to engender sympathy for the woman for whom Cook was attempting to raise funds, to make apparent her human suffering, but that the means of achieving these ends required her figurative mortification and the diminishment of her actual physical—not to mention emotional or mental—pain in order for readers to believe Reddy's and by extension Cook's and Wormeny's claims. The report's purposes are to distance medical observation from abolitionist sentimentalism while simultaneously supporting an antislavery agenda that relies on the reader's sympathetic physical response, usually tears.

In the medical account, the enslaved body loses a portion of its live, embodied humanness and by extension a measure of the subject's sense of self ("sense" here quite literally) even as we might assume the putative purpose of the foregoing slave narrative is to create and justify such an animate, sympathetic self. However, Reddy's description functions to (1) distance the reader from Wormeny, (2) further distinguish between black and white, and (3) secure a separation from the grotesque, debilitated body of the fugitive slave. All told, his account reifies demarcations that fear and pity inspire. The fugitive occupies an amorphous, uncertain place in the proto-nation, and her story emphasizes the elusive nature of her sense of self within the dominant culture, yet Reddy's professional account "corrects" the instability of Wormeny's embodied self through techniques at once culturally evocative yet professionally paratactic that remove it from the audience's own sense of self.

For example, Dr. John Reddy's report of Wormeny's physique reads almost like a postmortem examination. His account represents the third layer of interpretation of Wormeny's experience. First there is Wormeny's oral account, transcribed and then told using the third-person voice, which includes—as in Sophia Pooley's narrative—interjected notes verifying the existence of her injuries, after which (as in Prince's narrative) appears an appended report of her examined body, followed by an editorial note. Reddy's report "covers" Wormeny's body more thoroughly than Mrs. Pringle's account of Prince or Drew's interjection regarding Pooley. Whereas Mrs. Pringle focuses most detailed attention on the appearance of Prince's back, thereby presenting a kind of rhetorical replication of white supremacist violence, Reddy's examination is far more detailed—as one might expect in a physician's report—and beyond imitating a violence, it stylistically de-animates the subject in the process. Yet, to emphasize the dis-placement of Wormeny's body, his forensic anatomy is crucial to detailing the awfulness of slavery.

Scholarship on nineteenth-century medical case histories suggests that Reddy's work was in keeping with stylistic trends in medical literature. Harriet Nowell-Smith refers to Rudolph Virchow's *Post-Mortem Examinations* (1846), which argued that "'Pathological anatomy . . . is the most universal' of medical practices because it allows for the elimination of superfluous considerations, extraneous details, and erroneous causal suppositions" (51). Autopsy writing influenced the paratactic style of the case history. Nowell-Smith argues that in the latter, "details follow one after another, connected by the progress of either the disease or the medical intervention." Further, she contends, "Parataxis gives the impression of simplicity, of directness, and of immediacy and so promotes, by pretending to preserve, the truth of an account" (58). We can see Reddy's anticipation of such writing in his examination of Wormeny. The paratactic stylistic approach, however, largely removes the living Wormeny from the account. This is not surprising given the genre of autopsy writing from which the style derived. Furthermore, Nowell-Smith notes how statistics stripped away individuality in medical writing by 1840 to an even greater extent. She argues, "Much as autopsy had generalized the dead, the invention of statistics in the nineteenth century reduced the living to uniformity" as subjects such as "birth, death, and disease" were quantified (59). Therefore the conventions of medical writing apparent in Reddy's description function similarly to Mrs. Pringle's. They figuratively replicate the actual violence enacted on Wormeny's body in slavery. By multiply rhetorically fragmenting (or vivisecting) these physiques, the appended examinations reduce their living subjects to an almost lifeless state.

The dehumanizing effect of medical writing is a fairly common complaint about scientific objectivity in general, but here, there is something particular about the account's relation to the medical profession, to the colony's relation to the United States and most importantly, to slavery. During a time of anxiety about the status of the medical profession in colonial Canada and the qualifications of physicians, no doubt Reddy's own reputation was at stake in his support of the fugitive's story. Beyond that, the emergent medical establishment's interest in distancing itself from American empirics or quacks, not to mention its desire to remove itself from the republic's practice of slaveholding during the onset of the Civil War, all provide motive for Reddy's writing to be as consistent with the trends of his profession as possible and to convey the expected level of scientific objectivity that was associated with the truth. His testimony was crucial within the juridical model of antislavery literature and functioned to translate the possibility of abuse that Wormeny's body supplied into proof of it. His objectivity and separation from the sentimentalism of abolitionism were necessary as the validity of Wormeny's account and Cook's retelling of it rest on the authority of the doctor.

Following Reddy's description, Thomas Cook notes that Wormeny is still receiving medical attention from the doctor and continues to explain that "we [Cook and Reddy] have omitted many particulars communicated to us by the woman, the many *ruses* she practiced, counterfeiting madness, inability to walk &c., &c.," (Mackey 166).[8] The acknowledgment of Wormeny's performance of illness and disability reanimates her after Reddy's physical examination. It affirms her agency in her own escape and nods to the two ways of reading slave injury that Ariela Gross discusses: that scars can be read as indications of the owner/overseer's bad character or of the slave's.[9] By acknowledging Wormeny's capacity for cunning (which appears in her transcribed narrative), Cook potentially undermines the validity of the doctor's report. Such undercutting might also account for the removal of Wormeny's agency in Reddy's description, as the examination attempts to provide uncompromising proof of her injuries. Apart from these interventions, I believe Wormeny's inclusion of her ruses actually functions as a form of critique in the sense Gross outlines.

Deception has long been understood as a means for the enslaved to avoid work, and we might also recall its categorization under medico-legal designations of "vices of character." Deception's use attests to slaves' awareness of the commodified body's tactical potential. Wormeny's narrative reveals another dimension of such tactics. Her owner knocked her teeth out because she had bitten off part of his nose (164). This is the only act of violence against her owner that the narrative mentions. This form of equivocal resistance is symbolic. Historian Kenneth Greenberg, in his analysis of language and gestures of honor in the Old South, has demonstrated how a man's nose "was the most prominent physical projection of [his] character" (86). He explains, "One of the greatest insults for a man of honor, then, was to have his nose pulled or tweaked. Actually, nose pulling was just another, more aggressive form of accusing a man of lying. It was the ultimate act of contempt toward the most public part of a man's face, an extreme expression of disdain for a man's projected mask" (87). In this context, Wormeny's inclusion of this ruse, biting off a piece of her owner's nose, initiates (or perhaps responds in) a physical "conversation." She engages with southern codes of honor in which her gesture is the ultimate insult to the public image of her owner. Furthermore, her act is much more severe than the "pulling" and "tweaking" of noses among southern men of honor that Greenberg discusses. Wormeny has presumably scarred her owner, for she has bitten off part of his nose. Not only has she insulted the most public part of his face, she has "deformed" it. In doing so, she has invaded his flesh with her teeth. We imagine a mingling of their blood, mucous, and saliva during Wormeny's act that blurs the physical distinction between slaveholder and slave. Symbolically, her gesture not only insults her owner's public image but invades the security of his physical identity as separate from her as well. Furthermore, if we read his nose as part of a mask in the sense Esposito thinks about the distinction between human and person, Wormeny's gesture then works at reducing her owner's individual personhood to a disruptive comingling of their humanness.

Greenberg has emphasized that assaults on noses indicated less about the issue over which men might be in dispute and functioned more to insult character. The act's subtext of dishonesty and poor character perhaps speaks to Wormeny's inclusion of it in the narrative as her physical actions perform a critique, but they carry consequences for her: she loses her teeth, the instruments of her assault, which physically and symbolically challenge the distinction between owner and slave. Whereas there might have been a duel over the incident if Wormeny were a southern man of honor, she is an enslaved woman; there is no duel, just a physical retaliation.

I want to examine another way of reading Wormeny's gesture and the response it garners. The phrase "cut off his nose to be revenged of his face" dates back to the eighteenth century (OED). Of course, it is impossible to know if Wormeny was familiar with the saying, and it is possible that there is no more to this allusion than the simple fact that she indeed bit off part of her owner's nose, but it is worth considering how she may have interpreted the physical punishment she suffered as a result of her actions.

The phrase means "to disadvantage oneself in the course of trying to disadvantage another (usually with the implication that a person knows the likely consequences of his or her actions beforehand)" (OED). If we read Wormeny's act against this definition and consider that she bit off her master's nose to spite *his* face, we can interpret the defiant gesture as her understanding that master-slave physical abuse functions to the detriment of the slaveholder who requires the labor of that body he has abused and rendered, at times, unfit to work. We can also understand the act as representing her awareness that by injuring him she injures herself—indeed "to be revenged of *her* face"—as retaliation will undoubtedly follow in the form of physical punishment. Either way, Wormeny's act and the telling of it symbolize and thereby expose the slaveholder's somewhat paradoxical practice of injuring laboring bodies. It also underscores the limited recourse the enslaved had upon injury because retaliation brought revenge. The incident also alludes to the deliberateness with which owners injured their slaves. Wormeny's act did more than defy and injure her owner. The account of this symbolic gesture within the code of southern honor and in light of the phrase "cut off his nose to be revenged of his face" performs a critique of the owner and, by extension, the counterproductive and cruel practices of slaveholders in general, regardless of the southern medical writings that argued otherwise. If we accept Wormeny's violence as critique, we can see that she uses her body in this instance to enact both physical and analytical functions despite the corporeal price she pays for that critique.[10]

By responding to violence through a violent act, Wormeny demonstrates Walter Benjamin's contention that law is grounded in violence and that "all . . . lawmaking violence, which we may call 'executive,' is pernicious. Pernicious, too, is the law-preserving, 'administrative' violence that serves it" (252). Wormeny's act falls outside the law that was made to produce the possibility that slaveholders may legally enact violence upon slaves and which functioned to preserve the owner's protection from retaliation. Thus Wormeny's act represents an equivocal means of resistance, as it must accommodate punishment; however, the gesture's symbolism underscores that very equivocation and critiques the nature of legally sanctioned white violence by undermining the putative security it enjoys.

Despite the ruses to which Cook alludes and which appear in Wormeny's transcribed narrative, he yet renders her passive. He writes, "But we have given the recital in as tangible a form as we could from her account, which coming from a poor ignorant negress,—unable to read or write—was necessarily disconnected, but in which nevertheless after a thorough cross-examination, no contradiction could be discovered" (166). Immediately following Cook's description of Wormeny's "ruses," his editorial returns to familiar abolitionist tropes of the "poor ignorant negress" to characterize Wormeny and the juridical rhetoric of the "thorough cross-examination" to reassert the validity of the narrative and presumably to inspire pity (and generosity) in the readers of the *Montreal Gazette*.

Here, as in the narratives of Prince and Pooley, the medical reports read the enslaved female body and thereby uphold the abolitionist metanarrative of the moral crime of slavery. They also reveal, through layers of white authentication—as Frederick Douglass points out in the introduction to *My Bondage and My Freedom* (9)—that the slave is also on trial when recounting his or her stories. The combination of medical and juridical discourses applies familiar tropes to the enslaved body, which supplement the reporters' anatomization of suffering. As the narrators themselves do, the editors and doctors (both actual and lay) consider the body physiologically and metaphorically to support an abolitionist agenda; however, while purporting to advance the antislavery cause, the editors and doctors restrict the narrative agency of the formerly enslaved and through their techniques reify the arbitrary boundaries excluding her from full access to the privileges of personhood (even though at the time of narration she was legally entitled to them) in a similar way, rhetorically, as the institution and its supporters did.

But how is it possible to read defiance to such exclusionary techniques through narrators' mediated accounts of suffering? One way is to look for places where these narratives infuse medical discourse into the text and distinguish it from the interjected or appended accounts. In these instances the women's rhetorics of health carve out space to conceptualize an embodied sense of self.

Lavina Wormeny's transcribed account, of the three, focuses the reader's attention on herself the most; however, there is still an instance in which the physical suffering and deformation of another appears.[11] The part of the narrative referring to her husband explains: "The poor man had had on his legs for two years irons which had grown into the flesh; these impeded him in his flight and caused [his] capture" (163). The description of the leg irons that had grown into the man's flesh reminds us of the tangible fusion of the instrument of suffering and the bodily experience of it. For example, in Prince, we saw the fusion of product and producer in the salt's corrosion and consumption of her body. Here we can read the body as consuming the technology of captivity so that the restraint and individual become one. In this instance the body begins to incorporate the restraint. In contrast to the notion of work as a kind of prosthetic or extension of the body performing it, here the reverse seems to be the case. We can imagine the physique growing around the irons as a similar obscuring of distinctions between the self and the technology of work and confinement. As the restraint "deforms" the human body, the latter incorporates it, appropriates it.

Such a description parallels the account of Wormeny's experience in the "buck."[12] The narrative defines the term: "This was doubling her in two, until her legs were passed over her head, where they were kept by a stick passed across the back of her neck. This violence was the cause of the distortion mentioned in the doctor's statement" (163–64). The depiction of Wormeny's suffering as a result of the buck coheres with appended or interjected medical discourse: an account of pain and brutality, followed by an authenticating note that matches visible physical injury with the narrative account of it. However, when the "poor man" is the subject, there is no doctor or other white person to verify the man's wounds and subsequent illness—the reader must accept Wormeny's account and take her word for his injury and illness if he or she is to believe it. During the account of the man's physical injury and deformation, Wormeny acquires a narrative agency in which she testifies to another's pain in much the same way the doctors and editors have done in her narrative and others.

Sophia Pooley's narrative, by contrast, devotes much attention to descriptions of others and very little to her own suffering, which the editor further minimizes. The appearance of Joseph Brant and his mother is the subject of much detail: "Brant was only half Indian: his mother was a squaw.... She was an old body; her hair was quite white. Brant was a good looking man—quite portly. He was as big as Jim Douglass who lived here in the bush, and weighed two hundred pounds" (193). The narrative continues to describe Brant's dress, which alternated between Indigenous and Anglo depending on whether he was among aboriginals or whites: the "long silver ornaments" (193) he wore in his ears, and his bracelets. Here the body wears the racially and ethnically fluid identity, the self Brant performs. Furthermore, the recollection of Brant, in addition to obscuring racial and ethnic demarcations, challenges the stereotypes of the cruel slaveholder and brutalized slave as well as assumptions about the philosophical and political opposition of American and colonial Canadian approaches to slavery.

The focus on Pooley's owner represents a distinct break from the other narratives contained in Drew's collection, which generally depict examples of cruelty and suffering experienced in the United States after which emigration to colonial Canada seems for many a relief. In "'This Is No Hearsay,'" George Elliott Clarke has argued, "The success of such positive depictions of Canada has entailed the marginalization of slave narratives as essentially American literature by and for Americans, bespeaking an experience—slavery and slave resistance—supposedly alien to our 'Peaceable Kingdom'" (28). Further, he notes that Pooley's narrative is one of "a few admissions of the practice of anti-black or other racism in Canada West" (28), and I will add it is the only account in the collection that specifically depicts the practice of slavery in Canada. Moreover, the focus on Pooley's aboriginal captor, Brant, is also an uncommon aspect of the collection.[13]

By shifting the reader's attention from the enslaved to the physical appearance of Brant, the narrative racializes his person even as it unsettles the possibility of his "stable" ethnic identity. The reader, in order for the narrative to be successful—as in Wormeny's example—must believe in

Pooley as the narrator and believe in what the editors cannot or do not verify. Though the narrative does not specifically medicalize others as Wormeny's narrative does—and as we shall see Prince's does—it represents Brant through a kind of blazon that exoticizes him and potentially draws attention away from the characterization of Pooley as "I guess . . . the first colored girl brought into Canada" (192). For example, the narrative states, "When Brant went among the English, he wore the English dress—when he was among the Indians, he wore the Indian dress,—broad-cloth leggings, blanket, moccasins, fur cap. He had his ears slit with a long loop at the edge, and in these he hung long silver ornaments. He wore a silver half-moon on his breast with the king's name on it, and broad silver bracelets on his arms" (193). The ornamentation becomes a prosthetic extending from Brant's body and performing his identity. It marks and enhances his sense of self and his culturally invested personhood. The description concentrates on Brant's "Indian-ness"—or lack of any essential identification that is not performed—through the illustration of his clothing, jewelry, and the piercing of his ears. Such a description exoticizes him and unites owner and slave as physically marked and othered from the white dominant community despite Brant's control over Pooley. Further, there is an affectionate bond between them. The narrative details Brant's anger with his wife after the incident with the hatchet and his assertion that he "adopted [Pooley] as one of the family." She states, "I had no care to get my freedom" (194). We can read the focus on Brant as a tactic that defies not only an America hungry for tales of brutality against blacks but also colonial Canada which, Clarke argues, "was just as titillated by the tomfoolery and antics of burnt-cork-defaced blacks, terrified by the rages and outrages of cut-throat blacks, and entertained by the placid pastoralism of uncomplaining, choral blacks" (18).

The narrative embeds Pooley's racialized identity—apparent only in two short paragraphs discussing her experience of American slavery—into the remaining eight paragraphs of descriptions of Brant and his community. The account at once exoticizes and "civilizes" Brant and implicitly invites the reader to consider slave civility in the face of exoticization and otherness.[14] The antagonistic relationship between Pooley and Brant's third wife is consistent with the slave narrative trope of the cruel mistress, but the relationship between owner and enslaved undermines stereotypes of the brutal slaveholder. As such, the transcription affirms the brutality of slavery but complicates assumptions about the owner-slave relationship and asserts that otherness need not be inconsistent with civility. The narrative incorporates the savage and civil, depicting a sense of self as embodied, amorphous, and performed, and it undermines stereotypes about national and colonial politics of enslavement.

As I mentioned at the outset, two transcolonial African diasporic functions of Drew's collection of Canadian slave narratives, *The Refugee*, as a whole are (1) to support an American antislavery agenda and (2) to promote the notion that blacks are capable colonists, and that, in this case, the British monarchy is superior to the U.S. republic, bolstering as Van Gosse puts it, "England's claim to global leadership as a power both great and beneficent, a beacon of liberty versus the upstart Americans" (1005).[15] Pooley's narrative does not put the reader in the same position as Wormeny's does, for the editor's intervention in Pooley's account undermines her credibility. The purpose of authentication in this instance seems not so much to prove that Pooley was mistreated under slavery (in colonial Canada), but rather to promote the belief that her aboriginal owners were better than their white American counterparts. The editor, on remarking that he "saw many worse looking cicatrices of wounds not inflicted by *Indian* savages, but by civilized (?) men" (149), implies that Pooley's experience in colonial Canada was not really enslavement.

Prince's *History* offers the most successful example of the acquisition of such narrative agency and assertion of an ethical sense of self, perhaps ironically, by turning the focus away from herself, particularly toward the end of the narrative, which is set in England. More than that, though, we see Prince outline an ethics of vulnerability extending from the amorphous, decidedly non-autonomous human form she describes. Here we may productively recall the concepts of the postconventional and parahuman bodies that challenge the autonomous, whole, male ideal. Prince's text focuses much attention on the physical sufferings of other enslaved people, yet this attention neither the Pringles nor Ms. Strickland can verify for the reader. Through such descriptions, formerly enslaved narrators have much to tell us about the ethics of the vulnerable self and vice versa. One particularly violent account describes "old Daniel" who was "lame at the hip" (21). Prince's owner at the time, Mr. D—— stripped and beat Daniel "with a rod of rough briar till his skin was quite red and raw. He would then call for a bucket of salt, and fling it upon the raw flesh till the man writhed on the ground like a worm, and screamed aloud with agony" (21).[16] The narrative describes the skin tone and texture, evoking the images of ravaged flesh we have seen doctors and editors use, but what is different from such images is the attention to pain. The description, in contrast to Dr. Reddy's account of Lavina Wormeny's body, emphasizes Daniel's suffering through her depiction of his response to violence. The narrative's worm simile underscores the destabilizing effect of pain as behaviors distinguishing person from insect become unclear. Unlike Reddy's account, which I have argued de-animates Wormeny through the "anatomization" of her injuries, Prince's *History* places pain at the center of the questions about personhood and defies the reduction of the enslaved physique to an anthology of injuries and scars. The description of Daniel's pain continues: "This poor man's wounds were never healed and I have often seen them full of maggots, which increased his torments to an intolerable degree. He was an object of pity and terror to the whole gang of slaves, and in his wretched case we saw, each of us, our own lot, if we should live to be as old" (21). Here the physical person is far from a secure, enclosed entity. The physique is open; maggots invade it and again the putative borders demarcating self and other, human and nonhuman are questioned. Furthermore, symbolically for other slaves Daniel represents a future of pain and disability to come from brutal treatment and old age.

In this passage, Daniel metamorphoses from an example of human suffering to an almost Classical "object of pity and terror" whose purpose was to cast fear into other, younger enslaved people who are "doomed *to witness* and *to participate*" (Abdur-Rahman 237). Here according to the slaveholder's purpose, the physically wounded body transforms from individual physiological entity into biopolitical provocateur of fear. Pity as well functions as a disciplinary mechanism. His pain begins to function as an agent of the slave system as observer and observed fuse and pain and trauma transfer between the wounded person and witnesses to his agony. Nevertheless, Prince prompts us to think of another function of the connection between sufferer and observer and evades the disciplining aspects of pity and terror that brutality is meant to inspire. The narrative suggests the possibility that the experience and witnessing of pain produces a means of becoming with each other, a process that involves an ethics that eludes those who inflict such violence.

Echoing Levinas, Shildrick explains that "In place of the calculability of moral duty which theoretically at least treats everyone alike, an ethics of responsibility posits the other as a unique and irreplaceable individual. And moreover, it is precisely as the one called, the one who must respond to the vulnerability, the suffering, and the need of the other who meets me face to face, that I am instituted as a subject in my own right" (*Monster* 90). Prince suggests the potential of such a responsibility among the enslaved. Intercepting the abuser's triumph in the co-opting of Daniel's pain as an agent of slave regulation, Prince turns the point where experience and witness of torture meet into an ethical obligation to report abuse: "Oh the horrors of slavery . . . what my eyes have seen I think it is my duty to relate" (21). Prince takes the interrelation of pain among slaves and suggests the possibility of an ethical selfhood that results, uncomfortably, from responding to another's vulnerability and suffering. She says, "I have felt what a slave feels, and I know what a slave knows" (21). She implies that she does not have to have had Daniel's exact experience to know it. In witnessing it and testifying to it she becomes with him, to some extent feeling what he feels and knowing what he knows.

By extension, Prince demonstrates that the slaveholder and overseer who inflict pain and refuse to see anything but the barest (legal and moral) responsibility to the slave lose a measure of themselves in rejecting the call to respond to suffering. Though practically and legally it may make no difference for Prince and the other slaves, the text suggests that the slaveholder, in distinguishing himself from the enslaved other, undermines his own becoming. Furthermore, she exhorts England to "know it too"—what a slave feels and knows—to become with them and set them free (21). In recognizing, knowing, the other—the sufferer—as *an*other, the slave becomes a subject in his or her "own right"; the narrative suggests that colonial and imperial law have yet to catch up with such an ethics of responsibility.

Prince provides her readers with a glimpse of the potential for white people, even in the West Indies, to recognize a duty to the enslaved. When John Wood buys Prince, the narrative describes the pain she suffered as a result of the rheumatism that forced her to "lie in a little old out-house, that was swarming with bugs and other vermin" (25). There is reference to "a Mrs Greene" who "could not bear to hear my cries and groans. She was kind, and used to send an old slave woman to help me, who sometimes brought me a little soup" (25). In sending someone to help Prince, Mrs. Greene recognizes a responsibility to her, if indirect and only to relieve her own distress at hearing (being witness to) Prince's agony. By demonstrating Mrs. Greene's gesture of sending help for a pained woman, Prince reveals some recognition of white responsibility to the enslaved sufferer. She also suggests that it falls far short of the duty to each other that slaves understand. Prince continues, "When the doctor found I was so ill, he said I must be put into a bath of hot water. The old slave got the bark of some bush that was good for the pains, which she boiled in the hot water, and every night she came and put me into the bath, and did what she could for me" (25). The tender descriptions of Mrs. Greene, the "nurse," and the doctor, combined with depictions of Prince's physical suffering, propose a combined becoming with another through recognition of duty to acknowledge another's pain. Perhaps this is a step toward an interracial ethical sense of self.

Such an image challenges the replication of suffering exercised on her physique as it appears in the appended description of her brutalized body. Here, though, the narrative adopts a medical discourse contrary to that of the appendix. Rather, it suggests that self-constitution comes through an ethical responsibility to another who suffers. Prince may be anticipating the philosophy of Paul Ricoeur, for example. Dan Zahavi explains how "Ricoeur ends up arguing that the narrative take on selfhood must be complemented by a different perspective that includes the issue of *ethical responsibility*" (114). In witnessing Daniel's agony, Prince recognizes him, becomes with him, and ultimately realizes her duty to him. Her reporting of Daniel's pain transforms into a call for others, particularly whites, to fulfill their duty. She becomes with Daniel in a way that Mrs. Pringle does not become with her. Prince suggests the possibility that some whites in the West Indies on some level recognize a duty to—or are at least made uncomfortable by—black suffering. She implicitly emphasizes, through the depiction of Mrs. Greene's discomfort and attempt to help, that all whites in England have an ethical obligation, too, regardless of how removed they are from slave suffering. Through depictions of pain, suffering, and disability—her own and others'—Prince underscores the critical potential of the vulnerable self to reimagine humanness, personhood, and ethical becoming all toward a more interdependent society.[17]

Nationalism/Narration

Contrary to what would be Shadd's promotion of British potential to support the realization of an ideal black selfhood, Prince's *History* turns its narrative eye directly upon those who have the power to improve her condition to one of health, economic viability, and freedom, as well as those whom she believes hypocritically see themselves as ideologically separate and geographically distant from the goings on in the colonies because they remain in the empire's cradle. Such a shift in focus transforms the work from an account of slave life to criticism of white Christian abolitionism and English imperialism and nationalism. Here Prince reminds readers of both the inevitability of vulnerability and the promise of disability as a mode of critiquing colonial slavery.

Prince's narrative refocuses its rhetorics on white physicality, while the only significant mention of her own body appears when her rheumatism acts up severely, debilitating her upon arrival in England. Her physiological response to this nation reconfigures the place where she believed her freedom awaited: it is cast as a place of disappointment, of false hope—not the paragon of freedom that her U.S. counterparts believed it to be. Whereas more than twenty years later Shadd and Delany would infuse the promise of good health into their emigration propaganda and rhetorics of political autonomy, Prince's work articulates the stark reality of chronic illness and disability in the land where she is legally free. Shadd and Delany's single-minded determination to promote emigration, not to mention their experiences as free as opposed to enslaved or fugitive people, likely accounts for their ideal of the healthy self. For Prince, the colonial West Indies and England are not healthy places. Though earlier statements claim that "few people in England know what slavery is" and that Prince "would have all the good people in England to know [what a slave knows], that they may break our chains, and set us free" (21), the text reveals that England and some English fall short of her expectations. The return of her rheumatism physically and rhetorically emphasizes the material and conceptual disjuncture between the ideology of freedom and the realities of imperialism. Again she emphasizes recognition of and response to another's suffering as central to becoming an ethical subject. Her rheumatism in England, then, serves several critical functions as it challenges the empire to rise to its proclaimed potential.

The narrative's engagement with health, nation, and empire raises questions about the role of physicality in critiques of imperialism and colonialism. Traditionally in discussions of nationhood and nation-building, the body has functioned metaphorically. The concept of a national body and the question of what that body should look like figure prominently in all three of these transcolonial African diasporic narratives. Their rhetorics of physicality medically and metaphorically challenge ideas about who fits into the concept of an established or emergent national definition and who lies outside it. We can read the women in their respective transcolonial African diasporas—Prince in England and Pooley and Wormeny in colonial Canada—as Agamben's concept of the "limit figure . . . the radical crisis of every possibility of clearly distinguishing between membership and inclusion, between what is outside and what is inside, between exception and rule" (25). They reveal what Weheliye describes as the "different modalities of the human [that] come to light if we do not take the liberal humanist figure of Man as the master-subject but focus on how humanity has been imagined and lived by those subjects excluded from this domain" (8). Prince, Pooley, and Wormeny undermine the categories and demarcations of freedom, political sovereignty, and self from within the very geopolitical places that promise and prize such attainments.

Not only is the England section of Prince's narrative critical of her master and mistress. It also critiques England's economic state. When the Woods threaten to turn Prince out of their house without providing her with references, she says, "This was the fourth time they had threatened to turn me out, and go where I might, I was determined now to take them at their word; though I thought it very hard, after I had lived with them for thirteen years, and worked for them like a horse, to be driven out in this way, like a beggar" (33). Her disdain at being forced to beg and accept charity questions the merit and sovereignty of a country that benefits from, indeed requires, slavery for its economic sustainability. In Antigua she has no alternative to slavery, and in England—without the Woods' authority—her alternative is destitution. In terms of class, Prince moves from enslavement to indentured servitude and then to penury in her migration from the West Indies to England.[18] The narrative figures her first as a worker, then a beggar. The rhetorical contrast in physicality between strength and destitution questions the actual value of legal freedom and reveals anxieties about disability and work in nineteenth-century England.

Prince continues her critique by describing how she worked for Mrs. Forsyth who "had been in the West Indies, and was accustomed to Blacks, and liked them. . . . I was with her six months, and went with her to Margate. She treated me well, and gave me a good character when she left London" (36). Prince explains, "After Mrs. Forsyth went away, I was again out of place, and went to lodgings, for which I paid two shillings a week, and found coals and candle. After eleven weeks, the money I had saved in service was all gone, and I was forced to go back in the Anti-Slavery office to ask a supply, till I could get another situation. I did not like to go back—I did not like to be idle. I would rather work for my living than get it for nothing. They were very good to give me a supply, but I felt shame at being obliged to apply for relief whilst I had strength to work" (36). Of course, one could argue that this paragraph is an attempt to ensure her English readership that slaves do not wish to burden England financially; however, Prince's allusion to her physical strength in contradistinction to her position as a "beggar" asserts also her fortitude of character and questions the viability of the nation that subsists on slave labor in the colonies, yet cannot provide employment for a strong, middle-aged woman who is accustomed to working, so that she might support herself. Prince points to two economies in conflict here: slavery in Antigua and proto-capitalist wage labor in the imperial metropole.

The characterization of Prince in this instance as having "strength to work" is somewhat curious as it follows her repeated allusions to physical illness. In addition to assuring her readership that she will not be a "burden" on civil society, the change in her characterization may also imply that (as Shadd and Delany would later argue) with freedom comes a corresponding physical fortitude, which better working conditions not only physiologically motivated but psychologically inspired as well. And this certainly contradicts proslavery arguments about the health detriments produced by freedom in the northern states. Read another way, her emphasis on (perhaps exaggeration of) her health, strength, and ability underscores the ironic rigidity of an imperial nation whose demands on her during her enslavement in the colonies impaired her ability to exercise the freedom it ostensibly grants her on its own pure soil. Prince's rhetorics of physicality tell that England's sovereign purity is an illusion, and that practices of brutality in the colonies brought to the nation emphasize the falseness of any putative coherence of justice between the two.

Alternatively, though, or perhaps in conjunction with such possibilities, we can remind ourselves of the potential for Prince's performance of illness and a subsequent performance of health, whether conscious or not. In contrast to the potential use of illness as a means to resist abusive labor demands, perhaps the allusion to Prince's strength at the end of the narrative is a strategic acknowledgment of her engagement with such tactics. The text implies that if England offered adequate opportunities for a strong woman, Prince could contribute to its economy independent of slavery. Literature and disability scholar Martha Stoddard Holmes provides some context for anxieties surrounding the poor-law reforms of the early nineteenth century. She argues that figures of the "thieving beggar and the cherished image of the suffering child . . . were both screens for the truly threatening one of the disabled worker" (30). Prince's self-characterization as strong in the latter part of the narrative may have been an attempt at providing an image that is, perhaps ironically, less threatening than that of the rheumatic, debilitated—not to mention foreign, black, and female—worker on English soil. Within the nation she is in a state of exception. In Agamben's terms, she demonstrates the crisis of the imperial nation that allows her entry, grants her legal freedom, and then abandons her to a space of indistinction that it does not recognize in itself. Her status as the other within, a reminder of the amorphous categories of self and other, nation and colony underscores the reality of vulnerability despite political attempts to eradicate it from the national body.

Even when Prince wished to return to Antigua as a free woman, the lawyer who examined her case "told [her] that the laws of England could do nothing to make [her] free in Antigua" (35).[19] The text reveals that though Antigua is a British colony, English law is incapable of altering her status as a slave in the New World. Though literary critic Kremena Todorova has analyzed the debate Prince's publication ignited between West Indian colonists and the English living in England over what constitutes Englishness, it is clear that—perhaps unacknowledged by or unbeknownst to Thomas Pringle—it is not only the West Indian English who fall under the narrative's critical eye. Near the end of the text, criticism turns subtly from England's laws and economy to the English people living there. Here she asserts her critical presence most forcefully and directly.

Pringle footnotes Prince's last (and lengthy) paragraph to state, "The whole of this paragraph especially, is given as nearly as was possible to

Mary's precise words" (Prince 37). Possibilities abound in accounting for the motivation behind Pringle's footnote; however, it is this paragraph that is the most critical of some English. In this paragraph, Prince articulates what postcolonial theorist Homi Bhabha describes as an effect of hybridity. First, he defines the concept as "the revaluation of the assumption of colonial identity through the repetition of discriminatory identity effects," and then he explains its function: "It unsettles the mimetic or narcissistic demands of colonial power but reimplicates its identifications in strategies of subversion that turn the gaze of the discriminated back upon the eye of power" (154). Prince challenges the nation's ability to produce in slaves a colonial identity that cannot see or articulate injustice as it attempts—in Frantz Fanon's terms—to "*fabricate* the colonized subject" (*Wretched* 2).

She commences her conclusion by saying, "I am often much vexed, and I feel great sorrow when I hear some people in this country say, that the slaves do not need better usage, and do not want to be free. They believe the foreign people, who deceive them, and say slaves are happy" (37). In these two sentences, Prince targets some English people, white West Indians, and presumably U.S. proslavery southerners, whom she views as "foreign." Whereas the West Indian whites are deceptive, some English are gullible. She continues: "Since I have been here I have often wondered how English people can go out into the West Indies and act in such a beastly manner. But when they go to the West Indies, they forget God and all feeling of shame, I think, since they can see and do such things" (37–38). Again seeing, witnessing is crucial.

Here Prince does not distinguish between white English and white West Indian in the West Indies. Though she notes the gullibility of "some" English in England, she lumps together those in the West Indies and makes the geographical and tropical location the site of their bestiality. The rhetorics of physicality employ a trope that white writers commonly use to describe blacks and to profess the "degeneration" of whites in the colonies. When she argues that "they forget God and all feeling of shame," she recognizes the potential for such cruelty even in the God-fearing people, possibly implying that the pious abolitionists with whom she resides are susceptible to the same "beastly" impulses once away from England and their unifying goal to end slavery. Here, seeing such things does not result in an acknowledgment of duty to help the sufferer. In this sense, she underscores the capacity for moral degeneration in the English, West Indian, and abolitionist. Her rhetoric uncivilizes them. She transforms their soft, white human physiques into those of savage brutes. She undoes the classical body. She reveals that the other is within them. But Prince's argument is not necessarily geographically bound; in other words, some English who remain in England are vulnerable, too.

Midway through the paragraph, Prince attacks the duplicitous nature of a nation which relies on slavery from a geographical distance that allows them to justify its cruelty: "The man that says slaves be quite happy in slavery—that they don't want to be free—that man is either ignorant or a lying person. I never heard a slave say so. I never heard a Buckra man say so, till I heard tell of it in England. Such people ought to be ashamed of themselves. They can't do without slaves, they say. What's the reason they can't do without slaves as well in England?" (38). In this sense, Prince seems more critical of some English in England than of the white West Indian colonist and slaveholder. This section of her narrative critiques the source of the slave system that ironically had already abolished the slave trade and in 1569 declared itself "too pure an Air for slaves to breathe in," despite legal challenges to this over the next two centuries (qtd. in Salih xvii).[20] Her critique reveals a fissure not only between colonial and national laws but between the country's laws and its attitudes as well.

Furthermore, she continues that in England there are "no whips—no stocks—no punishment, except for wicked people" (38). The last lines of her narrative exclaim: "I tell it to let the English people know the truth; and I hope they will never leave off to pray God, and call loud to the great King of England, till all the poor blacks be given free, and slavery done up for evermore" (38). Again, "knowing" the truth, from Prince's utterance, is central to an ethical sense of duty to the other, to the sufferer. The subtext of this conclusion renders ironic the powers of king and country to end slavery. She has already established the falseness of some English people and the injustice of English law in the colonies. Prince's physicality disappears from this section as she trains the reader's attention on England. I want to suggest that this move implies that she has fully inserted herself into and revealed the vulnerability of the nation to the extent that we no longer can see her within her narrative. She has made outside and inside indistinguishable. This is the point of indistinction from which could have emerged the radical politics of inclusion for which we still wait.

In Pooley's and Wormeny's transcolonial African diasporic narratives, the question of a Canadian nationalism is anticipatory, yet both texts' editors convey an impulse to define colonial Canada in contradistinction to the United States and fit within a broader antislavery impulse to contrast the United States and Great Britain. As noted earlier, Pooley's text appears in an American publication titled *The Refugee; or, Narratives of Fugitive Slaves in Canada* sponsored by the Boston Anti-Slavery Society. The narrative portrays colonial Canada as a place where even enslavement is preferable to life in the United States under its brand of slavery. The portrayal of Pooley's owners as largely benevolent complicates the genre of the slave narrative but supports the publication's purpose. After seven years with an owner from Ancaster, she explains, "The white people said I was free, and put me up to running away. He did not stop me—he said he could not take the law into his own hands" (194–95). Here Pooley's potential escape from slavery in colonial Canada is an impulse of white abolitionists; the text acknowledges the law-abiding nature of her owner.

It is tempting to read Pooley's physicality as somewhat passive in contrast to other fugitives' assertions in the collection, which demonstrated determination to have freedom at nearly any price.[21] However, as I've noted, because the larger text has a role in presenting colonial Canada as superior to the brutal slaveholding society of the United States, it is not surprising that Pooley appears as such. Drew inserted himself into her narrative to qualify her suffering as less harsh than that which enslaved people in the United States suffered. Here we see the intervention of white U.S. abolitionists into colonial Canadian slavery not to promote immigration into the colony but rather as a means of bolstering the antislavery cause at home. Perhaps Pooley is a passive figure in the text, and perhaps her treatment was less cruel than the kind others experienced. Nevertheless, her text adheres to a project that promotes Upper Canada as the real "land of the free," as Shadd would have it, not even to endorse emigration but rather to underscore the backward, oppressive nature of the southern United States and of American republicanism generally. Here the figure of the refugee in the colony—though still enslaved—with the publishing arm of that nation's antislavery society holds a mirror to the slaveholding nation. Both U.S. and colonial Canadian activists define the two geopolitical places in opposition to one another—the former for self-critique and the latter for self-affirmation.

Wormeny's text heralds Lower Canada's espousal of black liberation and support. The *Montreal Gazette* article begins: "We have the account from the lips of the woman herself, who arrived in this city on Monday last, and we have also the statement, over his own signature, of Dr Reddy, under whose treatment she now is, which fully bears out every word of hers regarding the cruelty to which she had been subjected" (rpt. Mackey 162). As in Prince's narrative, ill health follows the formerly enslaved into freedom. Wormeny is under a doctor's care, and the text suggests that recuperation is possible and that good health may attend freedom in colonial Canada.

That the editors did not directly transcribe the narrative from her own lips but rather rendered it in the third person is curious because it deviates from the genre's traditional use of the first person and implies an amount of white mediation that editors, in the United States at least, typically minimized. Furthermore, they specify the narrative's fund-raising purpose, which relies on the goodwill of those who read the account. For example, after the narrative catalogues the horrific treatment Wormeny experienced in various American states, and prior to Dr. Reddy's examination, the article asks, "Need we commend the poor woman to the citizens of Montreal for their practical aid, after the history we have given of her? We feel that there will be an immediate response from all" (164). Such calls for assistance, paired with the appropriation of Wormeny's voice and Dr. Reddy's authentication of her story, beg the question: to what extent did Cooke and Reddy participate in a kind of anticipatory project of nation-building that defined Lower Canada—if not the colony as a whole—in stark contrast to the United States, and how do they use the medicalized, formerly enslaved, black female physique as a political tool for self-definition? By defining Canada against the United States, writers used slavery as a means of securing a proto-nationalism that articulated colonial Canada as morally superior to the United States, a nation which did not abolish slavery until long after Britain did and after a civil war.

It appears that Lavina Wormeny furnished Cook and Reddy with the means to create a portrait of proto-national sympathy for the oppressed that built on the work of white abolitionists like Benjamin Drew and endeavored to defy the colonial status of places like the West Indies as they appear in Prince. Ironically, perhaps, it appears that Prince makes the most successful transition from object to subject and offers the starkest critique of Anglo-European meanings of selfhood (firmly demarcated from otherness, distinct from nonhuman forms, autonomous, and whole) through rhetorics of physicality that manipulate discourses of the body and transfer the direction of the objectifying eye, even though by comparison she, of the three, purports to have felt the most severe physical abuses. Perhaps this is not surprising, though, as colonial Canada was in the midst of defining itself in relation to the republic recently divorced from its motherland. It seems the place that claimed to maintain an agenda of freedom for oppressed blacks may, in the context of the transcolonial African diasporic narratives in question, have exercised the greatest editorial control over its black voices and suppressed articulation of embodied black selfhood to serve its own attempt at self-definition. Enslaved women's expressions of selfhood through pain and debility are particularly revealing when read in light of editors' and authenticators' attempts at political/national self-definition; however, as the next chapter will demonstrate, enslaved women's articulations of self exhibit a drastic and desperate urgency when confronting the pain of sexual abuse.

→ 4 ←

The Protective Self

Slave Sexual Health, Crime, and U.S. Legal Personhood

CELIA'S MURDER TRIAL AND HARRIET JACOBS'S *INCIDENTS*

As sketched in the introduction, antebellum law recognized slaves as both persons and property, persons who could be criminally prosecuted and property that could be bought and sold. The two stories I address here involve instances of interracial sexual abuse of slaves and the lengths to which two enslaved women went to protect themselves. Indeed, one of the women explicitly stated she wanted to stop the abuse because she was sick. Their stories complicate the theory of mixed character that purported to explain and define slaves' status. Furthermore, enslaved women's responses to such abuse, particularly their criminal reactions, such as running away or killing the abusive owner, reveal how starkly brutal these legal definitions were and how detrimental to enslaved women's health and well-being despite the spirit of paternalism and benevolence the legal theorists claimed produced and upheld the notion of mixed character and U.S. slave law. This chapter addresses the gendered health problems attending the peculiar legal conundrum in which enslaved women found themselves when suffering the abuse of their slaveholders. Even more dependent in the period than a married woman whose legal existence was subsumed under her husband's, the slave's legal identity fell under that of the owners who theoretically were supposed to protect and care for their human property. Enslaved women's shifting legal subject-positions posed theoretical problems within this particular power relationship, as the boundary distinguishing the law's treatment of slaves as property and persons blurred. An enslaved woman's admittedly slender potential civil protection as property was eroded when her abuser was simultaneously her owner. This shift in her protections produced a rift in her legal subjecthood through which systems of terror could operate legitimately. Here the limits of personhood are bleakly devastating.

The concept of "double character" finds early articulation in *The Federalist* (1788), in which James Madison discusses the proportion of government representation for each state. He explains:

> In being compelled to labor, not for himself, but for a master; in being vendible by one master to another master; and in being subject at all times to be restrained in his liberty and chastised in his body, by the capricious will of another—the slave may appear to be degraded from the human rank, and classed with those irrational animals which fall under the legal denomination of property. In being protected, on the other hand, in his life and in his limbs, against the violence of all others, even the master of his labor and his liberty, and in being punishable himself for all violence committed against others—the slave is no less evidently regarded by the law as a member of the society, not as a part of the irrational creation; as a moral person, not as a mere article of property. (300–301)

Seventy years after Madison's explanation, the concept of slaves' "mixed character" resurfaced in proslavery legal theorist Thomas R. R. Cobb's *Inquiry into the Law of Negro Slavery* (1858), which used the term "double character" as a defense against abolitionist arguments that focused on slaves' status as chattels. Cobb argued, "In the Roman law, a slave was a mere chattel (*res*). He was not recognized as a person. But the Negro slave in America, protected . . . by municipal law, occupies a double character of person and property" (83). Cobb further argued that, as persons, slaves found protection in law: "In all of the slaveholding States, the homicide of a slave is held to be murder, and in most of them, has been so expressly declared by law. . . . Nor has the legislation of the States stopped at the protection of their lives, but the security of limbs and the general comfort of the body are, in most of the States, amply provided for, various penalties being inflicted on masters for their cruel treatment" (84–85). Cobb adds the "general comfort of the body," a condition to which the slave narratives from the previous chapter and the genre in general comprehensively offer a stark counternarrative to say the least.

Slaves did not singularly occupy the character of person, nor were they granted the same rights as white people under either criminal or civil laws. Such representational fluidity potentially benefited whites who could hold slaves as persons accountable for criminal acts, yet limited slaves' ability to act legally in their own self-interest. Legal scholar Cheryl I. Harris has demonstrated how slaves' "hybrid" categorization as property and person possessed "inherent instabilities that were reflected in its treatment and ratification by the law." She traces the problematical nature of such a hybrid designation through questions posed before the Constitutional Convention, the "legitimate" use of black women to increase property and the "use of Africans as a stand-in for actual currency" (1719–20). I interrogate the dual designation further to examine specifically how rape complicates the legal construct of "double character" and to determine its impact on representations of slaves' sexual abuse and their physical and mental health. While many states protected slaves, as property, from physical harm like maiming and dismemberment, lawmakers excluded rape from these protections. The law afforded such protections also to nonhuman property, such as livestock, and the exclusion of rape signals the limits of slave personhood, slave humanity only just separated from the livestock.

Distinguishing between sexual and other physical protections, Hartman points out, "The ravished body, unlike a broken arm or leg, did not bestow any increment of subjectivity because it did not decrease productivity or diminish value" (95). Hartman refers to Cobb's assertion that "The law, by recognizing the existence of the slave as a person, thereby confers no rights or privileges except such as are necessary to protect that existence. All other rights must be granted specially. Hence, the penalties for rape would not and should not, by such implication, be made to extend to carnal forcible knowledge of a slave, the offence not affecting the existence of the slave, and that existence being the extent of the right which the implication of the law grants" (86). Here his notion of "the general comfort of the body" has no bearing on the sexual and psychological health of the enslaved. Further, Cobb argued: "Another consequence of slavery is, that the violation of the person of a female slave, carries with it no other punishment than the damages which the master may recover for the trespass upon his property" (99). Therefore, according to Cobb, a master could seek compensation for his slave's rape because the act constituted a trespass on his property, and any physical injury incurred from such an attack fell under the same protection. Again, there is no recognition of harm beyond physical injury, and a slave abused by her owner was even more vulnerable.

There were two practical problems with this theoretical construction: First, incentive for an owner to seek reparations for the rape of his slave was negligible, since monetary compensation was typically minor, even for the murder of a slave.[1] Worse, such action drew attention to the sexual politics of slavery, attention which hindered the promotion of slaveholding's paternalistic ideology, an ideology prevalent among southern planters and in keeping with the South's code of "honor."[2] Second, the slave lacked protection from the sexual abuse of her owner because he could not trespass on his own property. It was, therefore, legally impossible for an owner to rape his slave. When addressing the situation of owner-slave rape among the Romans whose laws awarded to the slave "double damages," and among the Lombards,[3] who awarded freedom, Cobb argues:

> These laws are suggestive of defects in our own legislation. It is a matter worthy the consideration of legislators, whether the offence of rape, committed upon a female slave, should not be indictable; and whether, when committed by the master, there should not be superadded the sale of the slave to some other master. The occurrence of such an offence is almost unheard of; and the known lasciviousness of the negro, renders the possibility of its occurrence very remote. Yet, for the honor of the statute-book, if it does occur, there should be an adequate punishment. (100)

In the context Cobb describes, a raped slave was neither a person under criminal law nor property protected by civil law—whatever her human status. Further, his assertion of slaves' "lasciviousness" renders any consideration of owner-slave rape a matter only "for the honor of the statute book." Cobb all but negates the possibility of slave psychological harm. Thus enslaved women raped by their owners still maintained the "double character" designation: they could still be tried as criminals and sold as property, but as victims/survivors of slaveholders' sexual abuses, neither system of laws protected them, regardless of "the general comfort of the body" he theorized slave law to provide.

This chapter examines two situations in particular, one legal and the other legal and literary. The first involves Celia, a slave in Missouri convicted of murder in 1855. According to testimony presented at her trial,

Robert Newsom purchased Celia when she was fourteen years old, possibly raped her on the way back to his home, and subsequently sexually abused her until she killed him five years later.[4] His explicitly sexual enslavement of her resulted in the birth of at least one child and possibly that of Celia's third child, stillborn while she was in jail.[5] The second situation is that of Harriet Jacobs, whose experiences of her owner's sexual harassment in North Carolina culminated in the publication of her famous 1861 slave narrative, *Incidents in the Life of a Slave Girl, Written by Herself*, in which the author, portrayed as Linda Brent,[6] suffers the licentious attentions of her owner, the pseudonymous Dr. Flint, for approximately seven years before she escapes and hides herself in a crawlspace above her grandmother's house for another seven years, after which she flees a second time and goes to New York.

The women's experiences and the narratives that arise out of them, in different ways, critique each state's complicity in making slave women vulnerable to sexual abuse and highlight the effects of this complicity on women's health and well-being. Central to both women's engagement with the law are their own crimes. Celia murdered Newsom in her cabin, burned his body in her fireplace, and the next day invited his grandson to sweep away the ashes. Linda Brent flees Dr. Flint, hides herself above her grandmother's house that sits in close proximity to Flint's own home, and from this room surveys his actions. In response to their extralegal status as victims of their owners' sexual demands, these women break the law and subsequently censure their owners' lawful actions. Traversing the theoretical boundaries demarcating property and persons, both women take lives. Celia killed Robert Newsom and Linda Brent steals herself, the stolen property—thus pointing out another theoretical difficulty inherent in the concept of "double character." The narrativization of these incidents—Celia's through her trial and Jacobs's through her publication—suggests the fact of owner-slave sexual violence at a time when such abuse was theoretically impossible: not because interracial sexual relations were unacknowledged, but because legislation denied slaves the ability either to consent or refuse the sexual desires of white people. Buttressing such legislation was the notion that black women were too lascivious to make rape anything but a rarity. Therefore, because the law did not apply, enslaved women's experiences of sexual violation were effectively annulled.

Comparison of Jacobs's and Celia's stories underscores women's detailing of the effects of sexual and psychological abuse through their negotiations of nineteenth-century narrative conventions such as the use of juridical rhetoric and their engagement with literary traditions like sentimentalism and Gothicism. Through their representations in law and nineteenth-century American print culture, these two women's narratives employ literary and social constructs to produce, reproduce, and challenge their legal contexts and highlight issues particular to enslaved women's health. They engage with sentimental constructions of womanhood as they assert their notions of black women's selfhood and search for a legal character that would permit them to defend themselves against abuse; yet their ultimate inability to access such subjecthood potentially reinforces their marginality.

By foregrounding physical suffering and ill health in a discussion of law and literature, I want to complicate the prevalent understanding of the ultimate efficacy of literary uses of legal rhetoric and vice versa. The rift sexual abuse creates between enslaved women's assumed humanness as well as their designation as persons and property underscores the contradictions inherent in the category of black women for legal as well as medical purposes. The previous chapters demonstrated how black writers and orators conceived various senses of self, drawing from the classical Greek autonomous and healthy ideal that Shadd and Delany promote to the amorphous, interdependent, and vulnerable reality that Prince, Pooley, and Wormeny depict. Their attempts to define black selfhood, converse with medical discourses that recognized slave humanness on the one hand, but which hierarchized gradations of Man on the other, relegating all blacks to the bottom of the scale and claiming that free blacks were the most degraded type of human, discourses that worked very hard to demonstrate the difference between black and white but used black bodies for research and experiments to promote the health of white people. They engage with medical practices and theories that purported to promote "Negro" health, regulating black bodies in a southern or tropical slave system where climate, owner benevolence, and skilled doctors could protect them from disease, cold, and hunger. They complicate abolitionist medical interventions that anatomized, mortified, and undermined their individual accounts of brutality and "misread" the senses of self that black women sought to articulate. Here enslaved women engage with legal discourses' participation in similar projects of black definition and regulation but that as a result of the physical and psychological toll of sexual abuse seem to require from them a different, more urgent, and desperate response to subjugation.

Legislation extending protection to female slaves against rape would have undermined their dual role, outlined by Hortense Spillers, as producers and reproducers.[7] In Missouri and North Carolina, laws protected white women from rape but provided no shield for women of color and slaves. The legal language varies from state to state, but the import is the same. For example, the *Missouri Revised Statute, 1845* reads: "Every person who shall take any woman, unlawfully, against her will, with intent to compel her by force, menace or duress . . . to defile [her] upon conviction thereof shall be punished by imprisonment" (ch. 47, 29). The language in this statute is nonspecific as it refers to "any woman" and the act in question is defilement. Further, the statute allows that "Homicide shall be deemed justifiable when committed by any person [who is] resisting [attempts] to commit any felony upon . . . her" (ch. 47, 4). The inclusiveness of this general language did little, practically, to aid Celia in her murder trial. Her conviction for first-degree murder and the presiding judge's handling of jury instructions reveal that the court did not interpret the term "any woman" to include her; however, the statute was the foundation on which the defense counsel built her case, thereby indicating that though the jury did not interpret the statute to include Celia, her lawyers did. That the statute deemed homicide justifiable to prevent a sexual attack indicates the law's sense of the gravity of such an assault on a woman's well-being.

By contrast, the *Revised Code of North Carolina, 1854* specifies: "Any slave, or free negro, or free person of color, convicted by due course of law, of an assault with intent to commit a rape, upon the body of a white female, shall suffer death" (sec. 44). First, this section applies only to people of color—the articulated designation "person" reserved for free blacks—and specifies as its subject "a rape upon the body of a white female." Second, to ensure capital punishment, the rape itself was not necessary, only the "assault with intent to commit a rape" had to be proved. By contrast, there were no laws in either state protecting the slave from the sexual interference of her owner, whether the assault was actual or intended. Again, the statute acknowledges the severe harm that rape causes, even if it only recognizes its effect on white women.

Nonrecognition of slave rape meant that the owner could increase his "stock" by impregnating female slaves. The commercial value of such nonrecognition, paired with the impulse to hush slavery's sexual indignities and to attribute any sexual promiscuity to black women, not white men, meant that frequency of abuse and public knowledge of it did not coincide. Furthermore, it was openly perceived that black women's promiscuity and interracial sexual relations protected white women's virtue. Horsman quotes a letter from the 1860s wherein the author states, "There are few Southern boys who would not sleep with Negresses. These girls of mixed or African blood preserve the virtue of the white girls here, as women of loose character do in the North" (257). Not surprisingly, there are few recorded accounts of slave rape, but they are not an accurate indication of its incidence. Celia and Jacobs break the silence around a particular kind of slave suffering. A similar trend in American society today—where rape laws apply to all women regardless of race and status—reminds us of the continued discrepancy between incidences of rape and their reports.[8] Therefore, it is crucial to examine the role of female crime in establishing the existence of slave rape, despite the fact that this violence was a legal nonentity and furthermore most likely read as an indication of "vices of character" that acknowledge no actual injury to the well-being of that character. In the law's eyes, Celia was a murderer and Jacobs a fugitive; their criminal responses to their owners' assaults exposed gaps in paternalistic proslavery rhetoric through which they could reveal their physical and psychological suffering and question the law's legitimacy in order to complicate its notions of guilt and guiltlessness.[9]

A study of slave executions states, "Most slave women resorted to crime in retaliation for brutal treatment by their masters. A typical case of a murder by a female slave, for example, involved the killing of a white master after repeated sexual assaults and rapes" (Aguirre and Baker 23). Ironically, such analyses reveal that an enslaved woman's crime was necessary, first, to protect herself from sexual harm, second, for the law to view her as a person—though as a criminal, not a victim—and third, to suggest her owner's moral guilt. The function of Celia's and Linda Brent's actions then are twofold: first, they resist their owner's sexual demands and second, they recast Newsom and Flint in the role of perpetrator. Not only do they accuse their owners, but also those who uphold the laws, which forbid them sexual subjecthood. As literary scholar Christina Accomando points out with reference to Jacobs's narrative, "The keepers of the laws become the outlaws, and her allegiance is to some higher law, not made by white men" (241). Nevertheless, the rhetorical implications of Jacobs's narrative do not change the author's legal situation. That is to say that Accomando's own phrasing does not question what is at stake in conflating rhetoric and legality. For example, "the keepers of the laws" only "become the outlaws" rhetorically, regardless of Jacobs's allegiance to a "higher law." Accomando states, "The larger irony . . . is that it is Jacobs who ultimately lays down the law anew by deconstructing legal fictions in the course of her narrative, which long outlives Flint and his real-life counterparts. She recodes the law as criminal to undercut the legitimacy of legal practices in the South and North" (241). The danger of such hopeful readings, however, rests in their potential to diminish the importance of Jacobs's own crimes in the service of her health and well-being, and to forget that, ultimately, it was Jacobs who literally had to become an "outlaw" to exercise her rhetorical power.[10] Furthermore, outlaw status may have removed her from a sexually abusive situation, but it did nothing to benefit her overall health; in fact, as a fugitive her physical health declined substantially.

To reverse or at least complicate the confession's purpose to acknowledge the commission of a crime, the women had to counter paternalistic ideology that contended that slaves' betterment was a natural result of their owners' benevolent treatment. Prevalent and convenient to slaveholders were notions like Cobb's "remove the restraining and controlling power of the master, and the negro becomes, at once, the slave of his lust, and the victim of his indolence, relapsing, with wonderful rapidity, into his pristine barbarism. Hayti and Jamaica are living witnesses to this truth; and Liberia would probably add her testimony, were it not for the fostering care of philanthropy, and the annual leaven of emancipated slaves" (49–50). Here Cobb's own use of legal terms like *witness* and *testimony* appropriates conventional abolitionist rhetorical strategies in an attempt to reinforce a paternalistic argument about slavery's benefit to slave health and well-being.[11] Celia's and Brent's narratives demonstrate that slavery was severely detrimental to their physical, sexual, and psychological well-being *and* that their resistance contributed to new forms of ill health and, in Celia's situation, to her and her child's deaths.

Nevertheless, the perception of slave lust and master benevolence provided a scale on which slaveholders could balance conservative and liberal ideologies during a period of increasing scrutiny from northern abolitionists. Fugitives and violent slaves, however, countered proslavery propaganda that advertised the contentment of slaves. For example, Gross highlights the necessity of publicly distancing slaves' criminal behavior from any perception of ill-treatment. She says, "It became a trope to intone that a slave ran away 'without cause' or 'without provocation'" (*Double* 100). Such a trope attempted to establish a firm distinction between victim and perpetrator. For example, St. Louis's *Missouri Republican* printed that Celia's owner, Robert Newsom, had been murdered "without any sufficient cause."[12] Read in conjunction with the statute that deems homicide justifiable for rape, the newspaper's report seems almost an example of apophasis. Similarly, Dr. Norcom, the real-life Dr. Flint, wrote an ad for the capture of Harriet Jacobs that read, "This girl absconded from the plantation of my son without any known cause or provocation" (Yellin 237). Dr. Norcom compounded the emphasis by combining both phrases. The *Missouri Republican*'s and Norcom's employment of such disclaimers implies the social and personal anxiety attending public perception that the owner's ill-treatment could have been a motive for Celia's and Linda's actions. We see that the confession and the runaway advertisement both can function as attempts to invert notions of guilt and guiltlessness. This is the process Celia and Linda Brent undertake in committing murder, on the one hand, and escape on the other, and then confessing to their actions.

As noted, neither crime—even as it secures legal personhood and subverts the logic of rape law—wholly empowers the women or relieves their physical and psychological suffering. Celia ultimately is hanged for her actions; Brent confines herself to a crawlspace where her muscles atrophy, and then, after being purchased and having settled in the North, finds herself still in ill health and restricted by racist attitudes, poverty, and the Fugitive Slave Law. Though perhaps a seemingly small consolation, in the process of committing these crimes, the women disempower their owners. Celia killed Newsom and burned his body; Brent leaves Flint impotent to find her and enlists him as the object of her disciplining gaze and, by extension, the gaze of her readers. By constraining others, the women partly empower themselves; by committing crimes, they achieve legal status as persons, albeit as outlaws. Though physically injurious, their actions appear to be mentally, emotionally, and physically necessary for their physical and psychological protection (if not health). Temporarily, each slave woman asserted agency and expressed a particular kind of resistant black sense of self at the expense of the physicality, which previously identified her.

The court's formulaic language before Celia's arraignment—similar to the paratactic style of contemporary medical discourse we saw in chapter 3—emphasizes the corporeality of the accused when it orders the constable to take Celia's body and "bring her forthwith before the . . . Justices of the Peace . . . to answer the complaint." The identification of the accused with her body in this instance where the accused is also enslaved seems to reinforce the interpretation of Celia as a sort of physical entity devoid of emotional content—a body, not a person. Further, after her arraignment, the constable was instructed to "take the body of the said Celia a slave and forthwith deliver her to the keeper of the common jail" (file 4496). The corporeal identification of people in legal rhetoric is not uncommon, as the term *habeas corpus* ("that you have the body") illustrates. Further, legal historian Randall McGowen has argued, "The symbolism of punishment was employed to point beyond the body to relations within society, to the natural unity of society, and to its human and divine purpose" (654). In this context, though, it seems that Celia is very much separated from the body of social relations, as a rupture of that social unity. Therefore, partly in keeping with legal symbolism and partly as a result of the political context surrounding Celia's trial, her identity extended significantly beyond her corporeality, if mostly emblematic of social disharmony. As I demonstrate, building on the work of Melton McLaurin in the article version of this chapter, she came to represent a divide within the body politic between pro- and antislavery supporters. But more important for my purposes here, Celia's legal and social symbolic value emphasizes the court's disregard for her humanity, her physical and psychological suffering. In the context of small-scale Missouri slaveholding, historian Diane Mutti Burke notes that "White Missourians argued that [the] familiarity [of small slaveholdings] ultimately led to better treatment of the state's slaves" (143); therefore, her story contradicted this narrative of "domestic" slaveholding as ensuring slave well-being. Nevertheless, new evidence I have uncovered from looking at the original court documents at the Calloway County Courthouse since the publication of the article demonstrates the extreme lengths to which the presiding judge had to go in order to preserve the impression of Celia as a "mere body" and killer, not someone defending herself.

Laws that only protected slaves from physical harm and ensured their proper feeding and clothing underscore the corporeal preoccupation through which the dominant culture viewed the enslaved. For example, North Carolina's code stated: "In case any slave who shall appear not to have been properly clothed and fed, shall be convicted of stealing any corn, cattle, hogs, or other goods whatsoever, from any person not the owner of such slave, such injured person may maintain an action on the case, against the possessor of such slave, for his damages" (sec. 27). The code protected whites' property from theft by other owners' ill-treated slaves. Though the law referred to slaves' proper clothing and feeding, it did not so much enforce such care for the enslaved as it served to protect whites against damages resulting from slaves' abuse. Further, the same state shielded white people's characters from insult, embarrassment, and humiliation by racial others in addition to "protecting" their bodies: "It shall not be lawful for any slave to be insolent to a free white person; nor to utter mischievous and slanderous reports about any free white person, nor to willfully trespass on his property or person; nor to intermarry or cohabit with any free person of color; nor for any male slave to have sexual intercourse, or indulge in any grossly indecent familiarities with a white female" (sec. 31). The content of this section of North Carolina's code explicitly prohibits male slaves from having any sexual interaction with white women, but specifically only prohibits white men from intermarrying or cohabiting with free people of color. The law reveals an anxiety about relations between white *women* and slaves that it does not admit between white *men* and slaves. Further, where the code addresses interracial sexual relations, it deems that slaves do not require any sexual "protections." Again, the law overlooks the possibility that the power differential between male owners and female slaves could merit the latter some protections as sexual beings, their physicality, life and limb, comprising the extent of such legal protections.

The code identifies what Cobb later described as the law's responsibility to protect the "existence" of the slave. Legally unrecognized was any emotional hurt. The identification of slaves as primarily laboring bodies, known for their "lasciviousness," informed the legal and ideological situation of white and black women as opponents (Cobb 100). As Hartman argues, "Rape disappeared through the intervention of seduction—the assertion of the slave woman's complicity and willful submission. . . . The discourse of seduction enabled those disgusted and enraged by the sexual arrangements of slavery . . . to target slave women as the agents of their husbands' downfalls. The complicity of slave women displaced the act of sexual violence" (87). The logic of the slave code omits any recognition that for black women, rape can injure internally, both physically and psychologically. Furthermore, evidence of slave women's rape would have been difficult to obtain, and antebellum courts regarded circumstantial evidence as inferior to eyewitness testimony.[13] The sexual and therefore private nature of rape generally reduces the potential of witness availability, and the testimony of other slaves (against whites) was largely inadmissible. Moreover, the noncriminalized designation of owner-slave "intercourse" effaced enslaved women's psychology and reduced them to "mere bodies" on which evidence of sexual assault or injury was invisible. Such combined erasures, consistent with slaves' extralegal character as victims, potentially informs the difficulties survivors had in linguistically articulating the sexual harm they suffered from their owners.

In the press, Celia's story was reprinted—directly and paraphrased, and with various introductions—from the *Fulton Telegraph* in both pro- and antislavery newspapers in cities and towns of neighboring counties and as far away as Baltimore and New York.[14] Headlines like "FIENDISH MURDER" and "HORRIBLE MURDER. A MAN KILLED AND BURNED BY HIS OWN SLAVE" appeared in June and July issues of Missouri newspapers.[15] The longest articles detailed the mechanics of Newsom's murder and Celia's disposal of his body:

> She then washed the blood from the floor, which had flowed from the old man's head after the second lick, with cold water, and stirred the ashes so that the bones might be broken to pieces. Some of the bones which were not charred sufficiently to crumble, she took them up and threw the largest under the floor of the house, and put the smaller ones in a box to be carried out the next day, which she and a little boy did the next morning; the boy not knowing that he was carrying out anything more than ordinary wood ashes.[16]

This excerpt shows Celia's reduction of Newsom to inert matter. Rather than portraying Celia as a "mere body," the newspaper account focuses on Newsom's body, specifically the elimination of his personhood and his corporeal existence. Nowhere in the press—as far as I have seen—however, is there any direct reference to allegations of rape and forced concubinage. The closest implication of any potential sexual relationship rests in the *Telegraph*'s reporting that Robert Newsom was "an old gentleman who has been living by himself for sometime past." This phrase, along with descriptions of Celia, "a negress" or "negro woman about 22 or 23 years of age," appear in every reprint of the original *Fulton Telegraph* story.[17] The papers' inclusion of such information—Newsom's living arrangements being false, according to trial testimony, which stated that Newsom's daughter and grandchildren lived with him—hints at a potential motive for the crime. Celia's age, according to trial testimony, is overestimated in the newspapers. Of course, the errors may be just that, but it is possible to read Newsom's arrangement with Celia, as the papers describe it, as an example of concubinage—Newsom having been without a wife for some time. The difference between their ages combined with Newsom's prolonged solitude potentially suggest some impropriety. Of course, mention of his age and isolation may also serve to illustrate his inability to defend himself. The pro-slavery *Missouri Republican*, the only paper I found to have printed the story from one of its own correspondents, approximates Newsom's age to be "about sixty," does not indicate Celia's age and, as McLaurin noted, contradicted the other papers—and subsequent trial testimony—to state that the murder took place in the kitchen adjacent to the main house, not in Celia's cabin. The article also notes that "the murder was committed, without any sufficient cause, so far as I can hear."[18]

Despite the absence of motive in press accounts, Celia, by acting to defend herself, effectively transferred the ideological identification of her person with her body to a focus on Newsom's physique. Most newspaper coverage of the murder constitutes his body as "old," though the *Missouri Republican*'s correspondent also describes him as "active and energetic in his business." Further, the papers depict his injury: "the first blow struck him only served to stun him; and being about to rise after the first blow, she struck him a second time to keep him from getting up." The descriptions culminate in his reduction to ashes and "a few bones . . . found under the house" as well as "portions . . . that resembled the skull base" but that "were so small that they could not be certainly recognized."[19] The newspapers invite white male readers to identify with Newsom. They are also being asked to ponder the potential violence of their own black female servants and slaves.

Though Celia's body became the focus of the trial, both for the prosecution and the defense in opposing ways, her physique acquired significance beyond the individual. Celia's transition from "mere body" to cultural symbol both improved and hindered the status of her individuality during her trial, and so the court's decision reflected more than the "facts" of the case. Similarly, we must consider how the defense may have appealed to cultural symbolism when promoting its narrative to the court. Unfortunately, we do not have a record of the defense's questions, only the witnesses' responses to them, so we can only infer the approach of Celia's lawyers. Celia's representation as a sexually abused woman appealed to another culturally recognizable narrative structure that could have potentially recast her as the victim. Literary scholar Laura Hanft Korobkin argues, "Though it is often associated with female authors and female readers, in the nineteenth-century courtroom sentimentality was often the rhetorical tool of choice for male lawyers who . . . argued their cases to all-male juries and judges" (6). With Korobkin's argument in mind, we can read the defense's introduction into its case of Newsom's abuse of Celia as an attempt to appeal to a literary and, by extension, legal symbolism. It was an attempt "to construct a bond of sympathetic intimacy" through which the defense hoped jurors and the judge—familiar with the conventions of sentimentality—would identify her with a white archetype and therefore according to Missouri law acknowledge her as a woman, thereby admitting her right to self-defense (6). However, we can see that any plea the defense made to sentimental narrative ultimately failed. Despite the evidence presented, the judge admitted no mention of sexual intercourse into the final jury instructions, and thus the only significant grounds for Celia's defense were erased. An example of one of these instructions the defense submitted follows: "Although the jury may believe from the evidence that Newsom and another had had sexual intercourse with Celia, prior to the time of the said alledged [sic] killing, yet if they further believe from the testimony, that said Newsom at the time of said killing, attempted to compel her against her will to have sexual intercourse with him, they will not find her guilty of murder in the first degree, unless they further find that Celia killed Newsom feloniously, willfully, deliberately, premeditatedly, and of her malice aforethought" (file 4496). This instruction accounts for the fact that prior sexual involvement does not preclude rape—a sort of anticipatory "No Means No" approach to sexual violence. Regardless, the judge rejected the instruction along with nine others out of thirteen requested. Beyond the sexual abuse, testimony of witness William Powell also acknowledged Celia's illness—which may have been the way in which she characterized her pregnancy: "She said she threatened [him] that she would hurt him if he did not quit forcing her while she was sick. I don't know what her condition was as to health—had heard she was sick" (file 4496). Witness and daughter of Mr. Newsom, Virginia Wainscott, testified during cross-examination that "Celia had been sick. Took sick in February. [The trial was held in October.] Had been sick ever since. Had not been able to work since February" (file 4496). Neither the illness that prompted her to put a stop to the abuse, nor the abuse itself, factored into the possibility that Celia had any legal right to protect herself.

Beyond denying Celia a right to self-protection, the court drew attention to her bringing harm to Newsom. The prosecution and potentially even the judge seemed to have countered the defense's narrative of sentimentality with another literary genre: the Gothic. These symbolic literary registers produce rather opposite desires in witnesses and thus drastically different implications for the women they represent. Literary scholar Katherine Henry explains, "It is important . . . to distinguish between the effects of the Gothic and sentimental modes and the *desires* they produce: the Gothic effect is to entrap, producing the desire to escape, to externalize, to separate; the sentimental effect is to detach, thereby producing the desire to merge" (46). In keeping with this narrative logic, as the defense attempted to draw on the tradition that would inspire the jury's wish to "merge" on a sympathetic level with Celia and her suffering, the prosecution sought to distance the jurors as far as possible from her pain, to "other" her to the extent that they desired to "escape" her, which means to find her guilty and sentence her to death. Though they elicited testimony that cast a chilling brutality about the murder, it is evident that the prosecution's task was a difficult one. Though witnesses concentrated on the movements of Celia's body as she struck Newsom twice, they also discussed Newsom's movements as he entered her cabin after dark and indicated his lecherous motive. Even witnesses for the state mentioned Newsom's sexual relationship with Celia before cross-examination by the defense; however, as parentheses indicate, portions of the summary that potentially indicate Celia's intent to harm Newsom were subsequently added. The addenda appear to match Judge Hall's signature at the end of the summary and suggest his engagement with the prosecution's aim. The first witness for the state, Jefferson Jones, testified that Celia

> said the old man (Newsom, the deceased) had been having sexual intercourse with her. That he had told her he was coming down to her cabin that night. She told him not to come, and that if he came she would hurt him. {She then got a stick and put it in the corner.} He came down that night. {When she heard him coming she fixed the fire to make a little light.} There was very little fire in the kitchen cabin. She {said he was standing talking to her when she struck him.}

She said his face was towards her. He did not raise his hand when she went to strike the first blow but sunk down on a stool towards the floor. Threw his hands up when he sunk down. She struck him with one hand, her right hand. The stick with which she struck was about as large as the {upper part} of a Windsor chair, but not so long. She thought she did not kill him the first blow at the time of striking, but thought now that, the first blow must have killed him. She said she struck the second blow because he groaned. She {was afraid he} was not dead. (See figure 7.) (File 4496)

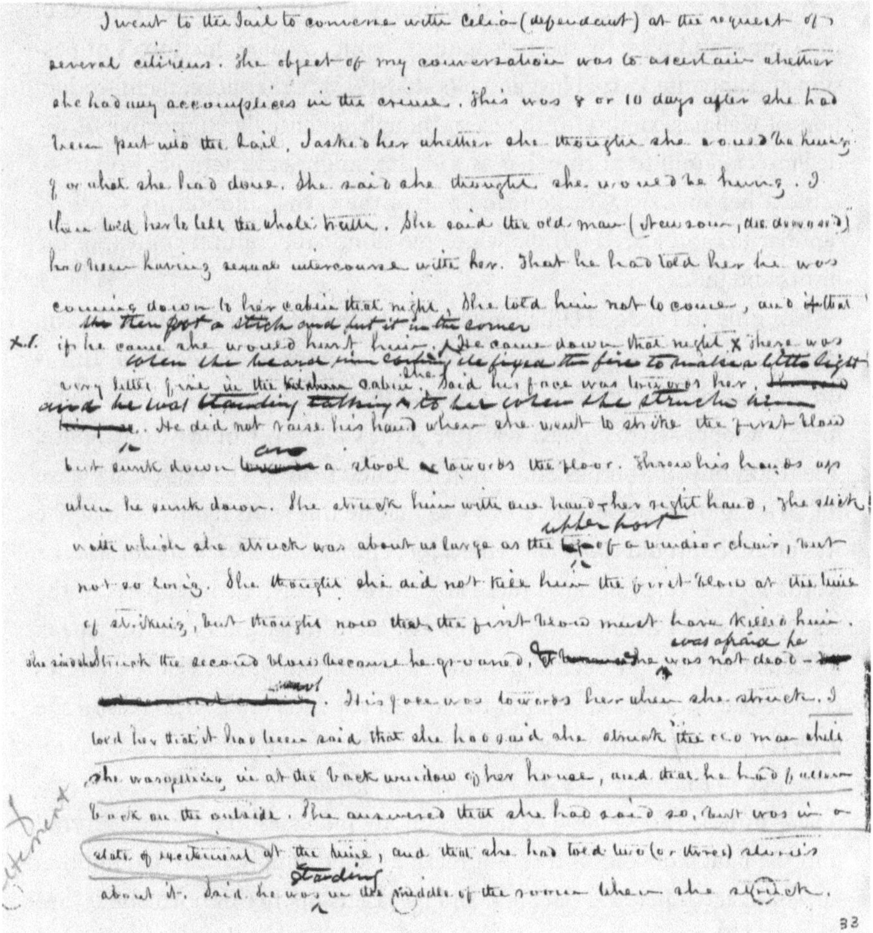

Figure 7. Addenda to trial summary, *Missouri v. Celia, a Slave*, 1855. Calloway County Courthouse.

Parenthetical information—namely Celia's positioning of the stick by the door, and increasing the light in the cabin—potentially indicates Celia's intent to harm Newsom, as does the mention of what he was doing when she struck him. Jones's testimony and the addenda situate Newsom securely as the passive victim in the encounter and emphasize Celia as exercising a calculated yet irrational violence. Further, the testimony underscores the racial anxieties to which historian H. L. Malchow refers in his discussion of Gothicism and race. He argues, "Both the gothic novel and racist discourse manipulate deeply buried anxieties, both dwell on the chaos beyond natural and rational boundaries and massage a deep, often unconscious and sexual, fear of contamination, both present the threatened destruction of the simple and pure by the poisonously exotic, by anarchic forces of passion and appetite, carnal lust and blood lust" (5).[20] Therefore, the introduction of Celia's sexuality to the case, though potentially supportive of the defense's attempt to portray her as a victim, might have actually worked to cement her into the Gothic/raced role of the carnal, bloodthirsty "other" familiar to (and feared by) the white and dominant cultural context of the jurors and judge.[21]

Not only did Judge Hall alter and add to the summary to imply intent; he also removed testimony that implied her actions in self-defense. This is the new evidence I have found recently from reading the original documents (as opposed to copies) available at the Calloway County Courthouse. The testimony of Thomas Shootman as edited reads: "The reason she gave for striking him the second blow, was that he threw his hands *up* that she was afraid he would *catch* her" (file 4496, emphasis mine). I emphasize the words *up* and *catch* because these are the most heavily edited parts of the testimony and which prior to what I assume is Judge Hall's editing, speak to Celia's attempt to defend herself. The testimony underneath the lines crossing out words and without the judge's addenda read: "The reason she gave for striking him the second blow was that he threw his hands up *toward her, to catch her that she was afraid he would hurt her*" (file 4496, emphasis mine). This version of the testimony indicates that Celia delivered him the fatal blow out of fear, not that he would simply *catch* her, but that he would catch her and *hurt* her, and by extension, her unborn child. (See figure 8.) The court concentrated on determining that she *intended* to kill Newsom and eliminated her right, while she was ill, to defend herself and her unborn child from harm.

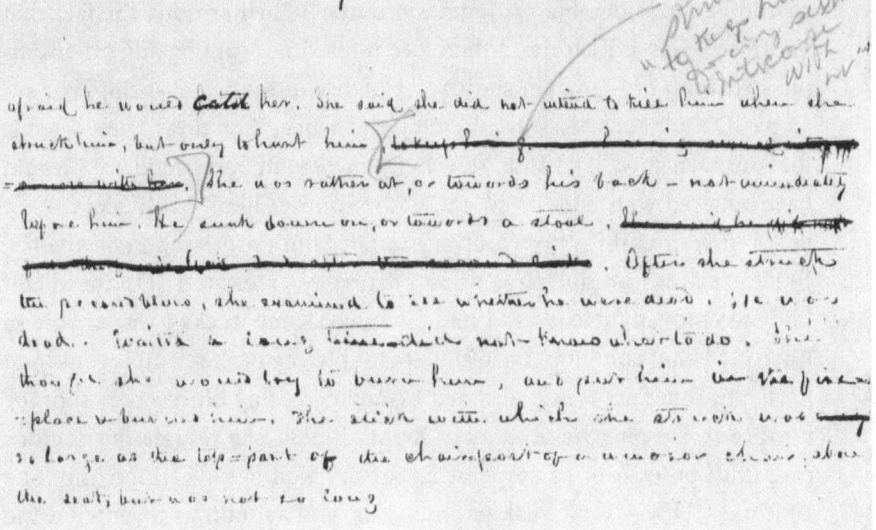

Figure 8. Addenda to trial summary, *Missouri v. Celia, a Slave*, 1855. Calloway County Courthouse.

Despite Celia's inability to transcend the limits of political, literary, and legal symbolism, her intentions became the focus of the trial, and in the process she became much more than a "mere" body, but a thinking—and according to the state, plotting—actor in the events, in behalf of whom the defense stated that "the greater portion of the community here [were] much interested."[22] However, she became so, politically, at the expense of her individuality and, individually, at the expense of her physical existence, and according to the court document, which records her stillborn child, at the expense of her child's life, too. As the cabin functioned metonymically to represent her body—owned and forcibly entered by Newsom—and the court debated her right to defend herself against sexual abuse, her body symbolized pro- and antislavery debates and engaged with traditions of sentimentalism and Gothicism. Because her physical signification was unsettling, however, the court added malicious intent and removed self-defense. The state sanctioned her execution, and her corporeality and agency were eliminated.

Linda Brent's actions also signify the increased deterioration of her body and emphasize the decline of her health as her narrative too engages with familiar nineteenth-century literary, social, and legal modes. Brent refers frequently to her ill-health, and like Celia's, her pregnancies also caused her considerable pain and discomfort. Furthermore, the fact that her owner was a doctor and therefore refused her care by any other emphasizes both pro- and antislavery use of discourses of well-being. For example, Dr. Flint chastises Brent with phrases like, "You don't know what is for your own good" (31) and "Your master was your best friend. . . . I would have bettered your condition" and with promises like, "I will take care of you and your child" (59). Contrary to Dr. Flint's professed benevolence, Brent explains how during her first pregnancy, "I was too ill in mind and body to enjoy my friends as I had done. For some weeks I was unable to leave my bed. I could not have any doctor but my master, and I would not have him sent for. At last, alarmed by my increasing illness, they sent for him" (60). Despite the severity of Brent's illness, she refuses the doctor's care until others out of desperation for her well-being call for him. She continues, "I was very weak and nervous; and as soon as he entered the room, I began to scream. They told him my state was very critical. He had no wish to hasten me out of the world, and he withdrew" (60). Far from having a beneficial effect on Brent's health, Dr. Flint's presence is psychologically and physically harmful to her. Medical historian Marie Jenkins Schwartz discusses the discrepancies between physicians and slaves concerning pregnancy: "While physicians and their slaveholder clients worried about shamming and deliberate abortions by enslaved women and inadvertent miscarriages initiated by doctors, slaves held different fears about the future of mothers and infants. Enslaved women were . . . likely to be deprived of sufficient material resources or subjected to harsh work regimens and physical chastisement during pregnancy" (132). To deprivation of resources and subjection to hard labor, in Brent's situation, we can add psychological torment. That her owner was also her physician *and* her abuser exacerbates the already complicated nature of slave pregnancy. Brent depicts her physical and emotional/psychological suffering as a result of Dr. Flint's "care."

It seems here that love for her child and the desire to protect him sustained her, indeed kept her alive. Brent gives birth to a premature baby weighing only four pounds, but the child lives. Her own life is threatened: "I heard the doctor say I could not survive till morning. I had often prayed for death; but now I did not want to die, unless my child could die too"

(60). On the flipside of the psychological torture she underwent, the love she has for her newborn and her determination to protect him seems to fortify her somewhat. "Many weeks passed before I was able to leave my bed. I was a mere wreck of my former self. For a year there was scarcely a day when I was free from chills and fever. My babe was also sickly. His little limbs were often racked with pain. Dr. Flint continued his visits, to look after my health; and he did not fail to remind me that my child was an addition to his stock of slaves" (61). Brent's and her child's ill health persist, and the doctor, while purporting to care for her, physically takes the opportunity afforded by his visits to inflict further psychological abuse on the already ill and weakened woman. As in Mary Prince's situation, Brent's condition does not improve when she's "free" from Flint. Ill health follows her as she becomes a fugitive.

Confined to the crawlspace above her grandmother's house and secretly surveying others' actions through a hole in the wall, Brent also watches her body atrophy. She recollects how she lived "with no space to move [her] limbs, for nearly seven years" (148). Another time she explains how she had to sneak into the storeroom in order to regain feeling in her limbs: "They were so numb and stiff that it was a painful effort to move; and had my enemies come upon me during the first mornings I tried to exercise them a little in the small unoccupied space of the storeroom, it would have been impossible for me to have escaped" (132). Linda Brent's identity as a sexual human being changes after her escape from Dr. Flint. As her health deteriorates and her muscles weaken, so does her corporeal identity. We might read this shift as similar to the one that occurs when Mary Prince turns her critique toward the English. Brent laments that "the laws allowed *him* to be out in the free air, while I, guiltless of crime, was pent up here, as the only means of avoiding the cruelties the laws allowed him to inflict upon me" (121). However, she also notes the satisfaction she feels in having outwitted Dr. Flint. When she hides in the anonymous "mistress's" house, she explains how she "could lie perfectly concealed, and command a view of the street through which Dr. Flint passed to his office. . . . Thus far I had outwitted him, and I triumphed over it" (100). As many critics have noted, her rhetoric of command and triumph underscores the potency she feels from the shifting power differential between herself and Dr. Flint. This time he is under her surveillance. Feminist historian Stephanie Camp has reworked Edward Said's notion of "rival geographies" for the slave South—"alternative ways of knowing and using plantation and southern space that conflicted with planters' ideals and demands" (7). For Brent, the crawlspace functions in this way, allowing her the ability to survey Flint's movements and words to reorient southern space and alter power dynamics. Later she explains how she "could hear much that was said in the street without being seen" (107) and that she "heard many conversations not intended to meet [her] ears" (117).

Michel Foucault's identification of the relationship between surveillance and discipline is a connection with which Brent reveals her familiarity.[23] Of course, at the time Brent secretly watches Dr. Flint, he is unaware of her presence; however, her ability to remain concealed from his view while surveying his actions lends to her an amount of power she previously lacked when constantly pursued by his gaze. By extension, her invisibility and Flint's visibility impart to the reader a similar measure of control so that we can read the publication of her narrative as an exercise in disciplinary power, even though it comes with a cost of increased physical pain and discomfort. By relaying the events she experienced during her enslavement, Brent exposes the "secrets of slavery" to her readers, and when narrating her surveillance of Flint from a place of concealment, she extends the experience to the reader whose gaze also falls on the unwitting, and now dead, slaveholder.[24]

Such transference of power, though physically constraining for Linda, also identifies her less with her body—again, a similar shift to that which we've observed in Prince's *History*. As Brent's focus shifts to the street she watches from her hiding place, Flint becomes the object of the narrator's eye, and her own physicality becomes less its focus. She exercises the power of surveillance and finds herself privy to information not intended for her. Such power also enables her to condemn Dr. Flint through a third party. In the conversations she overhears, she recounts one man who says, "I wouldn't move my little finger to catch her, as old Dr. Flint's property," to which his companion responds in opposition, "A man ought to have what belongs to him, [even] if he *is* a damned brute" (117). By reproducing the informal debate between the two men about property rights, Brent condemns Dr. Flint's character through a perspective other than her own and illuminates the ideological division among whites on the subject of rights where owner-slave sexual exploitation is concerned. Through these techniques, Brent transfers the focus of sexuality from herself onto Dr. Flint as she places him not only within her disciplining eye but also within her reader's.

Brent's "melting away" in a confined space suggests yet another religious narrative: the saint in a nunnery, the maiden who walls herself in to escape male lechery and exploitation. Her physical deterioration becomes symbolic of her rejection of sexual abuse. Of course, this construction is problematic in that Brent's identification as more than a "mere body" is contingent upon her body's desexualization and the further decline of her health. Like Celia, Brent begins to undergo a process of physical eradication when she attempts to define herself beyond her corporeality. When Celia escaped from jail just before the scheduled date of her execution, newspaper reports stated that she "had been out nearly a week, and during that time, as she states, she had lived on raw corn which she gathered from the fields.—She was driven in by cold and hunger. Being thinly clad and without shoes, and the night very cool, she must have suffered considerably during the time of her absence."[25] The papers reported that Celia returned to Robert Newsom's son as a result of "cold and hunger," not that she was "returned" by people aiding her as McLaurin has hypothesized—though reports of her escape are consistent with a letter to the Missouri Supreme Court in implying that she and her fellow inmate were "most likely assisted in their efforts to escape from the outside."[26] And indeed Camp has demonstrated that truants in general could not "avoid the material deprivations that would compel them to return to their quotidian lives" (54). The possibility that Celia returned to the Newsoms out of physical desperation corresponds to the type of physical decline Linda Brent suffers when she asserts her agency; we must also acknowledge Celia's agency in returning herself. Of course, the state-sanctioned execution of Celia and the injurious consequence of Brent's willful concealment do not represent identical physical responses to the lack of civil subjecthood they encounter in their abusive situations, but they do punctuate their difficulty by explicitly articulating sexual interference.

In order to disclose their abuse within such confined subjecthood, Celia and Brent manipulate one mode of testimony available to slaves: the confession. Foucault has delineated the causal relationship between the increasing prevalence and scope of discourses of sexuality and the religious confession (*Sexuality* 19). Furthermore, both women's confessed acts are attempts at protecting themselves from further physical, sexual, and psychological harm. In the Protestant context of the nineteenth-century United States, we see a similar scope of confession in Jacobs's narrative when Brent "confesses" her relationship with her white lover, Mr. Sands, "I will not try to screen myself behind the plea of compulsion from a master; for it was not so. Neither can I plead ignorance or thoughtlessness. For years, my master had done his utmost to pollute my mind with foul images, and to destroy the pure principles inculcated by my grandmother and the good mistress of my childhood. The influences of slavery had had the same effect on me that they had on other young girls; they had made me prematurely knowing, concerning the evil ways of the world. I knew what I did and I did it with deliberate calculation" (54). Brent chooses to disclose this relationship and her willing entry into it. By identifying the sexual sins of Dr. Flint in her own confession, she becomes the medium of a kind of vicarious confession in which she places the reader as silent hearer/confessor. The continuation of her statement regarding Mr. Sands reveals the increasing relationship between the discussion of sexuality (not named imprudently) and encompassing confession that Foucault discusses. Brent continues:

> So much attention from a superior person was, of course, flattering; for human nature is the same in all. I also felt grateful for his sympathy, and encouraged by his kind words. It seemed to me a great thing to have such a friend. By degrees, a more tender feeling crept into my heart. He was an educated and eloquent gentleman, too eloquent, alas, for the poor slave girl who trusted in him. Of course I saw whither all this was tending. I knew the impassable gulf between us; but to be an object of interest to a man who is not married, and who is not her master, is agreeable to the pride and feelings of a slave, if her miserable situation has left her any pride or sentiment. It seems less degrading to give one's self, than to submit to compulsion. (54–55)

In her descriptions of Sands, she somewhat adopts the conventional role of the seduction novel's heroine, but she downplays Sands's vice. Rather she uses him and her willingness to be seduced—or even her seduction of him—to underscore Flint's vice and to cast him in the literary role of the seducer.[27] She explicitly details her desire for attention, sympathy, and kindness, which she found in Sands. Furthermore, she expresses the gratification she experiences knowing that she is sexually attractive to him—all of these characteristics of this relationship seem to benefit her mental health, which suffered unspeakably under Dr. Flint's authority. She reworks the confessional mode to expose aspects of sexual and psychological health and well-being that Dr. Flint's behavior not only denied her but that actually did her injury. Brent gathers her readers together with black women under the umbrella of "human nature," regardless of legal constructions of personhood.

Both Celia's and Brent's "confessions" underscore motives of health and well-being for their actions. Trial testimony that "spoke" Celia's confessions addressed the sexual abuse she suffered as Newsom's slave. Witnesses noted her relationship with George, the slave who had been "staying with her," and who threatened to "have nothing more to do with her if she did not quit [Newsom]." Further testimony alleged that Newsom "forced" Celia to have sexual intercourse with him. Therefore, evidence presented at trial attested to the physical, sexual, and psychological harm Celia suffered under the authority of Newsom and to an extent George. Her second deposition, the only one bearing her mark, however, says nothing of the sexual abuse or of her relationship with George. It states that

> Celia a slave belonging to Robert Newsom being sworn says that she killed her master on the night of the 23rd day of June 1855 about two hours after dark by striking him twice on the head with a stick, and then put his body on the fire and burnt it nearly up, then took up the ashes in the morning after day light, after breakfast, the bones were not entirely burnt up. I took up the ashes and bones out of the fire place in my cabin where I burnt the body and emptied them on the right hand side of the path leading from my cabin to the stable . (See figure 9.) (File 4496)

Consistent with the edits and addenda I attribute to Judge Hall, this court document also excludes any motive for the killing that implies self-preservation/protection. Her deposition, testimony ostensibly less removed than the confessions provided in the trial summary, portrays her in a much less

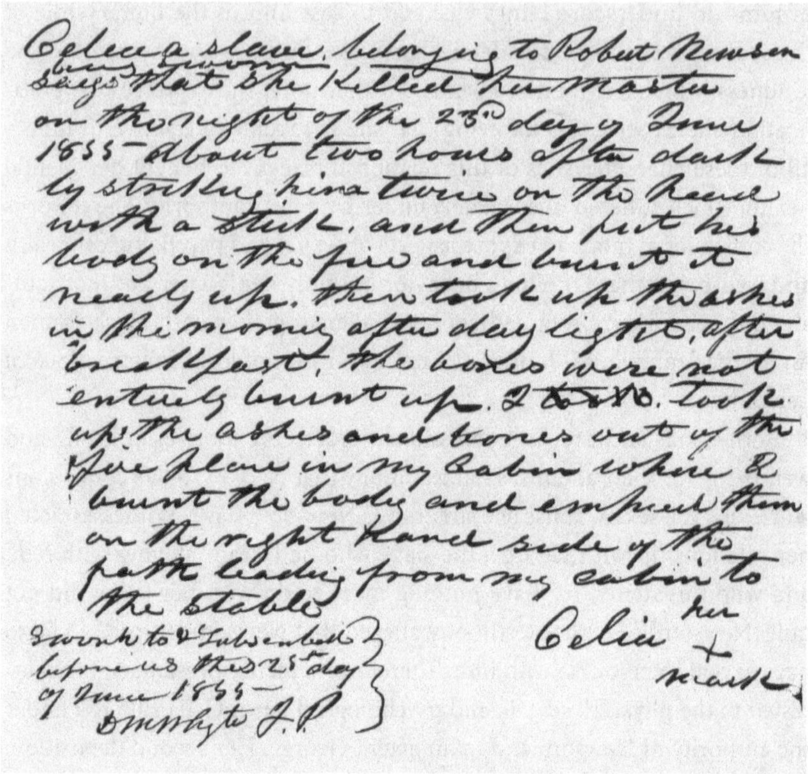

> Celia a slave, belonging to Robert Newson says that she killed her master on the night of the 23rd day of June 1855 — about two hours after dark by striking him twice on the head with a stick, and then put his body on the fire and burnt it nearly up. then took up the ashes in the morning after day light, after breakfast, the bones were not entirely burnt up. I took. took up the ashes and bones out of the fire place in my cabin where I burnt the body and emptied them on the right hand side of the path leading from my cabin to the stable
>
> Sworn to & Subscribed before us this 23rd day of June 1855 — D M Whyte J.P.
>
> Celia ✕ her mark

Figure 9. Deposition bearing Celia's mark, June 23, 1855. Calloway County Courthouse.

sentimental light as it describes her killing and disposing of Newsom. As a confession, the deposition, stripped of Celia's motives, preempted the "powerless victim" role with which the defense would attempt to furnish her; the document fashions the speaker as a calculated, reasoning murderer who carefully attempted to cover up her crime—a portrayal similar to the arguably Gothic representations that the prosecution (and potentially the judge) would elicit/invoke during the trial. However, in keeping with the defense that would be presented at trial, reprints from the *Fulton Telegraph* express doubt as to Celia's ability to have committed the murder and disposed of the body on her own:

> The short time allowed in which to dispose of him, the condition of the Negro, (who, we learn, had been unwell for several days) and the known physical ability of the old man, render it a matter of doubt whether or not his body had been consumed. . . . We think the whole

story very improbable, and believe that she must have had some assistance. She stoutly denied having any aid and says that she has disclosed all the facts of the case.[28]

Pregnant and sick, Celia no doubt would have had an extremely difficult time disposing of Newsom if not killing him as well. Nevertheless, the prosecution objected to the questions that Celia's defense intended to ask the testifying doctors, and the judge sustained the objections. There are three separate questions along these lines: "In your opinion, as an adept or scientific physician, what length of time would be required to destroy or consume the body of a man, in an ordinary fire-place, by a wood fire?" (file 4496). (See figure 10.) The defense seems to have wanted to imply that it was unlikely that the contents of the fireplace the day after Newsom's disappearance were actually his remains, perhaps casting doubt about how the sick, pregnant Celia could have disposed of the dead man on her own.

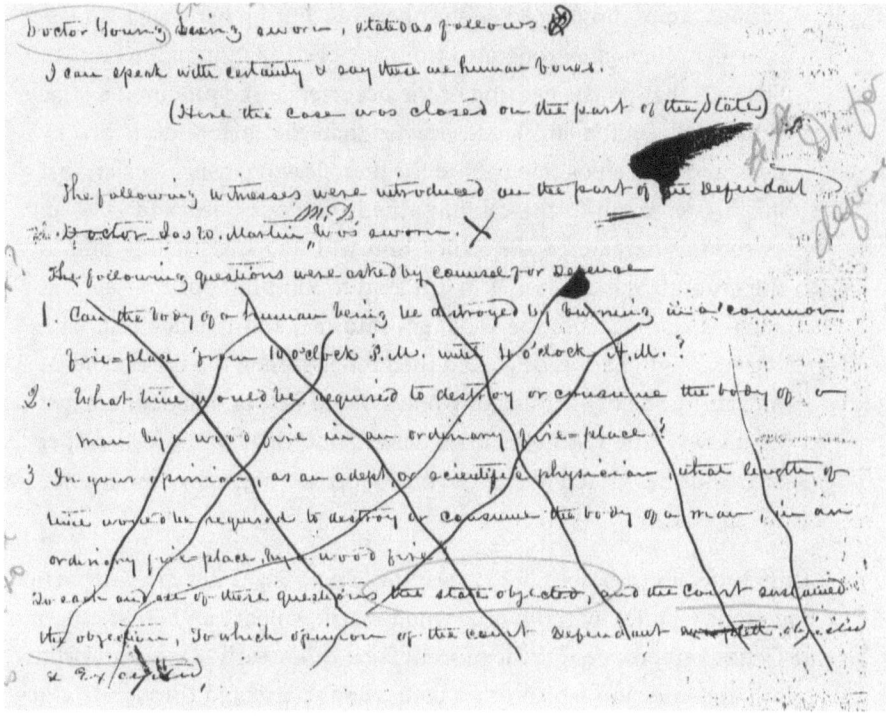

Figure 10. Questions for testifying physicians, prosecution objections, and objections sustained, 1855. Calloway County Courthouse.

Celia's "confessions," presented in the newspapers and at trial (even by state witnesses), are concerned with her motive and means, and thereby cast doubt on the extent of her guilt; only the deposition—and newspaper accounts taken directly from it—provided testimony omitting any statement of motive for the murder and denying any assistance in her disposal of the body. The accuracy of Celia's sworn statement can never be known, but the discrepancy between it and the press and public's hesitancy to accept it are noteworthy, as is the court's desire to suppress her motive and potential right to self-defense.

The confession taken on the eve of her execution, quoted in the *Fulton Telegraph* and reprinted in the *Daily Missouri Democrat*, the *New York Times*, and the *Baltimore Sun*, makes no mention of her sexual abuse, but alludes to the source of her physical strength and mental determination to kill Newsom and closes with an ambiguous sentence:

> The evening previous to her execution, and while under the gallows, she made what she said was a full confession of the crime. She has, at various times, implicated several persons, but by her dying confession all of them are exonerated from any participation in the murder. She said that on the evening of the occurrence she procured a large stout stick, (much larger and heavier than that before described by her), and took a position behind the door, leaving it slightly ajar; that her master came to the cabin, pushed the door open and entered; as soon as he entered she struck him with the stick, felling him to the ground. She did not at first intend to kill him, but she said, "as soon as I struck him the Devil got into me, and I struck him with the stick until he was dead, and then rolled him in the fire and burnt him up."[29] She denied that any one assisted her, or aided, or abetted in any way. She was hung at 2½ o'clock, on Friday, 21st of December last. Thus has closed one of the most horrible tragedies ever enacted in our county.[30]

This confession, as does her deposition, emphasizes her criminal action and omits mention of motive. Its emphasis on violence and on the absence of Celia's remorse renders it more typical of an early American printed criminal confession which other confessions presented through trial testimony do not; Celia's (or the journalist's) invocation of the Devil is also in keeping with traditional American gallows literature that functions as a warning to the religious community. Further, we can read her allusion to the supernatural as a gesture to the Gothic. If the piece accurately represents her own words, it is possible to read her previous confessions as not only rejections of the sentimentalist mode but also as direct invocations of the Gothic. From such a possibility, we must ask to what extent Celia may have participated in reinforcing her self-image of the Gothic other in response to her victimization. Furthermore, the absence of her abuse combined with her ill health might speak to her rejection of the victim's role, and given the extent and duration of her abuse, it is not difficult to imagine the accuracy of her statement, that if not the Devil, then perhaps the adrenaline rush and thrill after that first disabling blow could inspire her to finish off the man who terrorized her. Of course, we can only speculate that the omission of sexual references in newspapers, particularly after her trial, indicate Celia's unwillingness to report her exploitation or the reporter's censorship of it. However, the last sentence of the *Telegraph*'s final article on Celia is decidedly ambiguous. I have found reprints only in the antislavery *Missouri Democrat*, the *New York Times*, and the *Baltimore Sun*. That there are so few reprints is surprising given that numerous Missouri papers had reprinted stories regarding Newsom's murder and Celia's indictment, escape, and recovery. The absence of her final confession in most Missouri papers and its presence in out-of-state papers might suggest that the ambiguous "tragedy" to which the *Telegraph* refers might have been interpreted by some papers to have been Celia's own and that the newspapers either chose to print and therefore endorse such a sympathetic view or not.

Though Celia's and Brent's indirect reporting of sexual abuse is contingent upon their crimes, each verbal reenactment of the abuse signifies another violation of them. We can hypothesize that Celia and Jacobs adopted indirect means of reporting their experiences for both physical and psychological reasons. Celia's filtered testimony and Jacobs's allusive and euphemistic rhetoric refuse the listener or reader an explicit account of their victimization. Thus we must hear and read the owner's sexual "crimes" from the tongues and on the bodies of white people. Witnesses speak Celia's "confession" in court while Brent writes hers on the white faces of her listeners and the white spaces of her text.

Early in her narrative, Brent frames the confession as a "crime." Jacobs's rhetoric implies that in the context of owner-slave sexual abuse, revelation is "criminal." As Jeannine DeLombard argues, "Over the course of the narrative, Jacobs rejects a confessional posture in favor of a testimonial one: adopting the stance of a witness and testifying *against* the crime of slavery and *to* the trauma of sexual exploitation" ("Adding Her Testimony" 32). Brent recounts the plight of Dr. Flint's former slave who "had forgotten that it was a crime for a slave to tell who was the father of her child" (13). Here she conflates the woman's speech with legislated crime while simultaneously implying her owner's moral guilt. Later in the narrative, Brent describes how, as she grew older and Dr. Flint began "swearing by heaven and earth that he would compel [her] to submit to him," that the other slaves noticed, and knowing "too well the guilty practices under that roof... were aware that to speak of them was an offence that never went unpunished" (28). Her legal rhetoric here attempts to invert notions of crime. Speaking of the owner's guilt is a punishable offense. We can read such an inversion as Jacobs's attempt to draw on Puritan law, which indicted moral crimes and on the same conflation abolitionists would later infuse into their antislavery rhetoric about moral guilt. Against such notions of law and morality, she reflects nineteenth-century North Carolina law, which prohibited slaves from "utter[ing] mischievous and slanderous reports about any free white person" (sec. 31). The law's ability to encompass mischief *and* slander protected owners and white people generally from suffering implications of impropriety—whether true or slanderous. By combining moral and legal concepts of crime, Jacobs attempts to undermine the validity of the slave code. Legally, Brent was required to submit to Flint; however, Jacobs's rhetorical structure morally condemns the U.S. laws allowing this practice. Further, as Accomando duly notes, "Part of Jacobs's purpose in emphasizing law is to shift the focus to the *institution* of slavery, as it was designed and supported, as opposed to mere exceptions or excesses. Focusing at times on *national law* also helps reveal Northern complicity in Southern slavery" (241).

Not only does Jacobs inject Brent's rhetoric with allusions to law, but she does the same with Dr. Flint's language, as he terrorizes her by invoking the very laws that render her vulnerable to him. Brent recalls his accusations that she had "been criminal" toward him, that he said "on one condition [he] will forgive [her] insolence and crime" (58–59). In fact, in the state of North Carolina, insolence was a crime.[31] Hartman argues, "The repeated use of the term 'crime' throughout the narrative documents the displacement of culpability onto the enslaved and crime as a predominant mode of black subjection" (105). I argue, however, that Brent's rhetorical emphasis on "crime" also divests the word itself of its meaning and renders it ironic. Acts her society criminalizes, her narrative justifies, and conversely, acts her society justifies, her narrative criminalizes; however, her narrative does so only rhetorically. She was, in reality, neither free nor exonerated.

In keeping with such an inverted structure, Brent reveals her owner's "crimes" in an unsettling testimonial scene with Mrs. Flint, who becomes the text where we read sexual exploitation. As we have seen in Mary Prince's *History*, Brent shifts her rhetorics of physicality from depictions of herself to those of her mistress and thereby critiques the woman and her actions. Brent explains, "As I went on with my account her color changed frequently, she wept, and sometimes groaned. She spoke in tones so sad, that I was touched by her grief. The tears came to my eyes: but I was soon convinced that her emotions arose from anger and wounded pride. She felt that her marriage vows were desecrated, her dignity insulted; but she had no compassion for the victim of her husband's perfidy" (33). Here, as in Prince's *History*, the mistress's color change is the focus. Although critics have read this scene as a reenactment of sexual abuse and a violation of Mrs. Flint, I believe Brent's rhetorics of physicality also sexualize the mistress and implicitly question her sexual morality.

Literary scholars have interpreted the violence of this scene compellingly in different ways. First, Karen Sanchez-Eppler points out that "For Linda . . . this enforced act of recounting her sexual victimization repeats the scene of sexual abuse" (95). Further, Deborah Garfield has argued that Brent displaces the act of violence "into language"; therefore, possibly to resist a subsequent violation by writing it, Jacobs metonymically displaces the abuse onto the mistress whose reactions reveal to us the gravity of Linda's injury ("Speech" 30). Her confession also symbolically violates Mrs. Flint who, as Garfield points out, "must now remain the passive recipient of Linda's recitation of the Doctor's infidelities" (35).

As well as symbolically violating Mrs. Flint, Brent challenges the woman's sexual morality by casting her as a participant in Brent's sexual harassment. Mrs. Flint reenacts her husband's abuse of Linda by ventriloquizing his voice at night while Linda sleeps. Brent and her mistress verbally transfer the trauma of sexual abuse in a scene which, through suggestion, reveals the haunting severity of Dr. Flint's cruelty. Further, in the chapter "Jealous Mistress" in which the ventriloquized scene takes place, Brent testifies to another "crime." When Mrs. Flint speaks for her husband, she takes part in his sexual abuse of Linda. The sufficiency of Brent's assumption that Mrs. Flint does this to trap her into revealing her husband's sins can be debated. It is possible that the "jealous mistress" is such because she does not enjoy the extent of oppression over Brent that her husband does. Garfield has described the scene as "a re-creation of the Master's attempt to seduce Linda" and noted Mrs. Flint's inability to "sculpt a sexual persona outside his" ("Earwitness" 115). Thus Brent's depiction of the "jealous woman bending over [her]" (34) portrays the mistress exacting her own kind of sexual authority over the girl. If Brent's focus on Mrs. Flint's physicality demonstrates the woman displacing her husband's indulgences onto herself for her own sexual gratification, then perhaps the mistress's "jealousy" is directed at her husband and his ability to exercise a distinctly raced, authoritative sexual persona that she cannot enjoy but only imitate. Either way, psychologically both owner and mistress are sexually abusive.

In Celia's and Brent's accounts, we see practical and rhetorical distinctions between testimony and confession and the insufficiency of either mode to represent black women's sense of self adequately. The available modes of culturally symbolic self-representation are restrictive. The courtroom testimony of Celia's trial tried to emphasize her intention to defend herself from her owner's sexual advances and overtly called into question the dead man's character, which Celia's lawyers used as the foundation of her defense.[32] Illness and sexual and psychological abuse prompted her action to protect herself and her unborn baby from further harm. The published newspaper confession, on the other hand, underscored the sensational violence of Newsom's death, thus following in the tradition of nineteenth-century Gothic tradition and American gallows literature, which included publication of increasingly sensational criminal confessions and trial transcripts.[33] However, Celia's published "confessions" omitted the sexual details of the case despite the fact that, as Daniel Cohen points out, "One of the most striking aspects of . . . nineteenth-century [crime] literature, cutting across the different genres, was its preoccupation with crimes of sexual deviance and violence" (*Pillars* 36).[34] The popularity of such accounts in nineteenth-century American print culture and their absence in the *Telegraph* suggest that Newsom's race and social status may have influenced the omission of the confession's sexual content. In the *Missouri Republican*, under the headline "FIENDISH MURDER," Celia's character emerges as a female variation of what Cohen calls "the protoracist image of the black man as a cruel . . . murderer of white women and children already embedded in popular English print culture" ("Social Injustice" 489).[35] Therefore, Celia's sexual abuse exposed the gap in her legal subjecthood denoted as a "double character" that legitimated Newsom's use of terror. Further, her criminal response to such abuse, followed by testimonial and confessional representations of it, exposed a gap in her literary/cultural subjecthood onto which various agents attempted to fashion sentimental and Gothic conventions, but who ultimately situated her outside an established tradition of sexual assault narratives whose characters were mainly black male perpetrators and white female victims. In the end, it is tempting to read the last primary representation of Celia, her "confession" to the *Telegraph*, as an example of her coherence with the character of the Gothic murderer, racially "othered," possessed by supernatural forces, and therefore requiring amputation from the social body. Even so, her possible acceptance or even crafting of this retributive sense of self in defiance of her victimization and as a reclamation or representation of physical strength and vitality after years of abuse and at least eight months of ill health—though potentially reinforcing stereotypes of black criminality—does not obscure the complex legal and cultural ruptures that expose her status and context as abused, enslaved, and female.

Six years later, however, Harriet Jacobs reworked aspects of the criminal confession, testimonial, criminal biography, and the seduction novel—out of which grew the nineteenth-century woman's slave narrative. She demonstrates the dire lengths to which Brent had to go in order to remove herself from Dr. Flint's sexual and psychological abuse. Though she is successful, she still has to contend with the physical ill health resulting from that abuse. Ill health follows her into hiding where at one point she is unconscious for sixteen hours and where her friends fear she'll "become a cripple for life" (122, 127). Even though once in the North her "health was greatly improved, . . . [her] limbs continued to trouble [her] with swelling whenever [she] walked much" (168). The centrality of (ill) health and well-being to Brent's sense of self, her determination to protect herself from further sexual and psychological harm, as in Celia's case, undergirds her actions, some of them even at the expense of her health and wellness.

By crossing the borders demarcating the duality of slaves' legal subjecthood, Celia and Linda Brent reveal the sexual and psychological terror against enslaved women the slave system supported and demonstrate the extent to which owner-slave sexual abuse complicated the theoretically protective concept of "double character." By exposing gaps in their subjecthood, as constructed by the dominant legal and social discourse of their time, and by responding to interracial sexual abuse with state-defying actions, both women question the legitimacy of the laws by which they are bound to live and expose the limited conceptions of black women's selfhood those laws have crafted. The criminal responses of Celia and Brent demonstrate the dire defenses required against antebellum violent sexual victimization of enslaved women and the similarly dire effects such action has on their health. In the next chapter, men's fictional literary imaginings of masculine responses to women's sexual abuse as well as enslaved men's status as dependents of white males further emphasize the centrality of sexual identity in the articulation of Black American embodied selfhood. As we will see, men's novelistic depictions use the vehicle of revolution to imagine the avenging of wrongs commensurate with the enjoyment of a healthy, vigorous sexuality and the reclamation of manhood—heroic manhood—all crucial to their mid-nineteenth-century sense of black health and well-being.

5

The Promising Self

Sexual Expression, Heroism, and Revolution

FREDERICK DOUGLASS'S "THE HEROIC SLAVE"
AND MARTIN ROBISON DELANY'S BLAKE

Slave women's particular vulnerability to sexual abuse and coercion no doubt inspired not only women's desire to protect themselves and even seek retribution, but many a male revenge fantasy as well. Actual larger-scale reprisal in the form of revolt not only attempted the reclamation of stolen freedom but in fiction becomes symbolic vengeance for numerous wrongs committed under the protection of slave law as well. By the time Frederick Douglass and Martin Delany extended their literary talents to fiction, they were firmly established public figures and men of letters. Turning to a fictive form, they were able to expand their political imaginings and claim a place within a growing genre of Black American literature and participate in the novel's rising importance in American literature more broadly. This form in some ways offered greater possibilities for conceiving the project of self-making and articulating a potential black sense of self that conversed with white writers' portrayals of black revolutionaries, ancient and modern European, real or imagined or both. Black health and well-being—particularly healthy sexuality—are central concerns of these texts, which are as much about domestic happiness as they are about political upheaval and the making of the black hero. Shifting from enslaved women's personal narratives, sexual abuse, individual crimes, and self-expression, this chapter returns to a similar idealism we saw theorized in chapter 2 to uncover these two writers' exercise of political and individual reimagining through what we might understand as the fantasy of revolt, the taking back of stolen freedom, and the realization of a sexually healthy and robust, classically heroic, ideal black self.[1]

Frederick Douglass's novella, "The Heroic Slave" (1853), and Martin Delany's novel, *Blake; or, The Huts of America* (1859, 1861–62), are fictive representations of organized slave revolts.[2] This literature uses the trope of revolution figuratively to repair the black, particularly the enslaved, body, which nineteenth-century medical and legal theory had fragmented and categorized. The theoretical anatomization refers to contemporary notions of conceptualizations of hierarchically ordered human species, which relegated black people to the lowest rank, a mind/body split within humans that exaggerated black corporeality and dismissed intellect, and the slave's dual status as property and person. Reading Douglass's and Delany's fiction in the broader context of this book builds on recent scholarship emphasizing the centrality of the home and the family to the black radical's sense of self, a concern that had been given little attention previously and that offers new ways of understanding midcentury Black American masculinity.[3] I extend this scholarship in my consideration specifically of healthy, consensual, enjoyable sexuality and the ability to exercise sexual choice. Furthermore, I depart from previous scholars in my impression of these authors' expressions of gender, health, and power dynamics. Whereas these critics typically see Douglass's and Delany's fiction conforming to dominant cultural ideas about women's inferiority, I see them emphasizing women's integral roles in the project of black revolution. Douglass and Delany assert healthy black physicality to reveal the embodied experience of intellect and emotion in producing a concept of intimate black selfhood at once physical, intellectual, and sexual. Extending from this intimate black selfhood is the ideal hero who draws together classical values of civic responsibility, physical strength, virtue, manliness, and intellect.

Medical and legal divisions distinguished the enslaved body from the mind to diminish or to undermine the slave's mental capacity altogether. The result was the white intellectual tendency to conflate black selfhood primarily with corporeality. With regard to the fictive works addressed in this chapter, scholars have productively emphasized the relation between the eloquent black voice and intellect and demonstrated how Douglass and Delany defy discourses that de-emphasized black intellectual capacity.[4] But privileging the voice or assuming that the voice and body are somehow separate ironically replicates the dividing of the enslaved self that the "peculiar institution," its supporters, and discourses of medicine and law practiced on it.[5] Rather, these authors infuse in their characters what Eric Hairston identifies as "The Aristotelian intellectual virtues of wisdom and intuitive good judgment—combined with the moral virtues of courage, temperance, greatness of soul, gentleness, honesty, wit, friendliness, righteous indignation, and justice" (5).[6]

Douglass and Delany use the forms of the novella and novel to reclaim the enslaved physique from discourses that have attempted to subdivide it, categorize it, and separate it from its intellect. They confront the stereotypes of the "black savage" who is at once violent and ignorant, incapable of complex thought, and hypersexual—essentially a positive threat to white existence when allowed to lurk outside the dominant culture's rule and regulation. Both activist authors and intellectuals, Douglass and Delany chose the subject of revolution during times when the fear of slave revolt gripped the southern United States. Names of rebel leaders like Denmark Vesey and Nat Turner were either held up as examples of the potential for black-on-white violence and large-scale revolt and therefore the need for stricter regulation of slaves or they were uneasily downplayed as atypical disrupters of a typically peaceable South. David Walker's 1829 *Appeal to the Coloured Citizens of the World* sent ripples of alarm throughout the South to the extent that its distribution was illegal. In this climate, Douglass and Delany made their protagonists physically powerful and intellectually rigorous, capable of committing acts of violence—in Delany's work, on both individual and organized levels. Their protagonists are the leaders of the revolts and appear when such events—actual or possible—panicked and terrorized the white community. In other words, they chose for their heroes men who threatened to reify all the stereotypes of black savagery, criminality, and hypersexuality that white racism had produced; however, their appeals to classical heroic ideals function as a mode through which to critique slaveholding ideology that works so hard to separate black from white and remove the possibility of heroism outside a white, male elite context. They remind their readers of the heroic value of revolution and the response to injustice while emphasizing the importance of personal intimacy.

The authors portray this black self as consciously embodied; the body and mind work in concert as two components of the same form that cannot be separated and should be feared for its determination to remove itself from white subjugation. They show that black sexuality is a crucial component of a black masculine sense of self and of political relationships as well. Sexuality and marriage in Douglass and Delany are central to the way their characters understand themselves and their acquisition of political autonomy. Contrary to nineteenth-century representations of black sexuality that have mainly focused on criminality and subjection, for example, in *Missouri v. Celia, a slave* and in Harriet Jacobs's *Incidents*, Douglass and Delany present the possibility of black sexuality that is healthy, consensual, enjoyable, external to white rule, and unapologetic. The two authors regard such sexuality as a human right to which Black Americans are entitled, not a privilege that requires white consent or regulation or even a civil right that attends citizenship. As the previous chapters have demonstrated, both pro- and antislavery advocates approached sex and slavery in ways that severely limited black sexual expression. Proslavery theories, such as Cobb's, about black lasciviousness as well as white abolitionist "separate spheres" and "cult of true womanhood" ideology—as manifested in moral and legal codes—imposed restrictions on acceptable conjugal conduct among Black Americans and between black men, particularly, and whites. Furthermore, the denial of legally sanctioned marriage for slaves relegates black enslaved men to the status of dependents of white men rather than men with their own dependents. As quoted in this book's second epigraph, thinkers such as William Harper argued that men "should indeed regard [slaves] as wards and dependents on our kindness, for whose well-being in every way we are deeply responsible" (118). Douglass and Delany's rhetorics of physicality present to their readers a model black masculine sense of self that is complexly layered and rejects their relegation to a collection of measured body parts, as wards of white "masters" requiring the benevolent care of white planters to protect them from themselves. The heroes demonstrate the need to reject and subvert white domination by what they justify as the only effective means: violence—not random, but planned.

Literary critic William L. Andrews's analysis of the fictive voice is useful for this chapter because it applies to both texts and offers a way of discussing them that accounts for their movement between real and imagined realms, and it can emphasize the actuality of the potential that both writers propose in these texts. His celebrated essay "The Novelization of Voice in Early African American Narrative" addresses the inherent difficulty in distinguishing fact from fiction in several early African American texts, one of them being Douglass's "The Heroic Slave." He also mentions Delany's *Blake* as belonging to this tradition. Both works frustrate any clear delineation between what is "real" and what is "made up" as they rely on historical events and personalities for their subjects. It is this precise quality that Andrews argues makes such texts so useful to Black American/transcolonial African diasporic literature. He notes the problematical history of the black voice as authoritative and traces a shift in the 1850s when, as he says, "the voice of black narrative broke most profoundly with discursive conventions and white expectations in an attempt to find new ways of authorizing itself" (24). What he calls the "fictive voice" represents this mode of authorization. It takes for its subject a real person whom the author makes "fictive." Such a move preempts questions of authenticity that nonfictive character representation begs. By not claiming "truth" but by portraying the figure as representing "a fictive member of an identifiable class of natural persons," the author can "realize" figures whom history would otherwise forget (26). They are realized because they are "fictionalized." Andrews argues that such a mode is empowering because fictive discourse "does not depend on the authentication of what is asserted in that discourse" (30).

Douglass and Delany present to their readers not simply a recounted or imagined example of organized uprising, but the real possibility that the event they represent may come to future fruition. By framing such fictive accounts within a broader classical heroic context that draws upon contemporary American interest in Hellenism, they craft a distinctly Black American critique, which "celebrated the Greek revolt and independence from the Ottoman Empire" to demonstrate that whereas "Greek liberation was a national fascination, black liberation was paramount in the minds of African Americans" (Hairston 75).

The classical elements in Douglass's and Delany's texts situate them in the literary context Hairston describes, thereby creating within it a space for black-authored literature and depicting the classical ideals of a healthy body in a healthy state, for example, that Delany and Shadd theorized in their emigration propaganda. Ultimately both texts advise that revolution and the achievement of healthy black selfhood is possible, and just as the writers preempt doubts about their characters' authenticity, they also realize the potential of revolt that is its own authority.

Frederick Douglass's "The Heroic Slave" appeared in *Frederick Douglass'*

Paper and in a collection of antislavery writings called *Autographs for Freedom*, edited by white abolitionist Julia Griffiths (with whom Douglass was widely rumored to be having an affair). It is based on the 1841 slave revolt aboard the *Creole* that Madison Washington led. Douglass was a famous nineteenth-century former slave, orator, editor, and author of political writings and three slave narratives, *The Narrative of the Life of Frederick Douglass* (1845), the revised and expanded version of it, *My Bondage and My Freedom* (1855), and *Life and Times of Frederick Douglass* (1892). "The Heroic Slave" is his only fictive work.

Martin Delany's *Blake; or, the Huts of America* was serialized in the *Anglo-African Magazine*. It was not published in book form until 1970, and its conclusion is missing. Most scholars agree that the majority of the chapters were written while Delany was in Canada. Perhaps his residence there was influential as the transcolonial African diasporic novel, which depicts the character, Henry Blake, a fugitive who rescues his wife from slavery and eventually prepares to stage a slave uprising in Cuba, crosses numerous borders and disrupts the chronology of historical events.

The novel form dramatizes the possibilities that Mary Ann Shadd and Martin Delany promote. Combined, Douglass and Delany here draw from a variety of forms and genres: travel writing, the epic, the slave narrative, periodical print culture, medical and legal theory, sentimentalism, romanticism, and the Gothic. The diversity of these texts supports the politics of the dynamic self that they suggest is not only possible but crucial to the achievement of Black American liberation. The figure of the ship in both works further bolsters the expansiveness of black potential.[7] Gilroy has argued that ships "need to be thought of as cultural and political units rather than abstract embodiments of the triangular trade" (17). The ship in Douglass's and Delany's fictive works functions as an example of the potential for black independent political self-rule. If the enslaved can secure the cultural and political unit of the ship, it is possible that they might do the same on land. The capture and control of the slave ship provides a physical example of a space wherein cultural and political reform can take place; it becomes a prototype, potentially translatable to the geographical location on which it eventually lands. Furthermore, the concept of the "ship of state" from Plato's *Republic*—the ship analogous to the state that needs someone qualified to navigate it and a crew with their various duties—emphasizes the class divisions that Shadd and Delany understood the ideal society to require. In "The Heroic Slave" and *Blake* there is little question as to who will be at the helm of this literal and figurative nautical political entity.

Douglass's transcolonial African diasporic novella ends with the retelling of the successful capture of the *Creole* and the freed slaves' settlement in the Bahamas, whereas Delany's novel—as much of it as we have access to—concludes with the promise of revolution in Cuba. In different ways, both texts present examples of black self-rule and function as propaganda that promotes fear of slave uprisings for white readers and confidence in New World African political capabilities for black readers.[8] Both texts also centralize the hero's healthy, vigorous sexuality as a crucial aspect of black selfhood and self-rule.

"The Heroic Slave" and a House Divided

Douglass's novella portrays the historical character of Madison Washington, who leads the successful slave uprising aboard the *Creole* as a revolutionary figure in keeping with American national ideals. Douglass compares Washington's actions with those of the founding fathers who "loved liberty" (175). Indeed, as many critics have noted, the protagonist's name combines James Madison with General George Washington. In Douglass's portrayal of Madison Washington's pursuit of liberty, he unites the hero's physical, intellectual, and sexual qualities to assert a model black masculine self that, rather than being distanced from American ideals, is an extension of them. "[T]he slave named Madison Washington reserves the common and unsubtle irony of a slave's naming, whereby classical names like Pompey or Caesar were employed in *antiphrasis*, as the Greek rhetoricians put it, 'by contradiction' naming someone with a stature or quality the opposite of what their actual status is. He becomes a genuine embodiment of both a founding father of the Constitution of the United States and its first great general and president as well" (Cook and Tatum 75). Furthermore, I would add that the name also implicates these Founders as "fathers" of black revolutionary impulse.

Recent scholarship addresses the role of storytelling in the novella to posit that Douglass privileges the voice over the physical body.[9] This technique, scholars contend, emphasizes the intellectual work of Madison Washington in order to prevent him from conforming to stereotypes of black savagery associated with figures like Nathaniel Turner, the insurrectionary figure, whose actions and apocalyptic "Confessions" (1831) instilled terror among whites in the South. Literary critic Herman Beavers, for example, argues that "Douglass recognized that the racial gaze needed to give way to acts of listening" (212). He maintains that the author considered himself "an eloquent spokesman for the abolition of slavery" and that "more than this, he felt himself capable of articulating in no uncertain terms the humanity and worth of the slave" (212). Similar to Beavers, Marianne Noble has argued that the novella illustrates "the superior political power of the voice over the body for slaves" and that the voice leads listeners "into the speaker's interior, inviting speculation upon the full range of emotional and intellectual experiences of the speaker" (60–61). Furthermore, Eric Sundquist contends that "because revolution is both a psychological and a political act in Douglass's short story, his focus on Washington's solitude and his power to persuade others through the medium of his voice suggests that his hero is located at once in the private, Romantic discourse of revolution as an act of imagination and cognition, and in the pragmatic public discourse of Douglass's own antislavery career" (118). Washington's voice is at once disarming, intimate, and pragmatic. Rather than privileging the aural over the visual in an effort to articulate slave "humanity" and "worth," I contend that Douglass asserts black masculine physicality in a way that demonstrates the embodied experience of intellect and emotion to reveal that the body is not distinct from—nor is it subordinate to—intellectual and emotional components of selfhood. The sound of Washington's voice and the content of his words make the listener and reader want to *see* him.

Shelley Fishkin and Carla Peterson, with reference to Douglass's journalism, suggest that the relationship between Washington and Listwell "creates in his fiction a narrative situation that he must have desired in his journalistic career . . . : an interdependent relationship between black slave as speaking and experiencing subject, on the one hand, and the white abolitionist, who both listens well and takes an active role, on the other, guided by an authoritative black leader whose role it is to write the black back on the page of human existence" (199–200). Douglass emphasizes that Washington exceeds the role of "experiencing subject"; he is active. If he "write[s] the black back on the page of human existence," he does so in blood.

The mind and the body work in concert, but it is precisely attempts to divorce the two, and qualify the worth of each, that has worked against the promotion and acceptance of Black American selfhood as equal to that of whites. Though the voice plays an extremely important role in the text, it cannot be separated from the very physical portrayal Douglass provides of Madison Washington, of his "trusty legs" and "sinewy arms," for example, that will free him (178). To ignore this is to overlook the protagonist's embodied experiences of cognition and emotion that I believe are central to his character and to Douglass's realization of black political subjective potential, not to mention heroism. Indeed, "His whole appearance betokened Herculean strength, yet there was nothing savage or forbidding in his aspect. . . . He had the head to conceive, and the hand to execute. In a word, he was one to be sought as a friend, but to be dreaded as an enemy" (179). Washington's heroic character embodies the virtues, moral, intellectual, and physical. Furthermore, as Hairston argues, "Douglass [himself] had become the epitome of black humanity and the Aeneas of his race: virtuous, pious, and heroic to the threshold of demigod. Revelation, heroic transformation, and resurrection are no less suggested by Douglass" (105). These comparisons with classical ideals are less to map Douglass and Washington onto an ancient ideal, which European and Anglo-American thinkers came to use in the service of white supremacist ideology, than to present the heroic as a mode of critique of white supremacist appropriation of it.

When we first encounter the hero, we hear his eloquent words before we see his remarkable body; Douglass keeps the reader in suspense; as I mentioned, he builds the desire for a look at the man who, "like the gray peak of a menacing rock on a perilous coast, . . . is seen by the quivering flash of angry lightning, and . . . again disappears covered with mystery" (175). The novella begins rather in the tradition of Coleridge's Wedding Guest in his "Rime of the Ancient Mariner" (1798), with a narrator and a listener. As Madison Washington speaks, his eager listener is the traveler Listwell, whose name critics have noted is short for "listen well."[10] The name may also signify that politically he "leans correctly" in the direction/guidance that Washington provides. The author's allusion to Coleridge calls to mind the precarious nature of the sea and the trauma that can result from immoral acts, both of which loosely prefigure the slave mutiny of which we will hear.

There is a long critical tradition that regards the ship in Coleridge's "Rime" as a slave ship and the Mariner as a slaver. Alan Bewell, referring to the historical context of the "Rime," explains that the Mariner's story "explores how the racial violence directed toward blacks recoils on the enslavers." He continues to argue that the Mariner "undergoes a symbolic 'blackening' throughout the poem," one that "reinforces the contemporary expectation that such [tropical] spaces are pathogenic, for it is a depopulated world of corruption, disease, and death. Yet he also asserts that the institution of slavery has made this space what it is" (103). I believe Douglass reverses roles here to present the possibility of reparation. Washington takes control of the ship and tells his story to Listwell. If Washington is a Mariner figure, he has the capability to restore health to the infected place that the institution of slavery made. His retelling of the story may also make for "sadder, wiser" men, but it is crucial to the restoration of health, both physical and moral. Douglass's allusion draws on what I read as Coleridge's questioning of the sustainability of an economic system that relies on the importation of goods, particularly people, and corrupts in the process.

Building on medical readings of the poem, literary critic Debbie Lee has argued that the crew in Coleridge's poem most likely died of yellow fever, a disease that probably has also infected the Mariner himself—the Wedding Guest, for example, notes the old man's "yellow hand." The Mariner's seeming immunity to the disease could indicate his biracial or African ancestry as noted previously. Blacks' perceived immunity to the disease took on a severely exaggerated status regardless of the fact that black people contracted and died from it. The slave ship, as a cultural and political unit in Plato's and later Gilroy's sense, can and will be captured, and those who deal in the immoral trade will suffer. In Douglass's novella, Washington buttresses his lamentations about his enslaved condition with an acknowledgment that birds are his "superiors," that they "live free, though they may die slaves. They fly where they list by day, and retire in freedom at night. But what is freedom to me, or I to it? I am a slave,—born a slave, an abject slave,—even before I made part of this breathing world, the scourge was plaited for my back, the fetters were forged for my limbs" (177).

Washington's allusion to birds as "superior" evokes the image of Coleridge's Mariner who shot the albatross for sport and as a result (at least he sees it this way) suffers life-in-death. Washington, unlike the Mariner, appreciates the birds; in fact, he envies them their freedom. His embodied description of his political restraint is a common trope of antislavery literature. He refers to the scourge and the fetters, his back and his limbs. He feels the restraint in his body even though he is not literally scourged and fettered as he speaks. Douglass's allusion to the birds and his formal evocation of Coleridge asserts the protagonist's morality, literacy, and literariness and identifies the embodied experience of enslavement that is at once physical, emotional, and intellectual.

After deliberating aloud, Washington determines to flee to Canada, and he pairs his evocation of Patrick Henry's desire for liberty with a description of physical fortitude: "Liberty I will have, or die in the attempt to gain it. This working that others may live in idleness! This cringing submission to insolence and curses! This living under the constant dread and apprehension of being sold and transferred, like a mere brute, is too much for me. I will stand it no longer. What others have done, I will do. These trusty legs or these sinewy arms shall place me among the free" (178). In this example, the protagonist's intellectual and political capabilities are commensurate with his physical power. He alludes to American revolutionary history and the work of his legs and arms that will achieve liberty in keeping with national ideals. Implicit is the irony that he will have to do this in another country. Also ironic is that the revolutionary—an American identity—plans to remove to a monarchy. The evocation of Patrick Henry in the context of antebellum black literature highlights the celebration of Great Britain as a beacon of freedom in northern black activism and abolitionism, further critiquing the contradictions in U.S. republican ideals.

Subsequent to Washington making his decision, Douglass further emphasizes the character's healthy physicality—and here I'll quote in full the passage I briefly referenced earlier:

> Madison was of manly form. Tall, symmetrical, round, and strong. In his movements he seemed to combine, with the strength of the lion, a lion's elasticity. His torn sleeves disclosed arms like polished iron. His face was 'black, but comely.' His eye, lit with emotion, kept guard under brow as dark and as glossy as the raven's wing. His whole appearance betokened Herculean strength; yet there was nothing savage or forbidding in this aspect. A child might play in his arms, or dance on his shoulders. A giant's strength, but not a giant's heart was in him. His broad mouth and nose spoke only of good nature and kindness. But his voice, that unfailing index of the soul, though full and melo-

dious, had that in it which could terrify as well as charm. He was just the man you would choose when hardships were to be endured, or danger to be encountered,—intelligent and brave. He had the head to conceive, and the hand to execute. In a word, he was one to be sought as a friend, but to be dreaded as an enemy. As our traveller gazed upon him, he almost trembled at the thought of his dangerous intrusion. (179)

I quote this passage at length because it defies white appropriation and division of the body in captivity, in theory, and in literature. It refuses to de-emphasize physicality for fear that intellect will suffer. Rather, Douglass's union of them repairs the body|mind rift that abolitionists *and* proslavery supporters projected onto Black Americans and promotes the classical healthy mind in a healthy body ideal. Douglass experienced firsthand the abolitionist desire to downplay his cognitive and literary capabilities to authenticate his narrative. He lived through his owners' need to repress his intellectual growth and found resistance in both physical confrontation and speaking and writing. Douglass identifies Washington's character not only with classical Greek and U.S. "republican" ideals but with Anglo-Saxon/British chivalry and nobility as well. His description reflects the influence of Sir Walter Scott in its elaborate style. Indeed, Douglass's name comes from Scott's "Lady of the Lake."

An expansion of Douglass's autobiographical work, this text injects some of his own qualities into Washington and projects a kind of fantasy of powerful black masculine selfhood. He is at once animal, intellectual, and moral. Emotion appears in his eye—another union of interiority and exteriority—which his brow protects. The rhetoric of protection and the accompanying allusion to Hercules emphasize the physical superiority of Washington. Referring to the function of this allusion, literary critic Robert Reid-Pharr argues that "this black body is somehow so pure, classic, Herculean that it speaks to the reality of an ancient black humanity" (51), and I would add that it inserts black heroism into a nineteenth-century U.S. fascination with ancient ideals. Furthermore, Douglass's almost physiognomic descriptions of Washington's face, "his broad mouth and nose" that "spoke only of good nature and kindness" also assert the embodiedness of this classical black self in the nineteenth century. His descriptions recall the Greek ideal set out by Shadd and Delany in their emigration polemics published the year before, even if he didn't directly acknowledge these works until later.

Though such rhetorics of healthy physicality are problematic in that they allude to (and in some cases rely on) theories that equated character with appearance and therefore promoted notions of black inferiority, Douglass's appropriation of them implies that an outright rejection of the notion that the body can "wear" the mind threatens to bolster arguments that the two are separate and therefore support (and potentially further) white supremacist subdivision of black subjecthood. Rather, Douglass asserts the union of the two and in doing so presents an ideal portrait that, though it hints to the romantic racialism that George Frederickson has so helpfully articulated, vexes as well.[11] The figure of Madison Washington is to be feared. He kills, and he successfully organizes a full-scale slave ship revolt. As critics have rightly pointed out, he is no Uncle Tom—although he looks (physically) uncannily like him. However, Douglass reveals as well the sexually intimate side of the hero also central to his subjecthood.

Critics have addressed Douglass's tendency to relegate women characters to the background of his texts; however, I see his treatment of Washington's wife, Susan, in this work somewhat differently.[12] When the hero details his fugitive days to Listwell, he recounts how he lost his way en route to Canada and ended up back where he had started. He follows the description of his reunion with his wife, Susan, by detailing the subsequent need for them to separate so that her owners would not notice her absence from the kitchen. Washington uses a familiar trope of parting that is explicitly embodied: "Our parting was like tearing the flesh from my bones" (191). Despite the conventionality of the description, it reasserts that emotion is felt in the body as well as metaphorically revealed through it.

We can compare Douglass's simile to what we now distinguish as neuropathic pain. This sensation is pain whose root is located other than where the subject experiences it. Contrary to nociceptive pain, which one feels at the site of injury—imagine being kicked in the shins, for example—neuropathic pain can result from physical or psychic injury, but we can sense it in other locations. Psychogenic pain is an example; it does not require physical injury but can result in the experience of physical pain. Douglass uses a metaphorical medical description of a physical sensation to identify emotional injury. More than providing a comparison through which readers can better understand Washington's response to leaving his wife, the description locates emotional pain in the physical body. Furthermore, the simile figuratively unites not only the mind and body but Washington and his wife as well. She, metaphorically, becomes part of his body, beyond the fusion of bodies during intercourse, so that their parting is a tearing away of his flesh; they embody each other anatomically. Rhetorically, Douglass underscores the slave system's subdivision of black subjecthood, but his protagonist's purpose—in his determination to achieve liberty—is to reject and topple policies and people that would "carve up" a Black American sense of self. Furthermore, Douglass's rhetorics of physicality also allude to a split legal subjecthood (person and property). His imagery reminds the reader that legally sanctioned marriages (denied to slaves) treated the woman as part of, or one with, the husband. Under the legal fiction of coverture, husband and wife were one person. Douglass's conflation of medical and legal rhetoric in this scene exposes the processes of fragmentation operating on Black Americans and readies the reader for the process of reparation to come.

Ivy Wilson's very useful reading of Douglass's novella argues that Washington functions as a metonym for the nation (455). I believe the protagonist's metonymic quality underscores his physicality as he embodies national ideals, particularly liberty. Wilson refers to Washington's letter thanking Listwell for his assistance in getting to Canada where he "nestle[s] in the mane of the British lion, protected by the mighty paw from the talons and beak of the American eagle" (qtd. in Wilson 457). Wilson writes, "The manipulation of symbols here is deft: instead of insinuating that Washington is now a subject of the British monarchy, by using the more commonplace symbol of the crown, the author couches his critique of the United States through the metaphor of a struggle between animals of nature" (457). I argue further that the metaphor places Washington at the center of these animal struggles and creates an association between his and their physicality. Such references to animals and their political and sovereign connotations symbolically embody the monarchy and the republic in a way that gestures back to Douglass's initial description of Washington as "combining with the strength of a lion, a lion's elasticity" (179). By allying his protagonist physically with an animal of African origin and symbolic of the British monarchy—which the "American eagle" overthrew by organized revolution—the author simultaneously reminds the reader of the United States' revolutionary history and presents justification for black revolution. But he also suggests that America has ceased to be revolutionary (because it maintains slavery). As a false democracy, it is morally inferior to the British monarchy, which, as a global superpower, may indeed frustrate American slavery/imperialism and provide a bulwark for heroic Black Americans.

However, Douglass's symbolism is even more complex. The author reverses the position of Canada from the context of the Upper Canada Rebellion of 1837–38, during which time revolutionaries sought refuge in the United States. Figures like John Brown and Harriet Tubman—who used Canada West (Ontario) as both a refuge and a staging ground for insurrectionist politics—bring to mind the colony's potential as a site for libertarian agitation. Douglass's symbolic relation of Washington and the lion draws on this history. Nevertheless, it is impossible for Washington to make revolutionary use of the colony because his wife is absent.

When Washington is in Canada, he mourns the absence of his wife, and his embodied description of such emotional suffering builds on the parting scene during which he describes his return from his first attempt to flee. Washington explains, "On reaching Canada, and getting over the excitement of making my escape, sir, my thoughts turned to my poor wife.... She was in all my thoughts by day, and my dreams by night.... I was wretched. I lost my appetite. I could neither work, eat, nor sleep, till I resolved to hazard my own liberty, to gain that of my wife" (219). Washington's body's response to the emotional pain of his separation from Susan again emphasizes the union of the physical and psychological. Even after his wife's death, when he notes a distinction between body and soul and says, "With her in slavery, my body, not my spirit, was free," he underscores that one cannot be free without the other (220). The necessary coherence of body and spirit insists upon the understanding of the two as part of the same whole—whether or not legally sanctioned. Furthermore, it denotes the importance of conjugal union and consensual black sexuality that is crucial to health and to political self-rule.[13] Douglass suggests that the physical, intellectual, emotional, and sexual must be considered together. To privilege one over the others is to undermine the dynamism of the healthy self.

The hero's separation from his wife is instrumental in his recognition that he must secure freedom for himself, his partner, and ultimately his community. Part of his indecision regarding whether to flee is a result of his desire to remain with his wife, Susan. Rationalizing that he could be sold any day and separated from her, he makes his decision to leave, but when he loses his way to the North, he returns to her. So he decides to "make the woods my home, for if I gave myself up, I should be whipped and sold away; and if I started for the North, I should leave a wife doubly dear to me" (192). Washington describes how his wife made good on her promise to visit him in the woods once a week. I read these decisions as indications that Washington is determined to take whatever measure of control over his sexuality that he can. He wants to maintain his relationship with Susan, and the only way he can do that is to protect himself from recapture while remaining in the vicinity where she can visit him. Only after Susan dies can Washington become the revolutionary figure whom Douglass immortalizes. Gender studies scholar Maggie Montesinos Sale argues that the scene in which Washington is captured as he guards Susan's dead body "revises the earlier scene in which his fetters are broken by his determination to be free; this attachment asserts that the continuing slavery of loved ones compromises individual liberty—and that only a heterosexual union makes one fully a man" (*Slumbering* 184). I'm not sure Douglass implies that "*only* heterosexual union makes one fully a man" (emphasis mine). Rather, it seems Douglass demonstrates that black sexual self-mastery (more in the mode of the ancients as Foucault has described) and slavery are irreconcilable. He articulates such self-mastery as a crucial aspect of selfhood and, in Washington's example, heroic selfhood.[14]

Andrews details how publication of "new facts" about Washington's story in the *Liberator* (1842) signals the abolitionist desire for the addition of a romantic plot to his story. The "new facts" were acquired through a letter from Canadian abolitionist Hiram Wilson, who stated that Washington was living in the colony and planning to reenter the United States to free his enslaved wife. Andrews argues that the *Liberator* may have used this information to mitigate depositions it had printed earlier implying that Washington's "discovery in the slave women's cabin had led to the first violent acts of the slave revolt" and that the new information signals the paper's desire to "realize [Washington] as a powerful symbol of black antislavery heroism" (28). He argues that Douglass faced the same problems as the *Liberator* in having so few facts with which to create Washington's character that he relied on the fictive form through which he promised his readers only "marks, traces, possibles, and probabilities" (Douglass 176). As such, Douglass may have followed the *Liberator*'s lead in portraying Washington as monogamous. We do not know if Douglass believed his hero to be one or the other, but regardless, he chose to emphasize sexuality and slave marriage as crucial components of the revolt.

Wilson argues that Douglass "reduces the presence of the wife to accentuate Washington's heroism" (460) and Sale posits that "Douglass's model of rebellious manhood is constructed in opposition to a notion of passive womanhood" ("Critiques" 704). Despite the variety of critical opinions regarding Susan's role in the novella (her presence or absence has been a subject of debate), I think the issue is not so much her role as a comrade to revolutionary Washington but rather the importance for him of healthy, consensual sexual expression in the formation of his character and his political ideology. Washington's loss of Susan is central to his development as a hero embodying, expressing, and building on ancient heroic ideals very much focused here on the promise of healthy black selfhood and self-rule.

Though Wilson grants the novella a more "physical" reading than most critics, he argues, "Although the narrator will speak of Washington's strength, perseverance, and fortitude, none of these qualities are displayed; in fact, they have to be concealed to make him palatable to his reading audience" (463). Though I place more value on the physical descriptions of Washington and his narration of his actions as well as others' descriptions of him than Wilson does, I do believe that Douglass's understanding that a significant portion of his readership would be white perhaps militated against some of his descriptions of Washington's physical qualities—especially when we compare him to Delany's descriptions of Blake. First, at the beginning of "The Heroic Slave," during the scene in which Washington chastises himself over his indecision about how to free himself—the monologue Listwell overhears—Douglass introduces us to a narrator who convinces himself that he is brave. Washington's pep talk to himself reminds him of the time he saved a man from drowning while "others stood back in helpless horror" and how he kept "at bay with a single pitchfork" the "raging bull from whom all others fled, pale with fright" (177–78).

To a similar effect, he describes the fire that forced him out of the dismal swamps where he lived for five years as sparing nothing: "Bears and wolves, scorched from their mysterious hiding-places . . . ran forth, yelling, howling, bewildered" (193). By contrast, Washington is able to outrun the fire that the bears and wolves (among other animals) could not: "The very heavens seemed to rain down fire through the towering trees; it was by the merest chance that I escaped the devouring element. Running before it, and stopping occasionally to take breath, I looked back to behold its frightful ravages, and to drink in its savage magnificence" (193). Here he presents himself as possessing the instinct, intelligence, and physical stamina to save himself from the fire, and he emphasizes his recognition of the sublimity of it. Washington's description demonstrates not only his physical and intellectual fortitude, but his respect for nature as well. Such a respect for the land resonates with ecocritical readings of the classic slave narratives, which "offer an account of how oppression distorts one's relationship to the natural world" and the theory that "freedom and everything that word implies—free labor, secure property rights, social and political equality—is essential to establishing a healthy, productive, and positive relation to the land" (K. Smith 315, 324). Even beyond Washington's relation to the land he represents the classical "healthy body [that is] a well-balanced body, one that exists in harmony with cosmic laws and order" (Tountas 186). Douglass's description of the fire's "savage magnificence" rewrites the conventional use of the word *savage*. He draws on the typically pejorative descriptor—often applied to blacks—to describe something "magnificent"; by doing so he elevates savagery to the realm of the sublime. Washington's appreciation of power in the natural world implicitly critiques the unnatural authority of the slaveholders.

In the *Autographs* edition, Douglass highlights the different codes that existed for blacks and whites.[15] Washington says to Listwell (and implicitly to Douglass's white readers), "Your moral code may differ from mine, as your customs and usages are different. The fact is, sir, during my flight, I felt myself robbed by society of all my just rights; that I was in an enemy's land, who sought both my life and my liberty" (195). The emphasis here is on context and contingency: a free man/woman doesn't need to use violence normally; a slave who seeks freedom must.[16] This scene reminds readers that Washington's violent and unlawful acts are the product of his experiences of injustice. This gesture, an exculpatory/justificatory trope in antislavery writing, indicates Douglass's consciousness of the precarious task of depicting a heroic slave who achieves liberty violently, if valiantly. Unlike Delany, whose portrayal of Blake is far less apologetic, Douglass uses the frame of American revolutionary history to justify Washington's actions.

As a counterpoint to the justification of Washington's actions, Douglass includes a scene in which Listwell, mistaken for a slave trader, refuses to mention that he is an abolitionist even though "it was hard for him to admit to himself the possibility of circumstances wherein a man might, properly, hold his tongue on the subject" (214). In this scene Douglass reveals that the moral code between blacks and whites might not be so different after all: "Having as little of the spirit of a martyr as Erasmus, [Listwell] concluded, like the latter, that it was wiser to trust the mercy of God for his soul, than the humanity of slave-traders for his body" (214). Here he parallels Washington and Listwell in their reactions to slave traders and the physical threat they represent. Furthermore, Douglass enacts the same bodily division on Listwell's subjectivity that he rejects in portraying Washington. He states that for Listwell in this circumstance, "Bodily fear, not conscientious scruples, prevailed" (214). Though Douglass portrays the scene somewhat sympathetically, he draws a clear demarcation between the physical experiences of the two characters. Washington's body and scruples work in concert, whereas Listwell's function in opposition.

The division of white characters continues and is most obvious in Douglass's portrayal of Tom Grant, the southern first mate of the *Creole* whom Keith Miller and Kevin Quashie assert embodies "a House Divided" (206). "Detesting slavery but refusing to embrace anti-slavery, the ambivalent and unresolved Grant personifies a self-contradictory nation . . . in which destruction looms" (206). Grant experienced the mutiny aboard the *Creole* and in conversation with Jack Williams, a man whom he meets in a coffee house, finds himself defending the actions of the crew. The racist Williams makes typical arguments about how the crew should have controlled the slaves, for example, by showing no fear, and he argues that "the whole disaster was the result of ignorance of the real character of darkies in general. With half a dozen resolute white men (I say it not boastingly), I could have had the rascals in irons in ten minutes, not because I'm so strong, but I know how to manage 'em" (226–27). Here he de-emphasizes white physical power and privileges managerial/executive prowess. Grant attacks Williams's theory and defends the crew by asserting that Williams is ignorant of the practical and political differences between land and sea, of the effect of having both state and national government support and "physical force" (227). Again, this dispute is an argument over chivalric norms: no "manly" man can be a slave; thus enslaved blacks are cowards—and servile, manageable, controllable. Douglass argues that the enslavement is only possible because of superior arms.

The first mate's description of Washington during the mutiny demonstrates an amount of admiration for him. When Grant describes his attempts to stop Washington, he states how "he pushed me back with his strong, black arm, as though I had been a boy of twelve" (234). Washington bests the first mate with his strength and then explains that he is not a murderer, that "LIBERTY, not malice, is the motive for this night's work" (234–35). Whereas Williams identifies the assertion of white authority with knowledge over the possession of physical strength (or "know-how" versus "can-do"), Washington provides a model of both that in the end bests white authority. He distinguishes between murder and war. Grant admits that he "felt [himself] in the presence of a superior man; one who, had he been a white man, I would have followed willingly and gladly in any honorable enterprise" (237). Grant recognizes Washington's physical and mental superiority, yet he cannot control his own racism. He sees the congruence of Washington's values with those of 1776: "It was not that his principles were wrong in the abstract; for they are the principles of 1776. But I could not bring myself to recognize their application to one whom I deemed my inferior" (238).

The contradictions within Grant, as Miller and Quashie assert, represent what Douglass portrays as the disjuncture that underpins the hypocrisy of the republic unwilling to recognize the right of black revolution because it deems the race inferior. Douglass suggests that indecision and an incoherence of principle and action form the underlying problem that splits, and indeed will break, the self and the nation. The novella begins with Washington's anger with himself for his indecision, for remaining enslaved when he desires liberty. He chastises himself for yielding to physical cowardice when he knows his strength. When the two merge—strength and the courage of conviction—Washington begins to transform into the successful revolutionary. Washington represents the antitheses of the "House Divided," which white incoherence has produced and which, as a result, affords no room for a figure like him. Rather, in the end he commands the ship-state, "During all the storm, Madison stood firmly at the helm,—his keen eye fixed upon the binnacle. He was not indifferent to the dreadful hurricane; yet he met it with the equanimity of an old sailor. He was silent but not agitated. The first words he uttered after the storm had slightly subsided were characteristic of the man. 'Mr. mate, you cannot write the bloody laws of slavery on those restless billows. The ocean, if not the land, is free'" (237). The embodiment of the ideal heroic black self, Washington is incompatible with a politically divided United States; therefore, the revolution must occur offshore, and Washington must find liberty elsewhere. A liberal individualist, Washington takes freedom for himself but must eventually live in exile.

Blake; or, the United Huts of America

Martin Delany's novel, published in serial form beginning six years after the publication of "The Heroic Slave," expands in fictive form the notions Douglass introduced. Delany does not see the "House" quite as divided as Douglass does. For Delany, the North and South are two sides of the same profiteering coin. Black revolution cannot come only aboard a ship but must take place on land that will become the site of black national policy and self-rule. The eponymous character, Blake, murders—not randomly nor "savagely." But unlike Madison Washington, who reserves acts of violence for revolution, Blake must use force to prepare for revolution.

As does Douglass, Delany asserts black masculine sexual physicality as a crucial component of selfhood just as intellect and emotion are, but his portrayals are more explicit and less apologetic. *Blake* explores the role of the hero, the artist, the artist-intellectual, and the artist-intellectual activist as undivided from black physicality. In many ways, like Douglass's fictive work, we can read *Blake* as an iteration of fantasy as Blake, too, cuts an ideal form that provides a model of healthy black selfhood during a time when blackness in the New World was, generally speaking, the site of white subjection and subjugation. Similar to Madison Washington, Blake is a hero in the classical sense, both authors inserting black heroism into a nineteenth-century American literary, historical, and political context for the fulfillment of the individual and collective potential of that hero and his people.

Blake interweaves discourses of medicine, law, politics, and religion and travels through the United States, Canada, and the Caribbean. This transcolonial African diasporic novel combines historical and fictional figures, disregards the chronology of historical events, and presents the possibility of large-scale black revolution. Delany builds on his earlier emigration writings and uses the fictive form to "realize" the promise of black self-rule he advocated in those works. Eric Sundquist has articulated the importance of this novel: "Henry Blake spreads among the slave population of the South the simple belief that revolution is possible, that slave culture can nurture an African American identity invisible to the masters, that organized insurrection is not unthinkable. In this alone *Blake* is set apart from every other black text of the period, many of which advocated (or, in the case of slave narratives, recounted) individual acts of resistance but none of which suggested that large-scale nationalist political action was possible apart from emancipation and emigration—certainly not that it was possible, and had to be nurtured, within the most oppressive confines of the slave community" (199).[17] Furthermore, as we saw in Douglass, Delany, too, cannot or will not admit the possibility of a fulfilled black self in the antebellum United States, through a revolution or otherwise. The fulfillment of this ideal must happen elsewhere.

The discursiveness of his novel and his other writings on emigration, political destiny, and his explorations in Africa suggest that Delany—despite his decision to remain in the United States throughout and following the Civil War—during the time of these writings, did not think it necessary to secure an African American identity in the United States but rather to imagine a black identity somewhere else. For Delany, and as Douglass's novella demonstrates, there was no room in the "House" for black leaders who sought true political independence for their communities.

Critics largely agree that Delany wrote *Blake* while in Canada between 1856 and 1859.[18] I note this because unlike many of Delany's contemporaries, and as I have discussed in chapter 2, he did not see Canada as a viable permanent option for free or fugitive blacks. It is reasonable that Delany's restlessness in Canada informs Blake's continual movement across borders, but it is precisely this quest for a suitable location for black revolution in the New World that frustrates attempts to situate this novel as primarily African American.[19] Robert Levine usefully traces what I believe describes the transcolonial African diasporic nature of this text: "[Delany's] sense of the interrelationships among various sites in the Americas is adumbrated in the novel's opening chapter, which depicts Northerners and Southerners, Americans and Cubans, meeting in Baltimore to discuss their plans to make over the Baltimore clipper *Merchantman* into a slaver" (191). For Delany, the reality of such interrelationships among people, nations, and colonies demands a Black New World sense of self that is complexly layered and dynamic, that is neither divided by categories of physical/sexual and emotional/intellectual, nor even fully defined nationally until the right time and place are found. The novel reminds readers of Delany's appeal to classical ideals and virtues espoused in *Condition* and indeed Blake embodies many, if not all of these ancient, valorized traits.

Central to Blake's development as a hero in the classical tradition, as for Douglass's Washington, is a vigorous, healthy sexuality. Delany introduces us to Henry Blake—or Carolus Henrico Blacus, the name in keeping with the figure, somewhat hybrid and Latinized—the protagonist who arrives back in Natchez, Mississippi, to find that Colonel Franks has sold Blake's wife, Maggie. When we meet Blake, we hear his anger at his wife's sale, his disregard for religion, and his frustration at being told to wait for something better in the afterlife, ideas Delany promoted in *Condition*. Commensurate with Blake's knowledge of Maggie's sale is his determination to free himself. Like Washington, who becomes an insurrectionary figure after his wife's death, Blake becomes so after his wife's sale. As Peterson and others earlier and Adenike Marie Davidson more recently have argued, "Maggie's absence becomes the motivating catalyst for her husband's rebellious nature" (Davidson 33). Davidson further contends that Blake's broken family structure opens his eyes to the immorality of slavery and that "nation-building can only occur without the burden and responsibility of a family" (24). Furthermore, Peterson explains,

> The second half of *Blake* begins with the reappearance of both the *Merchantman* and Maggie. The sexual and economic plots conjoin here in a twin colonization—that of Cuba by American slaveholding interests, and that of Maggie by the black male. Much like Brown's heroine, Mary, the freed Maggie is privatized not by a white slaveholder but by the conditions of black patriarchy and capitalism, and disappears from the novel. (*Doers* 171)

And finally, Reid-Pharr contends, "Actual black bodies, at least the bodies of black misses, can never be trusted to act properly, to allow themselves to be placed securely in the service of black nationality" (126). Nevertheless, the centrality of women to the fulfillment of the hero's selfhood, of the ideal of healthy black manhood and by extension black political independence for Delany is clear.

Separation incites the desire to rebel; it also ratifies black men for the civil status of married white counterparts. Whereas Washington cannot fulfill his plan until after his wife's death, Blake cannot until he is reunited with Maggie. As Robert Carr points out, "Henry's turning point is his outrage that his wife, as his wife, has been sold: like David Walker before him, the state of the nation is here predicated on the ability of its people—to be 'men'—and it is this failure that sparks revolt. Maggie's sale is a sign of gendered political humiliation" (55). As Gail Bederman notes, "Framers of the state constitutions in sixteen northern and western states explicitly placed African-American men in the same category as women, as 'dependents'" (qtd. in Bay 40). In conjunction with the heroes' desire to be "men," however, both Douglass and Delany suggest that as effective as the prohibition of sexual and marital choice is for suppressing revolt, sexual and marital choice are just as crucial for the achievement of liberation. The characters' negotiations of their relationships with women are not so much a form of colonization, a lack of trust, or merely a sign of political humiliation, but rather Blake's sexual relationship with Maggie demonstrates a coherent black self whose involuntary as well as conscious responses function in concert and counter symbolically the contradictory logic of white supremacy.

Like Madison Washington, Henry Blake's freedom from indecision marks the beginning of his quest for self-possession. Similar to Douglass's listener who eavesdrops on Washington's soliloquy, we hear the hero's deliberations about his wife's sale and his frustration with religion and his subsequent resolve before we "see" a physical picture of him. The description is aligned with the hero's convictions:

> Henry was a black—a pure Negro—handsome, manly and intelligent, in size comparing well with his master, but neither so fleshy nor heavy built in person. A man of good literary attainments—unknown to Colonel Franks, though he was aware he could read and write—having been educated in the West Indies, and decoyed away when young. His affection for his wife and child was not excelled by Colonel Franks's for his. He was bold, determined and courageous, but always mild, gentle and courteous, though impulsive when an occasion demanded opposition. (16–17)

Blake represents a heroic ideal: he is handsome, intelligent, physically fit, not merely literate but literary as well, affectionate, bold, determined, courageous, and impulsive when necessary. Above all, he represents the classical ideal of balance and equilibrium. Blake's toned physique, in contradistinction to Franks's fleshiness, distinguishes the protagonist as superior to his owner, more capable of self-mastery and the practice of moderation, and this reminds us of Grant's recognition of his own corporeal inferiority in the presence of Washington. Rhetorics of physical superiority here are in keeping with Delany's considerations of the same in *Condition* emphasizing the physical potential of blacks in the New World—the Greek ideal of a healthy mind in a healthy body—suitable to a variety of climates and operating in concert with their intellectual promise.[20] The hero aspires to a Platonic ideal of a healthy state where he can be "in complete harmony with the 'universe'" (Tountas 186). Delany offers a picture of a protagonist whose sense of self is complex and dynamic and whose only limitations are external. Furthermore, Delany's characterization of Blake's "affection for his wife and child" as equal to that of Colonel Franks's for his demonstrates a rejection of black men's reduction to a condition of dependency on white counterparts. The rhetorics of strength in physicality and affection assert that black men have a role as heads of their own families.

Nor does Delany emphasize Blake's intellectual and artistic capabilities at the expense of his physical strength. Rather, the author emphasizes both to create a picture of superiority similar to that which he theorized in *Condition*. When describing Franks, though, Delany offers little other than a statement that he is "fleshy" and "heavy"—attributes that imply the laziness that is a common antislavery trope used to describe the southern slaveholder and that ran counter to the classical ideal of bodily balance and equilibrium. Franks is a figure of excess. His ideology is the focus of his depiction:

> The Colonel, as a husband and father, was affectionate and indulgent; but his slave had offended, disobeyed his commands, and consequently, had to be properly punished, or he be disrespected by his own servants. The will of the master being absolute, his commands should be enforced, let them be what they may, and the consequences what they would. If slavery be right, the master is justifiable in enforcing obedience to his will; deny him this, and you at once deprive him of the right to hold a slave—the one is a necessary sequence of the other. Upon this principle Colonel Franks acted, and the premise justified the conclusion. (13–14)[21]

Delany sets up a dichotomy within Franks that undermines the principles on which slavery is founded. Franks is an "affectionate" and "indulgent" husband and father, yet he sells Maggie because she refuses to yield to his sexual demands. Even in this we see Delany's commitment to the ideal. He presents a far less stark or more idealized (chaste) image of the enslaved woman as the owner's sexual focus than we read, for example, in Jacobs's or Celia's accounts. Whereas the slave narrative and court case detail the grave extremes to which each woman must go to protect herself and the ill health/death she suffers as a result, Delany has the owner sell Maggie when she refuses him. Delany though maintains the character's virtue and the hero's comfort in the knowledge that Maggie has not "disgraced herself" (15), a phrase likely frustrating to read on the heels of Celia's and Jacobs's narratives. At any rate, Franks must follow the underlying principle through to the end. He must sell Maggie or lose the respect of his other slaves, respect that is crucial so he can maintain his right to hold slaves and thus to uphold the "righteousness" of slavery. Delany demonstrates the sophistic logic of Colonel Franks and, by extension, slavery and slave law. Descriptions of the Colonel's body are absent from this passage, yet his sexuality looms implicitly behind it. For all the discussion of Franks's philosophy, his corporeal absence is conspicuous, for it is precisely his unfulfilled sexual desire that demands Maggie's sale and reveals the incongruity of white subjectivity that supports slavery. Contrary to Blake's physicality, which Delany explicitly describes and which embodies his ideals, descriptions of Franks's physicality are noticeably absent; as a result, that absence underscores the ideological contradictions that render his corporeal actions implicit, indeed perhaps unspeakable, and therefore unable to sustain his principles.

Nevertheless, likely as in any revolution—and within any revolutionary—there are disjunctures. The first of Blake's challenges in repairing (insofar as it is possible) such cleavages and fomenting revolution across the United States is to ensure the plan is uncomplicated and easily communicable. The transmission of information will be oral: "All you have to do, is to find one good man or woman—I dont care which, so that they prove to be the right person—on a single plantation, and hold a seclusion and impart the secret to them, and make them the organizers for their own plantation, and they in like manner impart it to some other next to them, and so on. In this way it will spread like smallpox among them" (41). Leadership and secrecy are crucial; gender is irrelevant. Delany crafts a particularly embodied simile using the rhetoric of disease to depict Blake's impression of the transmission of information that will ultimately devastate slavery and the white population that supports it. Such rhetoric calls to mind the decimation of aboriginal populations as a result of European contact as well as the perceived immunity of Africans to certain European and tropical diseases—resistance which contributed to the increased importation of African slaves. Delany's passage functions symbolically, using the threat of pathological contagion to posit that the "disease" which spreads through the black population will result in the destruction of white supremacist rule. The equation of knowledge and disease emphasizes the power and violence of both. If the enslaved can control the circulation of information and use it against the white population, they will eliminate the power of those who displaced the aboriginals and who imported Africans.

Indeed, Delany includes a meeting between Blake and an "Indian Nation" in Arkansas, which adds complexity to the hero's fashioning as he becomes associated with both classical Greek and aboriginal ideals, perhaps recognizing or even emphasizing the ancient histories and virtues of both. The chapter begins with a debate between Blake and Mr. Culver, the "intelligent old Chief of the United Nation," over the ethics of slaveholding among the aboriginal population (85). The latter distinguishes native slaveholders from their white counterparts—a similar gesture to that occurring in Sophia Pooley's narrative (see chapter 3). Once the untalented white physician leaves them (no doubt Delany's jab at the white medical community that shunned him), Mr. Culver explains that "Indians work side by side with black man, eat with him, drink with him, rest with him and both lay down in shade together; white man won't even let you talk! In our Nation Indian and black all marry together. Indian like black man very much, and Indian like 'im heap!" (86). Blake replies to this statement by lamenting that Africans are not united like the aboriginals are, but defends the former by reminding the Chief that the indigenous population was invaded by whites in small numbers whereas Africans captured other Africans and brought them to the New World in great numbers. The friendly debate between the two leaders culminates in the Chief's advice: "If you want white man to love you, you must fight 'im!" (87). At this point, Blake reveals his plot of insurrection and the Chief concludes that aboriginals did the same a long time ago, and he can't believe Africans haven't done it sooner. This hero and Black American heroism, generally, are in the making.

This meeting of leaders builds on the rhetoric of disease Delany uses in conjunction with revolution, which evokes aboriginals' and Africans' shared history of oppression and revolt. Whereas Douglass roots Washington's actions in the white American revolutionary, while alluding to classical tradition, Delany identifies his character with aboriginal warriors. Delany does not entirely fashion Blake with classical masculine ideals nor does he, as Douglass does, expand them to design his model of black masculinity; rather, he combines ideals of the classical and aboriginal hero. Such a move risks relating his hero to the trope of savagery, and indeed Delany does put Blake in violent individual circumstances. Nevertheless, Delany's association of Blake with aboriginal leaders also makes available to him the figure of the noble savage. When he tells the Chief about the insurrection plot, the Chief replies, "Ah hah! Indian have something like that long-go. I wonder your people ain't got it before! That what make Indian strong; that what make Indian and black man in Florida hold together. Go on, young man, go on! may the Great Spirit make you brave!" (87). The chivalric undertones of the Chief's argument and persona craft him as the noble savage figure; however, the aboriginal leader's use of dialect denotes a linguistic inferiority to Blake.[22] Here Delany at once valorizes the Chief and his community for their resistance to white authority, and presents the possibility that blacks, once enlightened—as Blake is—may even succeed the aboriginal community in this endeavor once they have committed themselves to it.

As Blake visits many plantations to "sow the seeds of insurrection," Delany is careful to demonstrate that Blake will not be a hands-off revolutionary. He has the courage and strength to execute personally the violence essential for successful, large-scale, organized rebellion. In the chapter "Henry at Large," Delany portrays his hero as cunningly traveling through many plantations, carrying with him a bridle, halter, et cetera, that will "testify" to his being on his master's business—a tactic Floyd J. Miller reminds us Henry Bibb, newspaperman in Canada West (Ontario), used when he was a fugitive. Delany presents Blake as a "scholar, [who] carefully kept a record of the plantations he had passed, that when accosted by a white, as an overseer or patrol, he invariably pretended to belong to a back estate, in search of his master's racehorse" (68). Blake here functions as a kind of questing hero visiting swamps and caves and meeting with conjurers, as well as a social anthropologist who gathers data on the cultures of the various plantations. Descriptions of his findings draw on the genres as diverse as travel writing and the epic; however, Blake, a fugitive, must travel with a cover story. Delany's characterization of Blake as simultaneously part of and apart from the populations he studies anticipates his *Official Report of the Niger Valley* (1861) and likely informed the writings of subsequent black anthropologists, most notably among them W.E.B. Du Bois, who studied various African and Caribbean cultures.[23] The writers are concerned with uplift, whether by improving the communities they study or by learning how they can improve their own through study of others. The concept of the "other," that is, the object of study, is not racial in these examples, and there is a sense of a unified or Pan-African purpose in Delany's work, one that at times he depicts as necessitating violent encounters with racialized others whose goal is to oppress, not uplift. After all, Blake is first and foremost a hero; social anthropology is his secondary pursuit, but one in keeping with his physical, intellectual, and moral virtues.

The author pairs Blake's scholarly character with his physicality. He explains, "Proceeding on in the direction of the Red River country, [Blake] met with no obstruction except in one instance, when he left his assailant quietly upon the earth. A few days after an inquest was held upon the body of a deceased overseer—verdict of the Jury, 'By hands unknown'" (68). Delany's account of the murder of the overseer is not physical. There are no graphic details such as appear in the newspaper accounts of Celia's murder of Robert Newsom. But Delany does allude to the print culture of the medico-legal inquest not only to depict Blake's act of homicide but to make explicit his stealth in carrying it out as well. As secrecy, courage, and mental and physical fortitude are necessary qualities of a successful revolutionary according to Delany/Blake, the author presents his protagonist as a most suitable hero in the making. Whereas Douglass does not include such individual acts of violence and portrays Washington as more Lockean/liberal in his rejection of the descriptor "murderer," we can see that Delany crafts the figure of the black revolutionary hero that embodies a broader combination of qualities that does not exclude the capacity to murder.[24]

Contextualizing the novel, literary critic Jeffory Clymer argues that beginning with the signaling of renewed "American attempts to acquire Cuba as a potential slave state," an allusion to the Ostend Manifesto of 1854,[25]

"Delany undermines the apparent distinction between civic and personal duties by intimating that, in fact, such differences do not exist" (711). This information also suggests that revolutionary action is an urgent requirement given the evidence of an imminent American expansion and consolidation of slavery concomitant with Manifest Destiny imperialism. Recall that Shadd is also alarmed by this threat/possibility. We can extend this assessment to Delany's portrayals of organized and individual acts of violence. Such a coherence of duties and ideologies, Delany suggests, is necessary if a black revolution of the scale Blake plans is to be achieved. Later when Blake explains to Charles and Andy (whom he has persuaded to seek freedom) how his idea for revolution was born, he explains how when he learned that Franks had sold Maggie, "the most I could take courage to do, was to leave [Franks], and take as many from him as I could induce to go" (128). But then Blake details the insufficiency of such an individual response to Maggie's sale. He says, "But maturer reflection drove me to the expedient of avenging the general wrongs of our people, by inducing the slave, in his might, to scatter red ruin throughout the region of the South. But still, I cannot find it in my heart to injure an individual, except in personal conflict" (128). By killing the overseer, he learned and taught "that mighty lesson: to strike for Liberty. 'Rather to die as freemen, than live as slaves!'" (128). Here the confluence of physical violence and individual political and personal pursuits underscores the strength of such private and public cohesion. The portrayal of consistency within individuals as extended to a larger organizational level represents a macro expression of the fulfilling black sense of self for which Delany strives. But still, Blake has much to accomplish and must address many difficulties among the enslaved population before his plan can take shape. It is tempting to conflate murder as a means to freedom with the notion of murder as an expression of freedom, but Delany articulates the injustice of violent acts in general. He regards slaveholder violence as an expression of the absolute freedom to oppress and slave uprising as an expression of forceful taking back of freedom that was stolen.

By introducing the promising Texas plantation character Sampson—likely named for the Samson of Hebrew scripture—Delany implies that there are other men capable of carrying out the insurrection. Sampson is "black, tall, stoutly built, and manly, possessing much general intelligence, and a good-looking person. His wife a neat, intelligent, handsome little woman, the complexion of himself, was the mother of a most interesting family of five pretty children" (83). Sampson embodies many of the same characteristics as Blake. He is at once physical, intelligent, virile, handsome, and married with children. Perhaps contra Douglass who denotes "The Heroic Slave," Delany suggests there could be more than one.[26]

Despite this optimistic meeting, however, Blake's trip to Louisiana reveals that for every Sampson, there are many who, as a result of their condition, lack the qualities necessary for success: "Light, of necessity, had to be imparted to the darkened region of the obscure intellects of the slaves, to arouse them from their benighted condition to one of moral responsibility, to make them sensible that liberty was legitimately and essentially theirs, without which there was no distinction between them and the brute. Following as a necessary consequence would be the destruction of oppression and ignorance" (101). Again, in keeping with the classical ranking system Delany delineates and promotes in *Condition* and which Douglass seems to convey through allusion to Plato's ship of state, the author is clear that slavery and white supremacy in general have stratified black people to an extent that large-scale insurrection is not yet possible. Even the leaders, of whom there are a good number, must educate the slaves before they can achieve liberty.

Knowledge of the legitimacy of liberty, Delany suggests, is the factor that cleaves human from animal. Here he disregards intellectual or artistic capability, brain size, approximation to apes—all the white supremacist arguments that attempted to define Africans as a separate, degraded species—as distinguishing features. Though enslaved Africans might share a condition with "brutes," they certainly do not share an identity distinction; we have seen Delany's rejection and resentment of such comparisons in his portrayals of black masculinity, sexuality, and marriage. Delany argues that it is the knowledge that liberty is just that makes one human, and in posing the argument this way, he delineates liberty as a human right available to blacks in the New World who recognize it as such. That it is not specifically enumerated in the Constitution for them does not matter; Blake, at this point in the novel, is determined to seize for blacks in America what he sees as their inalienable rights as persons.

In *Blake*, the commitment to inalienable rights fortifies the hero's determination for revolution within the United States, but his personal circumstances—his need to locate his wife—take him to another place. To forfeit this quest in favor of his revolutionary pursuits would be inconsistent with Blake's ideals. The personal and the political go hand in hand; for Blake, to be a man and not a dependent is to have his wife. The task is to repair the rift between the two, which his circumstances have created. But first, he must realize the first part of his plan and help his friends from the Franks' plantation secure their freedom in Canada. The novel didactically and strategically takes the reader to colonial Canada to point out the infectious racism in both colony and republic, to galvanize the need to revolutionize and acquire due rights, not to accept "charity."

Delany's view of the unsuitability of Canada as a permanent option for black settlement is developed in his *Condition* and in his other emigration writings, particularly his "Political Destiny" essay. But it finds articulation again throughout his transcolonial African diasporic novel. Delany underscores the discord between action and principle even in the British colony, which has become regarded propagandistically as the true "land of the free." When Andy drops to the ground in Canada West to kiss the soil, the narrator explains, "Poor fellow! he little knew the unnatural feelings and course pursued toward his race by many Canadians, those too pretending to be Englishmen by birth, with some of whom the blacks had fought side by side in the memorable crusade made upon that fairest portion of Her Majesty's Colonial Possessions, by Americans in disguise, calling themselves 'Patriots'" (152)—a reference to the War of 1812. Delany identifies white Canadians' racism as "unnatural," their hypocrisy as inconsistent. He uses the rhetoric of disguise to explain the disharmony between their outward appearance and inward conviction. He takes the same notion of contradiction between white colonial Canadian individual action and principle, the incongruity of their bodies and minds—characteristic of their notions of selfhood, which contrasts with those of the black heroes in this novel, and in Douglass's novella, and extends it to their greater level of organization, to that of policy and government. White hypocrisy is consistent on both micro and macro levels, the two authors suggest; they express their desire for the opposite in the formation of a coherent black community, regardless of how idealistic the notion of such an entity may be. Delany's recognition that blacks must empower themselves denotes the division between informed and uninformed blacks that he would like to repair. By underscoring the incongruities within white colonial Canadian communities, he works toward the reconciliation of disjunctures within the black communities.

Delany's use of "unnatural" to describe the feelings of whites in Canada West supports his notion regarding the narrator's discussion of black voting rights in Canada as a mere privilege and revealing of the colony's hypocrisy. Gregg Crane usefully argues that the meaning of "inherent," which "signifies the pre-legal moral authority for law in the liberal natural rights tradition of abolitionists such as Frederick Douglass and Harriet Beecher Stowe and the hierarchical order of nature in conservative natural rights diction of proslavery advocates . . . becomes in Delany's analysis a natural law metaphor for power. We call certain rights *inherent* because we are confident that we can enforce them. A privilege is a thing granted and thus withdrawable, but a right is something taken by force and guaranteed by the continuing possession of power" ("Lexicon" 546).[27] The use of "unnatural" implicitly supports the portrayal of black leaders, particularly Blake, in their consistency as "natural," and therefore claims for them the word and its connotations as applied in the discourses of natural history and natural law on which both pro- and antislavery advocates drew.

Delany's portrayal of Canada West as a consolation, not a solution, determines the need for Blake to travel again and emphasizes the hero's reluctance to be satisfied with anything less than the ability to self-govern. Freedom, as in the absence of enslavement, is not enough. He explains that Andy "knew not that some of high intelligence and educational attainments of his race residing in many parts of the Provinces were really excluded from and practically denied their rights, and that there was no authority known to the colony to give redress and make restitution on the petition or application of these representative men of his race, which had frequently been done with the reply from the Canadian functionaries that they had no power to reach their case" (153). In this exposition of colonial Canadian hypocrisy, the education the reader receives of which "Poor Andy" the slave is ignorant, reveals the severely limited access to rights in the colony, even for educated black elites.

Delany emphasizes the temporariness of a colonial Canadian solution for the fugitive slave, who may be simultaneously educated and elite, through Blake's reunion with his child, a meeting which primarily bolsters the hero's vow to find his wife: "By the instincts of a husband, I'll have her if living! If dead, by impulses of a Heaven-inspired soul, I'll avenge her loss unto death!" (156–57). The meeting of father and son marks the hero's desperation to find Maggie and reclaim his role as both father and husband, but the reunion of husband and wife must take place in a geopolitical location favorable to revolution—that is, not in Canada West. Again, Delany asserts Blake's willingness to commit acts of violence and his belief that such actions are "Heaven-inspired" and therefore moral. Blake's disappointed reaction to Canada West offers the reader a historical survey of the settlement at Chatham and the politics of the province.[28] Dissatisfied, Blake heads to Cuba.

It is there where Blake is reunited with Maggie. Cuba signifies the promise of revolution commensurate with the reunion of husband and wife. Contrary to the slaves in the United States who are still ignorant of their capabilities, those in Cuba are "ripe for a general rising" (173). Blake hears this from an old man he meets there who continues to wonder aloud, "but God only knew where they would find a leader" (173). This rather heavy-handed depiction of Blake's messianic or deus ex machina–style arrival in Cuba nevertheless demonstrates a coherence of time and place unavailable to the hero in mainland North America—whether the United States or Canada West. In Cuba, the huts are united in purpose. There, he also meets the historical rebel poet, Plácido, who turns out to be Blake's cousin.[29] It may seem ironic to say the time is right for revolution when we consider Sundquist's useful tracing of historical inconsistencies in the novel. He notes that the novel ends with Plácido still alive and awaiting insurrection in Cuba, while Narciso Lopez, leader of private American attempts to annex Cuba, is about to be executed. Historically, Plácido was executed in 1844 and Lopez in 1851. Literary critic Timothy Powell reads such disruptions productively through a postcolonial lens to argue that Delany is able "imaginatively to escape the constraints of what Anne McClintock calls the *imperial idea of linear time*" that "haunts" postcolonial texts which find themselves gazing back (361, emphasis in original). Powell argues that Delany leaves us looking forward. I believe this precise disruption of time and the inclusion of Plácido—despite historical inconsistencies—affords Delany the best means to articulate the role of the black hero—intellectual/artist/activist. Ifeoma Nwankwo argues that "Plácido becomes the medium through which all come to see the need for revolution, rather than the agent who issues the call to arms. Delany intensifies the threat he issues to whites throughout the novel by having an attack on Plácido be the impetus for the revolution" (79). By "realizing" the impossible according to historical "fact," Delany emphasizes the possibility of black self-rule through the actions of an intelligentsia who require no white support. The fictive form allows him to do this as it is its own authority. Here, if oddly, form and content cohere most usefully; place and time, no matter how disrupted, are right for revolution—the greatest disruption.

Contrary to his previous concern that the enslaved of the United States were not ready for revolt, Blake this time advocates the opposite. Plácido argues that they "have much left to learn to fit us for freedom," and Blake responds, "I differ with you, Plácido, we know enough now, and all that remains to be done is to make ourselves free, and then put what we know into practice. We know much more than we dare attempt to do. We want space for action—elbow room; and in order to obtain it, we must shove our oppressors out of the way" (197). Again, Blake pairs knowledge with physical force. Delany asserts Blake as a model of black masculinity when he is hired aboard the *Vulture* where he will plan an insurrection that fails, largely due to bad weather. However, I believe it really fails because Delany wants the revolution to take place on land. As he says, blacks "want space for action." I believe he means literal space, and the contained entity of the ship is insufficient.[30] The Portuguese first mate says to Blake: "I'm in want of just such a larky as you; a likely good-looking black to wrestle with the storms and untrip the hurricanes. By your looks a grin from you would fascinate a mermaid; the flash of your eye obscure the most vivid streak of lightning, and the sound of your voice silence the loudest clap of thunder" (200). This simultaneously erotic and religious assessment of Blake's powers at once sexualizes him in the eyes of the first mate and attributes to him the godlike powers that fit with Delany's messianic or divinely appointed portrayal of his hero. This combination of sexuality and power is crucial for Delany, as it is for Douglass—black selfhood demands free sexual expression.

Scholars are much more apt to recognize the importance of sexuality in Delany's novel than in Douglass's novella. Literary critic Lori Merish discusses the scene in which Judge Ballard, a northern white slaveholder who owns property in Havana, and Major Armsted, a southern slave trader, debate the relative laxity of Cuban social customs with regard to interracial interaction. Ballard is disgusted by the fact that in Cuba a black man might ask a white man on the street for a light from the white's cigar and therefore touch it: an object that the white man will then return to his mouth. Armsted is surprised that it never occurred to Ballard who was rolling his cigars in the first place. Merish uses this scene to relate American and Cuban commodity culture with the cigar's implicit phallic connotation to argue that Cuba represents the site where "fantasized interracial male union is consummated and nationally embodied," as the cigar in the novel "constitutes a sign of male homosocial cross-racial desire (marking the Anglo-American 'consumption' of the Afro-Cuban body) and marks the repression of that desire" (277). Here the discussion of sexuality in the novel is homosocial and repressed and occurs totally within the conversation of white male characters. If we accept Merish's reading, we can see Delany positioning black male physicality again as superior to that of these white males, if only by virtue of the repression of white homosexual desire for black men.

Even in this scene of seemingly hyper-physical|sexual masculinity, Delany presents a more encompassing portrayal of black selfhood. He does not shy away from offering the very embodied descriptions the Major gives of "black hands," kneading dough, the "arms full length immersed in molasses," and the sexual innuendo Ballard uses to describe how "Negro[es] swell so soon into importance" and how "[j]oking with a Negro is rather too large a dose [to swallow]" (63). Rather, Delany admits black masculinity, sexual physicality, and white impressions of it just as he allows the Major to state that the slave is "just like" him and Ballard. He argues that whites condemn in slaves that which they approve in themselves and that many are "warmhearted" and "intelligent" (63). Here again in the novel, we see—even focalized through potentially sexually repressed white male slaveholders/traders—a black masculine self that is physical, emotional, intellectual, and sexual.

But the primary focus of sexuality in Delany, as in Douglass, is heterosexual and relates directly to political self-rule.[31] First, when Maggie and Blake reunite, Delany acknowledges the sexual aspect of their reunion: "Gently laying her on the grass under the shade of a tree, the greathearted slave hastened to the rippling stream nearby from which to get water to lave her brow and temples to relieve her of the temporary insanity; when sitting over her in discharge of his duty of love and conjugal affection, he found solace by the intrusion of tears which freely fell from his eyes" (181). Delany creates a portrait of the couple that is sexually healthy, affectionate, and removed from white regulation or interference. His use of the words "discharge" and "tears" signifies Blake's body's involuntary or unconscious physical expression of emotion as the two function in concert, which Delany suggests is "natural." The coherence of Blake's embodied consciousness symbolically contrasts the incoherence of white characters' acts and thoughts and emphasizes the contradictory logic of slaveholding that must legislate what is "unnatural" in order to (re)produce white supremacy.

The symbolic value in this scene of reunion demonstrates a micro or intimate example of the sort of political autonomy that Blake, and by extension Maggie, desire. The sexual union of the two who had been previously unnaturally sundered serves as a metaphor for the classical ideal of autonomy, which "means that the political community provides its laws and that it does so excluding every idea of extra-social source of the laws and institutions, either natural or traditional, or metaphysical. This is the highest 'Kratos,' the highest power that exists in a society by giving ourselves, our laws and our institutions under which we live and the government with which we determine our direction" (Tountas 189). In *Blake* this scene of healthy sexual expression starkly contrasts the scenes of sexual violation and oppression we witnessed in the previous chapter or even in the white scrutiny of the Major's innuendos. The extension of this principle of autonomy we see in the sexual reunion of Blake and Maggie provides a template for the ideal black political self-rule and of black selfhood/manhood that Delany promotes. The symbolic value of this physical reunion between Blake and Maggie, the hero hopes, will find realization in the revolution plot.

This transcolonial African diasporic novel ends with the promise of insurrection, but not without demonstrating a final vicious sexual attack on a female character. The vengeance promised for this attack leaves the reader hopeful that the insurrection and attainment of the hero's desire for political self-rule will come to fruition. During the insurrection plot in Cuba, Delany brings together a coterie of revolutionaries, intellectuals, Plácido, and a banjoist and all-around accomplished musician (not to mention one of the most charming characters of the novel, Gofer Gondolier), all of whom gather, salon style, at the home of Madame Cordora to discuss their political philosophies and to plot their accompanying action. That Gondolier is a banjoist brings to mind the West African origins of the instrument as well as Thomas Jefferson's reference to the "banjar" in *Notes on the State of Virginia* when he explains, "In music [blacks] are more generally gifted than the whites with accurate ears for tune and time" (37).

Delany's interest in black superiority necessarily extends to the exciting character of Gondolier.

Emphasizing the connection between black political self-rule, marriage, sexual health, and fulfillment, the novel turns to the tradition of the wedding. Before the revolution can take place, two marriages among the rebels must occur: Gofer Gondolier will wed Abyssa Soudan and Juan Montega will marry Madame Cordora. Powell refers to the two weddings that occur at the end of *Blake* to suggest that "Delany consummates [his] black nationalist vision of pan-Africanism, which includes blacks of all shades, all classes, and from every corner of the black diasporic nation, with a double marriage, noting that 'the consummation of conjugal union is the best security for political relations'" (361). Nevertheless, the attack on Ambrosina Cordora, Madame Cordora's daughter, leaves the reader nervous as to the security of political relations without insurrection and a pan-African overthrow of white supremacist rule: "When in a thronged part of the thoroughfare, Ambrosina accidentally came against a lady with whom there was a gentleman. Politely bowing she made acknowledgments for the balk, which the lady acknowledged with a bow and passed on. The man, however, gave her a rude push with an oath and other hard language" (311). Later, when Ambrosina passes by the man in his shop, he runs out to attack her: "Snatching up a horsewhip, which seems to have been secured for the purpose," the whip metonymical of the violence of slavery, "running out and seizing her by the breast of the dress rendering it in tatters," also alluding to the stripping of enslaved women prior to whipping, "he dealt upon her person over the arms, neck, head, and face the most cruel punishment, to the sad disfiguring of her features for the time. Her cries brought no white persons to her relief—the blacks dared not have attempted it" (311). This scene of public sexualized violence and the insurrectionist group's promise of vengeance reinforces the centrality of sexual health and well-being to black political self-rule and the necessity for the fulfillment of the insurrectionist plot for the securing of that self-rule. Probably as many critics have lamented the incompleteness of the text as have regarded it optimistically in that the available ending provides what Powell terms the "forward looking" conclusion that most postcolonial novels cannot achieve because of their "perpetual present marked only as 'post'" (361–62).

The last line of the novel reasserts the relation of sexuality and selfhood and political independence for black men and women in the New World.

It signifies the beginning of the revolution and the collective union of realized black selfhood ready to claim the right to self-govern. It realizes the power Delany demonstrates is within blacks in the New World to recognize and secure their true liberation, and it makes explicit why he believes revolution—and not integration—is necessary. The line belongs to Gondolier, who is outraged at the savage and sexually charged beating of Ambrosia Cordora: "Woe be unto those devils of whites, I say!" (313).

Gondolier's words resurface in Black American literary traditions and history into the present century. Douglass and Delany present the coherent interrelation of violence and liberation in contrast to the incoherent logic of white supremacy. They assert a sense of self of a sexually robust, healthy, embodied, heroic consciousness whose logic and actions, voluntary or otherwise, cohere. As long as white oppression persists in the New World, we will continue to hear Gondolier's call: "Woe be unto those devils of whites, I say!"

Conclusion

Black Intellectuals, Black Well-Being

QUESTIONS ABOUT THE FUTURE OF BLACK AMERICAN LITERARY STUDIES

Rhetorics of health form a central register for black intellectuals' resistance to white oppression and the creation and expression of black selfhood in the nineteenth century and beyond. Informed by and conversant with dominant discourses of medicine and law, the black thinkers discussed here expose incongruities of white classificatory categories and hierarchies emerging in the early to mid-nineteenth century. They produced their works during a time of rapid professionalization, racialized medicine, and the increasing popularity of abolition. Print was cheaper to produce than it ever had been, and black intellectuals understood and commanded the power of publication. Whether penning their works themselves, relating events to amanuenses, certifying documents with an *X*, or accounting incidents to court clerks and neighbor witnesses, the black thinkers featured in this book all exercised rhetorics of health and well-being to theorize selfhood. Propagandistic polemics, complexly layered critiques, accounts of criminal acts, and imaginative works—every text here contains elements of each. This literature reveals the limits of legal personhood and the incoherence of nineteenth-century republican, colonial, and national ideals.

The literature here illuminates ways of reading black acts beyond those requiring conventional literacy and emphasizes that there were black intellectuals operating outside the realm of traditional composition—more in the vein, perhaps, of Antonio Gramsci's organic intellectuals. Scholarship has emphasized literacy in early Black American print culture, but studies of conventional literacy (that is, the ability to read and write) tend to reconstitute white hierarchical notions about intelligence and humanness. This is where I think rhetorics of health can help us resist the reproduction of such measures of worth even as we interrogate the medium of print that we know is so important, particularly for blacks in the early to mid-nineteenth century. There is something about each author's approach to health and well-being that challenges the hierarchical ordering that is so central to the period's ways of thinking.

Historian of reading Jennifer Monaghan posits, "In a free society, to be fully literate is also to be fully human." She refers to Frederick Douglass's literacy and the relation between composition and self-formation. The full paragraph reads, "Today, literacy—particularly the ability to compose—still marks a boundary between full involvement with one's own humanity and a feeling of exclusion from the human race. In a free society, to be fully literate is also to be fully human" (341). Though I do not doubt the relationship Monaghan draws between "liberty and literacy," and I respect the impulse to privilege printed works over other forms of resistance and self-formation, I question the centrality of composition, of authorship to the sense of humanness she describes. Distinguishing concepts of human from person and self complicates such assumptions.

The women featured in this book, for example, prompt us to ask: What is the meaning of Lavina Wormeny's biting off her owner's nose? What is the intellectual currency of this violent act, and how is it related to her well-being? What of Celia's clubbing Robert Newsom to death through her window? These women encourage us to ask. But never, I submit, do they suggest that they understood themselves as less human than, say, Frederick Douglass, Martin Delany, or Mary Ann Shadd, who relied less on their teeth and arms than their pens and presses and who drew on classical virtues to present ideal characterizations of black selfhood. Nor, for that matter, do they suggest that they saw themselves as less human than their white supporters or oppressors.

Eric Gardner proposes that the X marked on legal documents denotes both self-identification and a kind of literacy.[1] Reading such literacies as lesser and equating them with an experience of lesser humanity overlooks what might be gained by reading them as merely different literacies and different notions of what constitutes humanness. Reading rhetorics of health in a similar manner, across all of its forms and formulations in Black

American literature, we interrogate the limits of the very categories of human and person that we so often use loosely—as though they held a coherent meaning for nineteenth-century Black Americans.

The kinds of black selfhood the thinkers in this study imagine and explain through their rhetorics of health are holistic and discursive, conflicting, and complexly layered. They reveal dreams, desire, fantasy, pleasure, pain, peace, and violence—not necessarily, exclusively, or consistently with positive or negative connotations attached to them. Rather than sensing themselves as somehow less human, these thinkers question definitions of human and person and prompt us to ask what is at stake in distinguishing between the two in projects of self-formation, for slaves were understood as human but as both person and property. In these authors' diverse, often divergent approaches to black selfhood, they challenge the notion of a print-generated black counterpublic and suggest rather that we imagine black counterpublics—equally diverse and often in disagreement.[2]

A radical rethinking of the category of the human can reshape the ways in which we understand black selfhood during the period of New World slavery and beyond. The task of defining the human, locating its uniqueness, has proved through history to be no easy feat. Philosophical, biblical, theological, scientific, political, legal, medical, and computational perspectives have entered debates about and contested definitions of humanness. Beyond the question of the capacity of any of these disciplines to define the human "accurately" is the seeming insufficiency of language to articulate the definition.

As legal scholar Adam Sitze argued at a panel discussion on rethinking what it means to be human, "the language we use to talk about science is itself not scientific." We rely on metaphors of families, of games, of romance, et cetera. Even our relationship with technology, he continued, is really one of faith—evocative of religion. Thus the language of religion really is the language of our scientific and technological culture. For example, when I board an airplane, I rely on my faith that the technology will get me safely to where I'm going. My relation to this technology is one of faith in its "soundness." If we believe these observations, then linguistically and philosophically humans' relation to science is for the most part not scientific. This assessment speaks to the discursive nature of description. Here the language of faith is the medium of science. For the black intellectuals of this study, the rhetoric of health is the medium of self-interpretation, governance, and even at times mastery.

At the same panel discussion, biologist Michael Hood further troubled the concept of humanness by recalling that the number of parasites and pathogens is twelve times greater than the number of what we might call "free living things." Genetics tell us that we are no different than parasites and pathogens—65 percent of our DNA is made up of parasitic DNA. Furthermore, what are considered animals can behave in what are considered human ways. On the flip side, Hood noted that humans can have experiences of not being human—phantom limb sensations like the experience of feeling pain in a missing limb or experiencing one's arm as no longer one's arm as stroke victims might. Further complicating the putative borders of the human is Allewaert's consideration of the parahuman and Weheliye's concept of racialized assemblages.

I recount these examples because they complicate ideas about humanness from biological, linguistic, and philosophical perspectives. So what does it mean and how can it help us think through black literary self-formation? Elizabeth Grosz situates the human in a broader context, returning to Darwin and positing that evolutionary theory provides a way to understand humanity as fleeting, as part of a process of becoming (as opposed, perhaps, to being): "There are as many forms of political and social organization as there are collections of large numbers, populations. If these inventions are forms of self-transformation . . . then reason, language, culture, tools, and other distinctly human accomplishments must now take their place, not as the overcoming or surpassing of an animal ancestry but as the most recent elaboration, as one of the many possible lines of elaboration that life has enabled" (24). She sees the human not as half of a binary category that positions the human and animal in opposition, relegating the latter as inferior and thus to be "got over" or "surpassed," but as part of a continuum of "becoming." Here the human is continually becoming, elaborating lines of life.

Grosz continues, "The human, when situated as one among many, is no longer in the position of speaking for and authorizing the analysis of the animal as other, and no longer takes on the right to name, to categorize, the rest of the world but is now forced, or at least enticed, to listen, to respond, to observe, to become attuned to a nature it was always part of but had only aimed to master and control—not nature as a unified whole, but nature as ever-striving, as natural selection, as violence and conflict" (24). Placing the human in this continuum strips it of authority to order and classify or to master and overcome. What Grosz depicts is a much more dynamic concept of a constantly becoming entity that *becomes* in much the way the rest of nature does, not necessarily without violence and conflict, but not necessarily *in* conflict with nature. In Grosz's reading of Darwin, the self/other binary breaks apart in the concept of human.

But how is it possible to rethink evolutionary logic along the lines of elaboration that Grosz refers to as something *other* than denoting progression or advancement—discourses that have typically situated black people as somehow lagging or even retrograde? Here the concept of person relates to, relies on, and reconfigures the notion of human. Esposito argues, "On the one hand, person is the more general category since it encompasses the entire human species. On the other hand, it is the prism through which the human species is separated in the hierarchical division between types defined precisely by their constitutive difference" ("*Dispositif*" 22). The twofold constitution of the person is simultaneously encompassing and separating. For Esposito, the prism of the person at once identifies (inclusively) and categorizes (hierarchically) humans—legally, historically, and biopolitically. The modern era basically understood the person and the human as two extreme conditions with a "series of intermediate steps" in between. This is the sort of logic that understood the slave as human yet unable to occupy the same status of personhood as white people because they were also property.

Esposito further explains, "At its apex one finds the healthy adult, to whom can be awarded the title of being truly and properly a person; next there is the infant, who is considered to be a potential person; and then the elderly invalid, who has been reduced to a semi-person; to the terminally ill to whom the status of non-person is given; to finally the madman who has received the role of anti-person. A consequence of this classification is subjugating 'defective' persons to whole persons, who are free to dispose of the former as they will on the basis of medical or even economic considerations" ("*Dispositif*" 26). Recall also Weheliye's argument about the function of racialization in demarcating the human from the not-quite-human and the nonhuman. We know the implications of these gradations of personhood for the enslaved. Esposito's and Weheliye's assessments are helpful not only in thinking through the centrality of health to the project of black self-formation in the first half of the nineteenth century, but for such projects in general and in our own time as well. As such, it becomes clear why a rhetorics of health is such a promising and productive mode of political critique and why Black American literature continues to rely on it so heavily.

Recollect the prominence of the body, health, and well-being in the poetry, novels, and drama of Black American writers through the twentieth century and into the twenty-first. Diabetes in poet Dionne Brand's *Land to Light On*, loving one's hands in Toni Morrison's *Beloved*, and mental health in playwright August Wilson's *Pittsburgh Cycle* are three examples that readily leap to mind. There are countless other literary explorations of Black American embodiment, health, and well-being in circulation by prominent as well as emergent black authors. Carla Peterson reminds us that "among traditional African peoples no clear separation is made between body and spirit; rather, the body is conceived as the material form of it" (*Recovering* ix–x). Keeping in mind the traditional relationship between materiality and spirituality that Peterson mentions as we investigate its manifestation, articulation, and interrogation in writings and orations of black thinkers in the New World shapes our readings of the centrality of physicality in these works.

Informing this focus on physicality no doubt is the proliferation of assaults on black health and well-being that continue into our own time. Legal scholar Vernellia Randall recounts a devastating history of medical abuses from prison and military experiments to racial barriers to care and violence as a public health issue. She notes the Black American dimension to prison abuses, as blacks represent 40 percent of all prisoners. Her history of medical abuses includes the 1962 injection of live cancer cells into nearly four hundred inmates at Ohio State Prison, as well as a similar study a few years later in the Oregon State Penitentiary in which more than one hundred prisoners' testicles were injected with radioactive thymidine. The first project tracked the progression of disease; the second sought "to see whether the rate of sperm production was affected by exposure to steroidal hormones" (199–200). Add to this a 14 percent higher infant mortality rate than European Americans, racial discrimination and segregation in nursing homes, hospital privatization, or closure in Black American communities, doctor dismissal of CPR treatment for blacks, decreased use of drug therapies to prevent pneumonia in HIV cases, and the FDA's approval of the long-acting contraceptive Norplant, which all fifty states have incorporated into their welfare systems through reimbursement or cash bonus. The picture Randall presents is bleak, to say the least. And these are only a few of her examples.

Looking toward the future of Black American literature studies and of analyses of self-formation generally, I think there is much more we can consider regarding concepts of self-definition and our investments in notions of human worth. The relation of these ideas to concepts of race, health, illness, and disability offers fruitful ground for imagining the just and ethical society we want. As new technologies and theories continue to prompt the reimagining of what it means to be human, what will be the implications for legal personhood? How will race and histories of racism factor into future legal rubrics? How will such changing definitions influence or manifest themselves in future medical theory and practice, and how will literature influence these theories and practices as well as be influenced by them? How will dynamic definitions of humanness continue to shape and alter literary production and our discussion of literary history? What effects will these definitions have on issues of canonicity? And what will Black American literary history look like as boundaries separating human and animal and technology, for example, are continually challenged?

By questioning the categories that continue to rank us, we can challenge the power structures that reinforce the hierarchies that historically have ordered America. At a time now when revolutionary rhetoric and claims to the reassertion of republican ideals are making a forceful political comeback, combined with recent multiple killings of unarmed black people at the hands of white police officers, such investigations are crucial. I hope that *Black Well-Being* has offered some registers for reimagining how race and self-formation might structure America in more just and humane ways.

Notes

Introduction. Human, Person, Self: Blackness and Well-Being

1. A note on capitalization: *Black* is capitalized when the word modifies a group's geopolitical organization, e.g., Black American, Black New World, etc. For more general uses of the descriptor, *black* appears in lowercase.

2. For sources of these definitions, see "Mental Health: A State of Well-Being," World Health Organization online, http://www.who.int/features/factfiles/mental_health/en/, and "Health Related Quality of Life," Centers for Disease Control and Prevention online, http://www.cdc.gov/hrqol/wellbeing.htm.

3. Along these lines, it's also been useful to think about Hannah Arendt's tracing of the path by which commonsense reasoning relies on separation from the animal senses and reduces difference to measurable variations in mental power, calibrations that often carry terrifying—if not merely limiting—social and political consequences.

4. See in particular Mae Ngai's *Impossible Subjects*.

5. I want to note and adhere to Weheliye's cautioning about white European thinkers' presumed theoretical preeminence, particularly around concepts of bare life or state of exception: "Foucault's and Agamben's ideas are frequently invoked without scrutinizing the historical, philosophical, or political foundations upon which they are constructed, which bespeaks a broader tendency in which theoretical formulations by white European thinkers are granted a conceptual carte blanche, while those uttered from the purview of minority discourse that speak to the same questions are almost exclusively relegated to the jurisdiction of ethnographic locality" (*Habeas Viscus* 6). Furthermore, Allewaert proposes that the concept of the parahuman "suggests an alternative to Agamben's analyses of states of exception that, whether they attend to anthropocentrism or structures of sovereignty, depend on a reification of the identity and category of the human that stops short of accounting for colonialism or ecology" (*Ariel's Ecology* 110). *Black Well-Being*'s chapter 3 regarding colonialism, disability, and national identity, though it does not take up the term *parahuman* per se, demonstrates the interrelation of human and nonhuman species and substances to destabilize the modern valorized category of the human.

6. See Gardner, *Unexpected Places*.

7. See Rhodes, *Mary Ann Shadd Cary: The Black Press and Protest in the Nineteenth Century*.

8. In the wealthiest country in the world, access to health care is heavily mediated by one's economic status, that is, one's ability to pay (or for one's employer to pay) for it. Indeed, health care costs are *the* prevailing cause of personal bankruptcy.

9. See Valerie Smith, Deborah Garfield, and Saidiya Hartman for some examples.

10. For a superb study of black outlaw testimony and the assertion of civic authority, see Jeannine DeLombard, *In the Shadow of the Gallows*.

11. See Maurice Wallace, *Constructing the Black Masculine*; Robert Reid-Pharr, *Conjugal Union*; Carla Peterson, *Doers of the Word*; and Robert Carr, *Black Nationalism in the New World*.

Chapter 1. The Ruled and Regulated Self: Medicine and Race Science in the Black New World

1. Another reason for such increases in African enslavement was "humanitarian." Sixteenth-century Spanish priest and historian Bartolomé de las Casas detailed the mass death of "Indians" in the Spanish/Portuguese colonies. One response to this genocide was the replacement of "Indians" by African slaves.

2. I use (and want to emphasize) variations of the word *seem* here because as medical historian Harriet Washington points out, immunities "were usually partial and sometimes imaginary." Planters' beliefs in various immunities were sometimes just convenient myths (40).

3. See, for example, the narrative of Solomon Northup.

4. Such an example is part of the larger rhetoric of professionalization common throughout Canada and the United States, but the value of licensing laws was a particular point of debate. Rainer Baehre has recently complicated Canniff's history on this issue.

5. It is possible that in light of the recent rebellion in Upper Canada (1837–38), the officer in question may have been a sympathizer.

6. Both physicians and owners, Savitt explains, complained that "the enslaved ... waited too long before seeking medical assistance and often misdiagnosed illnesses. Owners permitted blacks a small amount of freedom in treating minor ailments at home, but lost their patience when sickness got out of hand," *Race and Medicine*, 74.

7. As Daniel Coleman points out in *White Civility*, there was also a shared interest in white supremacist discourse.

8. In *The Brain Takes Shape*, Robert Martensen traces the medical "emergence of the word 'constitution' and its cognates in many English contexts, not only medical, from the 1680s on" and acknowledges that seventeenth-century usage of it recalled Hippocrates (184–89).

9. See Warner, "The Idea of Southern Medical Distinctiveness," 203.

10. Frederick Douglass's *The Claims of the Negro, Ethnologically Considered*, one of a number of black ethnologies dating back to at least the 1820s, also appeared in 1854, the year *Types of Mankind* was published.

11. See Nott, "Acclimation," 369.

12. See Gross, "Pandora's Box," 305–6.

13. Recent medicine at times still contemplates the scientific usefulness of racial categories in, for example, attempting to detect higher incidences of pulmonary afflictions among people of African descent than other groups, and medical sociologists emphasize the importance of place (specifically geographical and social determinants of health) in such studies. Furthermore, popular print continues to imagine the interest of such findings to a general readership. See the following studies which address the rise in rates of lung disease in the United States, particularly among African Americans: "African Americans Vulnerable to Lung Disease"; Gathuru et al., "Differences in Rates of Obstructive Lung Disease"; Gathuru, "The Role of Socioeconomic and Environmental Factors"; and Starling, "What's behind the Asthma Epidemic in Black America?"

Chapter 2. Ancient Ideals and the Healthy Self: Mary Ann Shadd's *Plea for Emigration* and Martin Robison Delany's *Condition, Elevation, Emigration, and Destiny*

1. These refer specifically to Catherine Parr Traill's 1836 book *The Backwoods of Canada* and Susanna Moodie's 1852 *Roughing It in the Bush*. Literary critic Richard Almonte has attempted to read Shadd's *Plea* in this larger tradition of early Canadian literature, and I applaud his consideration of the text from a literary perspective. It's somewhat an uneasy fit, though, because *Plea* follows more the genre of the almanac, not to mention polemic, and lagged in popularity behind the tremendously successful examples from English emigrants partly because it had no home audience in England. Nevertheless, Almonte's reading challenges critics to see *Plea* as traversing colonial Canadian, British, and U.S. literary traditions, not just as a historical document. It is also noteworthy that before emigrating to Canada West, Moodie (née Strickland) served as amanuensis for Mary Prince's *History*. Moodie in a sense embodies some of the intimate connections between imperial, colonial, and national literatures on the issue of slavery and immigration.

2. Delany was not alone in his promotion of black physical superiority. Henry Highland Garnet, for example, along with Delany recognized "the reality of the rampant racialism of their day" and believed that "blacks needed to employ it on their own behalf." See Rael, *Black Identity and Black Protest in the Antebellum North*, 51.

3. A notable exception is Richard Almonte's introduction to *A Plea for Emigration*, 73n30.

4. Perhaps Eric Gardner's call for critics to look for African American literature in "unexpected places" might inspire scholars to pay more literary attention to the *Provincial Freeman*.

5. Of course Ethiop, whom I note in one of the chapter epigraphs, describes Shadd in a flattering light in the same paper where Delany disparages her. Levine identifies Ethiop as one of Douglass's contributing editors, William J. Wilson. See *Martin Delany, Frederick Douglass, and the Politics of Representative Identity*, 75. Despite Shadd's complimentary appearance in Wilson's letter, I think that Delany is focusing his critique on Douglass's individual silence about Shadd's accomplishments.

6. In part informing my reading of the role of women in Delany's novel *Blake* is his

public support of Shadd, as well as their lasting friendship solidified in Canada West. See Rhodes, *Mary Ann Shadd Cary*, 50.

7. I want to acknowledge three other readings of these works. One situates Delany's *Condition* as promoting capitalist entrepreneurship (Wallace) and Shadd's *Plea* as espousing a neo-Jeffersonian agrarian model (Peterson, *Doers of the Word*). Another argues that "Delany turned to law, rather than other readily available discourses such as Christianity or sentimentality, to make his case against slavery and foster a consolidated African American community." See Zuck, "Martin R. Delany and Rhetorics of Divided Sovereignty," 40. Within these excellent analyses of the two writers' models of becoming, health and rhetorics of physicality are largely overlooked.

8. See Marcus Wood, *The Horrible Gift of Freedom*. Wood describes emancipation as a second theft: slavery stole black people's freedom and emancipation stole blacks' ability to revolt and reclaim their own freedom. As Wood duly notes, the iconography of emancipation suggests it was a gift from white people, when in fact they were really just returning what they took in the first place.

9. For more on diseased societies, see Gay Wilentz's *Healing Narratives*.

10. Rhodes goes so far as to say, "*Notes of Canada West* consistently romanticized British rule, and elevated white institutions to the pinnacle of civilization" (*Mary Ann Shadd Cary* 44). Perhaps we can see the profound effect of colonial Canadian civilization rhetoric, particularly in contradistinction to portrayals of a backward, if not savage, United States (as we saw nineteenth-century physician and medical historian William Canniff promoting in chapter 1) operating on and through Shadd. We'll see similar civilizationist rhetoric embedded in Benjamin Drew's celebration of colonial Canada in chapter 3.

11. See Van Gosse, "'As a Nation, the English Are Our Friends.'"

12. See also Zuck, "Martin R. Delany and Rhetorics of Divided Sovereignty," on divided sovereignty in Delany, another (legal) iteration of his sense of brokenness.

13. Again, we see Shadd's susceptibility to the appeals of such rhetoric common in Canada West. See chapter 1.

14. Indeed, Shadd did become a Canadian citizen just before the conclusion of the Civil War. For historical interpretations of Shadd's decision, see Jane Rhodes, *Mary Ann Shadd Cary*, and Rinaldo Walcott, "'Who Is She and What Is She to You?'"

15. For more on this, see Samuel Cartwright's rhetoric of mastery/lack of physiological mastery in his discussion of the functioning of "negroes'" lungs, "Slavery in the Light of Ethnology," 693.

16. Walcott acknowledges Shadd's preference for the term *complexional character* over *race*. See "'Who Is She and What Is She to You?'" 140.

17. We might consider here a distinction Shadd may be making between actual monarchy and a republicanism that is little more than a disguise for an underlying monarchy that persisted even after the revolution. See Paul Downes, *Democracy, Revolution, and Monarchism in Early American Literature*, and Judith Shklar, *American Citizenship: The Quest for Inclusion*.

18. Though I don't go into Delany's post–Civil War writings, it is worth noting here that his *Principia of Ethnology* (1879) reasserts central tenets of mid-nineteenth-century

racial science but for the purpose of promoting black rather than white superiority. As noted, the appearance of black ethnologies extended back to the earlier part of the century.

Chapter 3. The Self in Pain: Colonialism, Disability, and National Identity—Mary Prince, Sophia Pooley, and Lavina Wormeny

1. Dea Boster's new study of African American slavery and disability is an important and much needed contribution to disability studies and race. Here I build on her history of disability in the antebellum United States through close readings of the works of black women during the period who wrote about their and others' disabilities.

2. George Elliott Clarke has argued that Moodie structures *Roughing It in the Bush* like a slave narrative, with Moodie playing a Mary Prince victimized not by whip-wielding hypocrites but by mosquitoes, etc. See Clarke's "'This Is No Hearsay,'" 13, as well as Kristina Kyser's interview with him in the *University of Toronto Quarterly* 76, no. 3 (2007): 864.

3. See Van Gosse, "As a Nation, the English Are Our Friends."

4. Sara Salih identifies Turks Island as the Turks and Caicos Islands in her introduction to *The History of Mary Prince*, 74, cf. 30.

5. See Mason et al., "Insulin-like Growth Factor (IGF) I and II, IGF-Binding Proteins, and IGF-Binding Protein Proteases Are Produced by Theca and Stroma of Normal and Polycystic Human Ovaries," and Wade, Schneider, and Li, "Control of Fertility by Metabolic Cues."

6. See Mbanya and Cruickshank et al., "Standardized Comparison of Glucose Intolerance in West African-Origin Populations of Rural and Urban Cameroon, Jamaica, and Caribbean Migrants to Britain."

7. Of course, it is possible that the tenderness he describes is Wormeny's sensitivity to his touch, but there is nothing else in the examination account that alludes to her pain or any other sensory experience. We might think it would be in the collective effort's best interests for Reddy to testify to the continuation of her physical suffering in this report, yet he does not describe her pain. I maintain that his interest, which serves that of all three involved in the narrative, is in remaining objective in accordance with his profession's understanding of the concept. Instead, Cook alludes to the necessity of Wormeny's continued medical care.

8. Cook's introduction to the narrative does not give any indication that Dr. Reddy was involved in the narrative's production, just that he supplied a statement "which fully bears out every word of hers regarding the cruelty to which she had been subjected." See Mackey, *Black Then*, 162. It is not until the very last comment that Cook refers to a second editor.

9. See Gross's chapter "Masters' Character" in *Double Character*.

10. Chapter 4 considers these issues also in legal terms.

11. The third person point of view of this particular narrative may account for its consistent focus on Wormeny's body as it is common in narratives "written by" or

"related by" former slaves (i.e., "in their own words") to contain many descriptions of others' suffering.

12. It is worth noting here the use of the same term "buck" to denote a male slave. Syntactically, the fusion of instrument and human emerges.

13. See Winfried Siemerling, "Slave Narratives and Hemispheric Studies," for his situation of Pooley's narrative in a call for the study of slave narratives and hemispheric studies.

14. I mean "civilize" here in terms of the rhetorical accounts of the putative savagery of the "American races." See Morton and Nott.

15. Note the resonance here of this second objective with that of Mary Ann Shadd's *Plea* and a more general Northern black association of Great Britain with freedom.

16. Here again the fusion of product and producer emerges as Daniel, too, worked in the salt ponds of Turks Island.

17. Boster contends, "African American slaves conceptualized health and physical well-being as a spiritual and community issue rather than as a matter of individual soundness, and felt a strong obligation to care for disabled individuals, such as the blind and elderly" (*African American Slavery and Disability* 28). I think we see something similar here with Prince, but I really don't think that it comes particularly from a sense of spirituality. In fact, I'm suspicious of the sincerity with which Prince adopts Christianity. I mention this a bit as I analyze the end of the narrative. At any rate, Prince's reimagining of ethical becoming extends slaves' communal concept of health and well-being beyond U.S. borders.

18. I want to note here Prince's emphasis on having *chosen* to travel to England to cure her rheumatism. Such agency contrasts with her history of forcible migration, but the point is that her decision results in the recurrence of illness while working for the Woods and her realization that freedom from enslavement in England places her in another class of dependency. Furthermore, returning to her home and her husband after achieving legal freedom in England, she will simultaneously return to a state of enslavement.

19. The Mansfield ruling of 1772 did not emancipate slaves in Britain, but it allowed them the right to live as free people there. Returning to the colonies would mean reenslavement.

20. Some significant rulings include the Grace Jones case of 1722, the Yorke and Talbot judgment of 1729, and the Mansfield decision of 1772.

21. See, for example, Benjamin Drew's anthology of the accounts of Christopher Nichols, 67, Sam Davis, 115, and Williamson Pease, 123.

Chapter 4. The Protective Self: Slave Sexual Health, Crime, and U.S. Legal Personhood—Celia's Murder Trial and Harriet Jacobs's *Incidents*

1. See Thomas D. Morris, who notes that in *Richardson v. Dukes* (1827) the South Carolina court set damages for a murdered slave, said to have been "of bad character," at one dollar. *Southern Slavery and the Law, 1619–1860*, 207.

2. See Ariela Gross's chapter "Honor and Dishonor" in *Double Character* and James Oakes's *Ruling Race*. See also John Fraser's *America and the Patterns of Chivalry*.

3. Cobb's reference to the Lombards specifies a situation where the raped woman is the master's slave's wife. According to Cobb, *An Inquiry into the Law of Negro Slavery*, damages awarded to the slave included procurement of his and his wife's freedom.

4. Melton A. McLaurin, in *Celia, a Slave* (96), notes that counsel for the defense "forc[ed] Jones [the first witness] to admit that Celia had told him that Newsom had raped her on the return trip from Audrain County immediately after his purchase of her"; however, according to the court file (*State of Missouri versus Celia, a Slave*, file 4496, Callaway County Court, October Term, 1855, Callaway County Courthouse, Fulton, Mo.), Jones said under cross-examination that he could not "say positively whether Celia said that the deceased had forced her, on the way home from Audrain county," that he had "heard that he did" but did not "know with certainty whether she told me so." The summary implies that knowledge or at least suspicion of Celia's rape was common to the extent that the witness could not identify positively where he had heard of it. Such a statement, further complicated by the legal and corporeal penalties enslaved people faced for accusing whites of sexual improprieties, implies that the possibility that Celia was "forced" on the way home after her purchase may have been the subject of discussion among whites in the area. Further references to court file 4496 will be made parenthetically.

5. A "Bill of Costs" in file 4496 indicates that Celia received medical attention "during sickness, delivering her of dead child."

6. As I move into a more specific analysis of the narrative, I use "Linda Brent" to denote the character as distinguished from Harriet Jacobs the author.

7. See Spillers, "Mama's Baby, Papa's Maybe."

8. According to the U.S. Department of Justice, Bureau of Justice, *Criminal Victimization in the United States, 2014*, "Only 33.6% of rapes and sexual assault are reported, down from 35.1% in 2005." See www.bjs.gov/index.cfm?ty=pbdetail&iid=.

9. I use *guiltlessness* here instead of *innocence* because the law recognizes guilty or not guilty in its verdicts. Innocence is reasonably not something on which the court rules.

10. It is useful here to consider Beth E. Richie's theory of gender entrapment as an extension of earlier American examples of black women's use of crime as a defense against violence. She uses "gender entrapment to describe the socially constructed process whereby African American women who are vulnerable to men's violence in their intimate relationships are penalized for behaviors they engage in even when the behaviors are logical extensions of their racialized gender identities, their culturally expected gender roles, and the violence in their intimate relationships." See *Compelled to Crime*, 4.

11. Such paternalism, as we've seen, is not exclusive to legal theory. Recall Nott's, Patterson's, and Cartwright's arguments in chapters 1 and 2 advocating the health benefits of slavery for the "Negro."

12. *Missouri Republican* (St. Louis), June 28, 1855.

13. Sarah E. Chinn, in *Technology and the Logic of American Racism*, argues, "In the

1840s, circumstantial evidence was indirect and inferential, inferior to the testimony of an eyewitness." She quotes William Wills and notes that "whereas eyewitness evidence 'applies directly to the fact which forms the subject of inquiry' . . . there was 'no necessary connection between the facts and the inference [from circumstantial evidence]; the *facts* may be true, and the *inference* erroneous'" (13).

14. See the *Baltimore Sun*, January 17, 1856, and the *New York Times*, January 16, 1856.

15. See the *Missouri Republican*, June 28, 1855; the *Randolph Citizen* (Huntsville), July 5, 1855; the *Boonville Weekly Observer* (Boonville), July 7, 1855; and the *Weekly Missouri Statesman*, July 6, 1855.

16. *Boonville Weekly Observer*, July 7, 1855; *Weekly Missouri Statesman*, July 6, 1855.

17. Because there are no extant copies of the *Fulton Telegraph* for the period in question, only reprints from other papers are available. As previously mentioned, these reprints are often varied; some are identical to each other and therefore potentially direct reprints of what appeared in the *Telegraph* while others at times use exact quotations and paraphrasing as well as appended introductions and conclusions.

18. *Missouri Republican*, June 28, 1855. All accounts include information taken from depositions—including one signed with Celia's mark—and indicate that she confessed to the crime.

19. See *Boonville Weekly Observer*, July 7, 1855; *Weekly Missouri Statesman*, July 6, 1855; *Missouri Whig* (Palmyra) July 12, 1855.

20. See also Teresa Goddu, *Gothic America*.

21. Another narrative, lurking behind this one, is of Salomé—the tempting exotic—whose actions result in the beheading of John the Baptist (Mark 6.14–29; Matthew 14.1–12; Luke 9.7–9).

22. Letter from Celia's defense attorneys to A. Leonard, Supreme Court, December 6, 1855. This letter requests a stay of execution for Celia arguing that "the court gave illegal instructions as well as refused such as were plainly the law, [and] indeed cut out all means of defense." Supreme Court Case File 356, Missouri State Archives.

23. Michel Foucault, in *Discipline and Punish*, argues: "Disciplinary power . . . is exercised through its invisibility; at the same time it imposes on those whom it subjects a principle of compulsory visibility. Their visibility assures the hold of the power that is exercised over them. It is the fact of being constantly seen, of being able always to be seen, that maintains the disciplined individual in his subjection" (187).

24. See Karen Sanchez-Eppler, *Touching Liberty*, and Deborah Garfield, "Speech, Listening, and Female Sexuality in *Incidents in the Life of a Slave Girl*" and "Earwitness: Female Abolitionism, Sexuality, and *Incidents in the Life of a Slave Girl*."

25. *Daily Missouri Democrat*, November 27, 1855; *Weekly Brunswicker* (Brunswick), December 1, 1855.

26. *Daily Missouri Democrat*, November 27, 1855; *Weekly Brunswicker*, November 24, 1855; *Weekly Missouri Statesman*, November 23, 1855. McLaurin, using the defense's letter to the Supreme Court and newspaper coverage of Celia's escape surmises that "Celia's benefactors were not prepared to ignore Missouri law totally, so once her original execution date had passed and it appeared that the supreme court would have an

opportunity to hear her appeal, Celia was returned to jail" (*Celia, a Slave* 126). However, articles from the *Democrat* and *Brunswicker* suggest that Celia returned herself; they do not hypothesize that she was hidden and then returned by those who attempted to help her. The validity of the newspaper reports can be debated, and as McLaurin notes, the letter to the Supreme Court does note that Celia was "taken out" of prison by someone (Supreme Court file). The papers also suppose that Celia was aided in her escape; however, reports of an earlier jail break, that of Thomas Carlisle, stated that Celia—imprisoned with him—had aided in his escape. Regardless, it seems possible that Celia, whether aided in her escape, potentially hid and returned herself, and that while in hiding, she "suffered considerably." For information on Carlisle's escape, see the *Daily Missouri Democrat*, November 20, 1855.

27. See Jean Fagan Yellin's introduction to Jacobs's *Incidents*.

28. *Weekly Missouri Statesman*, July 6, 1855; *Boonville Weekly Observer*, July 7, 1855; *Missouri Whig*, July 12, 1855.

29. She has, metaphorically speaking, dispatched Newsom to Hell.

30. *Daily Missouri Democrat*, January 9, 1856; *New York Times*, January 16, 1856; *Baltimore Sun*, January 17, 1856.

31. The North Carolina Code of 1854 postdates Jacobs's experience but coincides with the composition of her manuscript.

32. In *Scenes of Subjection*, Saidiya Hartman reminds us that the file remained in a courthouse drawer for 145 years.

33. The shadow of Nat Turner's confession for his mass murder of whites also falls upon this reportage.

34. See also Karen Halttunen's *Murder Most Foul*.

35. Cf. Nat Turner.

Chapter 5. The Promising Self: Sexual Expression, Heroism, and Revolution—Frederick Douglass's "The Heroic Slave" and Martin Robison Delany's *Blake*

1. See Rael, *Black Identity and Black Protest in the Antebellum North*: "Increasingly, African American spokespersons believed they were to play conspicuous and active roles in the impending apocalyptic contest. James McCune Smith told his readers, 'We live in the heroic age of our country, and the negro is the hero'" (273).

2. In "The Novelization of Voice in Early African American Narrative," William L. Andrews uses the term *fictive*, as distinguished from *fictional*, to denote a work that combines history and fiction. For Andrews, the "fictive voice" is a mode of authorization in black literature. I critique the term more fully, and with specific reference to each text, as the chapter progresses.

3. See Reid-Pharr, *Conjugal Union*, Peterson, *Doers of the Word*, Carr, *Black Nationalism in the New World*, and Davidson, *The Black Nation Novel*, for examples.

4. See Best, *The Fugitive's Properties*, Beavers, "The Blind Leading the Blind," and Noble, "Sympathetic Listening."

5. Here I distinguish between slavery ideology's ordering of intellect and physical-

ity and the mind/body hierarchy that Derrida, for example, has argued was built into Western metaphysics. Perhaps the former drew on the latter, but the manifestations of such hierarchical ordering took on a significance particular to slavery in the antebellum United States. It functioned to exaggerate blacks' physicality, equating the slave with his/her corporeality at the expense of his/her mental capacity.

6. For an extended treatment of classicism in Douglass's nonfictive writings, see Hairston, *The Ebony Column*, chapter 2.

7. Whereas Maurice Wallace argues, "The black masculine fondness for the home, the shanty, the underground room, the crypt, and the closet, then—as opposed to the Oedipal dread of them as domesticating, even emasculating, constructions (inasmuch as our cultural logic of sex and space renders the inside place feminine)—speaks for a longing to abscond from the neurotically uncanny experience of social spectragraphia by a retreat away from the public sphere where the gaze tyrannizes into the remote interiority of that other construction of space: consciousness" (*Constructing the Black Masculine* 123), I see the ship and sea—expansive as they are—as the preferable option for Douglass's and Delany's heroes. As I will demonstrate, this figuration is different from the home they may want to retreat to with their partners and does not rely on a movement away from a public gaze. Rather, the ship coheres with expansive notions of the potential for expansive black self-rule and governance.

8. Examples of revolution by this time included the United States, Haiti, and, to a somewhat less useful extent, France. There was also revolutionary ferment in Europe (1848) as well as proto-nationalist movements in Italy, Greece, Germany, etc., and the revolutionary war-born creation of many South American states as a result of Bolívar. There was also the establishment of "free" Liberia via revolt.

9. I want to note here Stephen Best's consideration of the voice as property in the antebellum United States and the influence of this demarcation on phonographic reproduction. The elusiveness of the voice and the law's conception of people as things preoccupied nineteenth-century American legal thought. It is tempting to read such legal problems retrospectively and to privilege, in literary study, those very intangible forms of property that the law sought to concretize. The danger, I believe, lies in creating even greater divisions within black subjecthood.

10. See Robert Stepto, "Storytelling in Early Afro-American Fiction."

11. Fredrickson, *Black Image in the White Mind*.

12. See Wilson, "On Native Ground," and Sale, "Critiques from Within."

13. See Reid-Pharr's use of the term *conjugal union* in criticism on Delany.

14. Though Reid-Pharr takes up a similar question with regard to Delany, I believe it resonates with Douglass's Washington as well: "able to imagine a world in which the emphasis was placed squarely on the body, in which a man might literally grab hold of his destiny, his subjectivity, and make something of them, something that could be touched. The workings of this particular discursive project are made most apparent in Delany's novel *Blake*" (*Conjugal Union*, 177).

15. We've seen that Harriet Jacobs would make this same claim in *Incidents*.

16. Larry J. Reynolds has "locate[d] [the novella's] composition within the trajectory of Douglass's career as an abolitionist and show[n] how it combines his early pacifism

with his growing belief in the justice of black slaves killing white masters" (*Righteous Violence* 87).

17. Actually, some nineteenth-century African American poets *do* counsel widespread rebellion/revolution, taking Byron as their inspiration. See Joan Sherman, *Invisible Poets*.

18. Robert Levine traces scholarship on this point. See *Martin Delany, Frederick Douglass, and the Politics of Representative Identity*, 177.

19. According to a tale in which an explorer asked an aboriginal what Canada was called, the definition the latter gave was "a collection of huts."

20. Carr argues that "Henry's Pan-African manhood, and thus his natural leadership, is constituted in comparison to Colonel Franks's masculinity, just as Maggie's femininity, and thus her status as a suitable object of pity, is constituted in relation to Mrs. Franks's femininity" (*Black Nationalism in the New World* 42). I hope to complicate these parallels.

21. The Colonel's language here alludes to Justice Ruffin's in *State v. Mann*: "the power of the master must be absolute to render the submission of the slave perfect. . . . This discipline belongs to the state of slavery. They cannot be disunited without abrogating at once the rights of the master and absolving the slave from his subjugation," qtd. in Tushnet, *Slave Law in the American South*, 24.

22. Dialect serves this function in scenes portraying "unenlightened" blacks as well.

23. See Du Bois's *Darkwater: Voices from within the Veil* and Carbonella and Kasmir's "W.E.B. Du Bois's *Darkwater* and Anti-colonial, Internationalist Anthropology."

24. It is noteworthy, however, that Douglass does specify Madison Washington as "*The* Heroic Slave," and not "*A* Heroic Slave," thereby suggesting that the character is atypical.

25. This document articulated the argument behind America's attempts to secure Cuba from Spain without, as Clymer puts it, "angering the other European nations" ("Martin Delany's *Blake* and the Transnational Politics of Property" 725). Clymer summarizes President Pierce's distancing of himself from the document as elements of it were leaked and abolitionists pressured him. Such discord in the politics of the president resonates with Delany's general portrayal of white political inconsistency.

26. Recall that Samson is effective brute force, but easily ensnared by superior wiles. He needs (divine) direction to apply his strength successfully against the Philistines. See the book of Judges.

27. See Crane's essay "The Lexicon of Rights, Power, and Community in *Blake*" for a detailed assessment of problems in Delany's theory which he sees as "threaten[ing] to collapse into a positivistic vision of legal rights as the privileges and licenses granted and enforced by the dominant political power within a society . . . [or as] reinstating the . . . vision of rights as the perquisites of the powerful" (546). Perhaps Delany is performing a conservative critique of the liberal rhetoric of rights.

28. I'll note here that Chatham was the final publication place of Shadd's newspaper, the *Provincial Freeman* from 1855 to 1857 (having moved from Windsor and Toronto) and recall that Delany was a frequent contributor to the paper, resident of the area, and friend of Shadd.

29. Plácido's poet status supports the earlier note, that appeals for revolution were voiced by African American poets who often took Europe (Greece) or Haiti as examples. Delany is most likely appealing to that literary tradition, too.

30. Also, ship-borne revolution/mutiny is easily—and literally—contained, especially once the ship docks. See Amistad.

31. Furthermore, note Reid-Pharr's contention that "Conjugality not only steers us away from the fact of the palpable homoeroticism that the combined figures of Blake and Plácido reflect but also helps settle the issue of how one might wed a peculiarly Black American body to the principles of (black) bourgeois universalism" (*Conjugal Union* 126). While I don't entirely agree with this assessment, I want to acknowledge Reid-Pharr's belief that the novel credits and then disavows the potential of homoeroticism and, I would add, sexual choice more broadly.

Conclusion. Black Intellectuals, Black Well-Being: Questions about the Future of Black American Literary Studies

1. See Gardner, *Unexpected Places*, chapter 1.
2. See Joanna Brooks, "The Early American Public." We might think of Nancy Fraser's critique of the hegemony of the Habermasian public sphere and resist the same hegemonic impulse when imagining a black public. See also Michael Warner's *Publics and Counterpublics* (New York: Zone Books, 2002).

Bibliography

Primary Sources

Bachman, John, D.D. *The Doctrine of the Unity of the Human Race Examined on the Principles of Science*. Charleston: C. Canning, 1850. Reprinted as vol. 5 of *American Theories of Polygenesis*. Ed. Robert Bernasconi. Bristol: Thoemmes Press, 2002.
Brand, Dionne. *Land to Light On*. Toronto: McClelland and Stewart, 1997.
Canniff, William. "An Historical Sketch of Canadian Medicine and Surgery." Canniff Papers, G3-2, Archives of Ontario (OA).
——. *History of the Settlement of Upper Canada*. Toronto: Dudley & Burns, 1869.
——. *The Medical Profession in Upper Canada, 1783–1850*. Toronto: William Briggs, 1894.
Carlyle, Thomas. "Occasional Discourse on the Negro Question." *Fraser's Magazine for Town and Country* 40 (1849).
Cartwright, Samuel A. "Introductory Address." *New Orleans Medical Journal* (May 1844): i–vi.
——. "Philosophy of the Negro Constitution." *New Orleans Medical and Surgical Journal* 9 (1853): 195–208.
——. "Report on the Diseases and Physical Peculiarities of the Negro Race." *New Orleans Medical and Surgical Journal* 7 (1851): 705.
——. "Slavery in the Light of Ethnology." 1852. *Cotton Is King, and Proslavery Arguments*. Ed. E. N. Elliott, LLD. Augusta, Ga.: Pritchard, Abbot & Loomis, 1860. 691–706.
Carey, Matthew. *A Short Account of the Malignant Fever, lately prevalent in Philadelphia: with a Statement of the Proceedings that took place on the subject, in different parts of the United States. To which are added, accounts of the Plague in London and Marseilles; and a list of the Dead, from August 1 to the middle of December, 1793*. 4th ed. Philadelphia: published by author, 1794.
Casas, Bartolomé de las. *An Account, much abbreviated, of the destruction of the Indies*. Ed. Franklin W. Knight. Trans. Andrew Hurley. Indianapolis: Hackett, 2003.
Cobb, Thomas R. R. *An Inquiry into the Law of Negro Slavery in the United States of America*. Philadelphia: T. & J. W. Johnson, 1858.
Coleridge, Samuel Taylor. "The Rime of the Ancient Mariner." *Lyrical Ballads*. By William Wordsworth and Samuel Taylor Coleridge. 1789. London: Methuen, 1968.
Combe, George. "Phrenological Remarks on the relation between the natural Talents and Dispositions of Nations, and the Developments of their Brains." Appendix in *Crania*

Americana; or, A Comparative View of the Skulls of Various Aboriginal Nations of North and South America: to which is prefixed An Essay on the Varieties of the Human Species. Illustrated by Seventy-eight Plates and a Colored Map, by Samuel George Morton, M.D. Philadelphia: J. Dobson, Chestnut Street; London: Simpkin, Marshall, 1839. Reprinted as *American Theories of Polygenesis*, vol. 1, ed. Robert Bernasconi. Bristol: Thoemmes Press, 2002.

Delany, Martin Robison. *Blake; or, The Huts of America*. Boston: Beacon, 1970.

———. *The Condition, Elevation, Emigration, and Destiny of the Colored People of the United States*. 1852. And *Official Report of the Niger Valley Exploring Party*. 1861. Amherst, N.Y.: Humanity, 2004.

Dew, Thomas Roderick. "Abolition of Negro Slavery." *American Quarterly Review* 17 (1832): 189–265. Rpt. *The Ideology of Slavery: Proslavery Thought in the Antebellum South, 1830–1860*. Ed. Drew Gilpin Faust. Baton Rouge: Louisiana State University Press, 1981. 23–77.

Douglass, Frederick. *The Claims of the Negro, Ethnologically Considered: An Address before the Literary Societies. Western Reserve College, at Commencement, July 12, 1854*. Rochester: Lee, Mann, 1854.

———."The Heroic Slave." *Autographs for Freedom*. Ed. Julia Griffiths. Boston: John P. Jewett, 1853. 174–239.

———. "The Heroic Slave." *Frederick Douglass' Paper*, 1853.

———. *Life and Times of Frederick Douglass*. 1892.

———. *My Bondage and My Freedom*. Ed. Brent Hayes Edwards. New York: Barnes and Noble, 2005.

———. *Narrative of the Life of Frederick Douglass, an American Slave*. Boston: Anti-Slavery Office, 1845.

———. *A Systematic Treatise, Historical, Etiological, and Practical on the Principal Diseases of the Interior Valley of North America*. Cincinnati: Winthrop B. Smith, 1850.

———. "To the Editor." *British American Journal* 3.6 (October 1847): 164–65.

Drake, Daniel. "Diseases of the Negro Population of the Southern States." *British American Journal* 1.3 (June 1845): 73–74.

Drew, Benjamin, ed. *The Refugee; or, The Narratives of Fugitive Slaves in Canada. Related by Themselves*. 1856. Toronto: Prospero, 2000.

Easton, Hosea. *To Heal the Scourge of Prejudice: The Life and Writings of Hosea Easton*. Ed. George R. Price and James Brewer Stewart. Amherst: University of Massachusetts Press, 1999.

Equiano, Olaudah. *The Life of Olaudah Equiano; or, Gustavus Vassa the African, 1789*. London: Dawsons, 1969.

Fugitive Slave Act, 1850.

Gray, Thomas Ruffin. "The Confessions of Nat Turner." 1831. In *Nat Turner's Slave Rebellion* by Herbert Aptheker. New York: Humanities Press, 1966. 128–32.

Harper, William. "Memoir on Slavery, Read before the Society for the Advancement of Learning of South Carolina at Its Annual Meeting at Columbia, 1837." 1838. Rpt. *The Ideology of Slavery: Proslavery Thought in the Antebellum South, 1830–1860*. Ed. Drew Gilpin Faust. Baton Rouge: Louisiana State University Press, 1981. 78–135.

Jacobs, Harriet. *Incidents in the Life of a Slave Girl, Written by Herself.* 1861. Ed. Jean Fagan Yellin. Cambridge: Harvard University Press, 2000.
James Somerset v. Charles Stewart. Lofft 1–18; 11 Harg. State Trials 339; 98 Eng Rep 99–510; King's Bench, 22 June 1772. Rpt. 20 Howell's *State Trials* 1, 79–82.
Jefferson, Thomas. *Notes on the State of Virginia.* 1781–82. New York: Library of America, 1984.
Jones, Absalom, and Richard Allen. *A Narrative of the Proceedings of the Black People, during the Late Awful Calamity in Philadelphia, in the Year 1793: and a Refutation of some Censures, thrown upon them in some late Publications.* Philadelphia: for the authors, by William W. Woodward, 1794.
Meigs, J. Aitken, M.D. "The Cranial Characteristics of the Races of Men." *Indigenous Races of the Earth, or New Chapters of Ethnological Enquiry.* Ed. Josiah Clark Nott and George Robbins Gliddon. Philadelphia: J. B. Lippincott; London: Trübner, 1857. Rpt. *American Theories of Polygenesis.* Vol. 4. Ed. Robert Bernasconi. Bristol: Thoemmes Press, 2002. 203–352.
Melville, Herman. *Moby Dick.* New York: Norton, 2002.
Moodie, Susanna. *Roughing It in the Bush.* 1852. Toronto: McClelland and Stewart, 1989.
Morrison, Toni. *Beloved.* 1987. New York: Vintage, 2004.
———. *Playing in the Dark.* Cambridge: Harvard University Press, 1992.
Morton, Samuel George, M.D. *Crania Ægyptiaca; or, Observations on Egyptian Ethnography, Derived from Anatomy, History and the Monuments. From the Transactions of the American Philosophical Society.* Vol. 9. Philadelphia: John Penington, Chestnut Street; London: Madden, Leadenhall Street, 1844. Rpt. *American Theories of Polygenesis.* Vol. 1. Ed. Robert Bernasconi. Bristol: Thoemmes Press, 2002.
———. *Crania Americana; or, A Comparative View of the Skulls of Various Aboriginal Nations of North and South America: to which is prefixed An Essay on the Varieties of the Human Species. Illustrated by Seventy-eight Plates and a Colored Map.* Philadelphia: J. Dobson, Chestnut Street; London: Simpkin, Marshall, 1839.
Nott, Josiah Clark, M.D. "Acclimation; or, The Comparative Influence of Climate, Endemic and Epidemic Diseases, on the Races of Man." *Indigenous Races of the Earth; or, New Chapters of Ethnological Enquiry.* Ed. Josiah Clark Nott and George Robbins Gliddon. Philadelphia: J. B. Lippincott; London: Trübner, 1857. Rpt. *American Theories of Polygenesis.* Ed. Robert Bernasconi. Bristol: Thoemmes Press, 2002. 4:353–401.
———. *An Essay on the Natural History of Mankind, Viewed in Connection with Negro Slavery: Delivered before the Southern Rights Association, 14th December 1850.* Mobile: Dade, Thompson, Printers, 1851.
———. *Two Lectures on the Connection between the Biblical and Physical History of Man. Delivered by Invitation, from the Chair of Political Economy, etc., of the Louisiana University, in December 1848.* 1849. Rpt. New York: Negro University Press, 1969.
———. "Two Lectures on the Natural History of the Caucasian and Negro Races." Mobile: Dade and Thompson, 1844.
Nott, Josiah Clark, M.D., and George R. Gliddon. *Types of Mankind; or, Ethnological Researches, Based upon the Ancient Monuments, Paintings, Sculptures, and Crania of Races and upon Their Natural, Geographical, Philological, and Biblical History illus-*

trated by selections from the inedited papers of Samuel George Morton, M.D., and by additional contributions from Prof. L. Agassiz, LL.D.; W. Usher, M.D.; and Prof. H. S. Patterson, M.D. Philadelphia: J. B. Lippincott; London: Trübner, 1854.

Plato. *The Republic*. Trans. Desmond Lee. 2nd ed. London: Penguin, 2007.

Pooley, Sophia. "Sophia Pooley." *The Refugee; or, the Narratives of Fugitive Slaves in Canada. Related by Themselves*. Ed. Benjamin Drew. 1856. Toronto: Prospero, 2000.

Prince, Mary. *The History of Mary Prince, a West Indian Slave*. Ed. Sara Salih. London: Penguin, 2000.

Revised Statute. Mo. 1845.

Slave Code. N.C. 1854.

Smith, James McCune. *The Works of James McCune Smith: Black Intellectual and Abolitionist*. Ed. John Stauffer. Oxford: Oxford University Press, 2006.

State of Missouri versus Celia, a Slave. File 4496, Callaway County Court, October Term, 1855. Callaway County Courthouse, Fulton, Mo.

Supreme Court Case File 356. Missouri State Archives.

Traill, Catharine Parr. *The Backwoods of Canada*. 1836. Montreal: McGill-Queen's University Press, 1997.

Winder, William. "On Indian Diseases and Remedies." *British American Journal* 1.10 (1846): 255–57.

Wormeny, Lavina. "Narrative of the Escape of a Poor Negro Woman from Slavery." *Montreal Gazette*. 1861. Rpt. Frank Mackey. *Black Then: Blacks and Montreal 1780s–1880s*. Montreal: McGill-Queen's University Press, 2004.

Secondary Sources

Abdur-Rahman, Aliyah. "'This Horrible Exhibition': Sexuality in Slave Narratives." *The Oxford Handbook of the African American Slave Narrative*. Ed. John Ernest. Oxford: Oxford University Press, 2014. 235–47.

Accomando, Christina. "'The Laws Were Laid Down to Me Anew': Harriet Jacobs and the Reframing of Legal Fictions." *African American Review* 32.2 (1998): 229–45.

"African Americans Vulnerable to Lung Disease." *Alcohol and Drug Abuse Weekly* 16.8 (2004): 2–23.

Agamben, Giorgio. *Homo Sacer: Sovereign Power and Bare Life*. Trans. Daniel Heller-Roazen. Stanford: Stanford University Press, 1998.

Aguirre, Adalberto, Jr., and David V. Baker. "Slave Executions in the United States: A Descriptive Analysis of Social and Historical Factors." *Social Science Journal* 36 (1999): 1–31.

Alexander, Michelle. *The New Jim Crow: Mass Incarceration in the Age of Colorblindness*. New York: New Press, 2010.

Allewaert, Monique. *Ariel's Ecology: Plantations, Personhood, and Colonialism in the American Tropics*. Minneapolis: University of Minnesota Press, 2013.

Almonte, Richard. Introduction. *A Plea for Emigration; or, Notes on Canada West, in Its Moral, Social, and Political Aspect: with Suggestions Respecting Mexico, West Indies, and Vancouver Island*. By Mary Ann Shadd. 1852. Toronto: Mercury Press, 1998.

Andrews, William L. "The Novelization of Voice in Early African American Narrative." *PLMA* 105.1 (1990): 23–34.

Baehre, Rainer. "The Medical Profession of Upper Canada Reconsidered: Politics, Medical Reform, and Law in a Colonial Society." *Canadian Bulletin of Medical History/ BCHM* 12 (1995): 101–24.

Bakare-Yusuf, Bibi. "The Economy of Violence: Black Bodies and the Unspeakable Terror." *Gender and Catastrophe*. Ed. Ronit Lentin. London: Zed, 1997.

Ball, Erica L. *To Live an Antislavery Life: Personal Politics and the Antebellum Black Middle Class*. Athens: University of Georgia Press, 2012.

Bankole, Katherine. *Slavery and Medicine: Enslavement and Medical Practices in Antebellum Louisiana*. New York: Garland, 1998.

Baron, Jane B., and Julia Epstein. "Is Law Narrative?" *Buffalo Law Review* 45 (1997): 141–88.

Baumgartner, Barbara. "The Body as Evidence: Resistance, Collaboration, and Appropriation in *The History of Mary Prince*." *Callaloo* 24.1 (2001): 253–75.

Bay, Mia. *The White Image in the Black Mind: African American Ideas about White People, 1830–1925*. New York: Oxford University Press, 2000.

Beavers, Herman. "The Blind Leading the Blind: The Racial Gaze as Plot Dilemma in 'Benito Cereno' and 'The Heroic Slave.'" *Criticism and the Color Line: Desegregating American Literary Studies*. Ed. Henry B. Wonham. New Brunswick: Rutgers University Press, 1996. 205–29.

Benjamin, Walter. "Critique of Violence." *Selected Writings*. Ed. Marcus Bullock and Michael W. Jennings. Cambridge: Harvard University Press, 1996. 1:236–52.

Bennet, Michael, and Vanessa D. Dickerson, eds. *Recovering the Black Female Body: Self-Representations by African American Women*. New Brunswick: Rutgers University Press, 2001. ix–xvi.

Bernier, Celeste-Marie. "A Comparative Exploration of Narrative Ambiguities in Frederick Douglass's Two Versions of *The Heroic Slave* (1853, 1863?)." *Slavery and Abolition* 22.2 (2001): 69–86.

Best, Stephen M. *The Fugitive's Properties: Law and the Poetics of Possession*. Chicago: University of Chicago Press, 2004.

Bewell, Alan. *Romanticism and Colonial Disease*. Baltimore: Johns Hopkins University Press, 1999.

Bhabha, Homi K. "Signs Taken for Wonders: Questions of Ambivalence and Authority under a Tree outside Delhi, May 1817." *Critical Inquiry* 12 (1985): 144–65.

Boster, Dea H. *African American Slavery and Disability: Bodies, Property, and Power in the Antebellum South, 1800–1860*. New York: Routledge, 2013.

Brereton, Bridget. "Text, Testimony, and Gender: An Examination of Some Texts by Women on the English-Speaking Caribbean from the 1770s to the 1920s." In *Engendering History: Caribbean Women in Historical Perspective*. Ed. Verene Shepherd, Bridget Brereton, and Barbara Bailey. Kingston, Jamaica: Ian Randle, 1995. 63–93.

Brooks, Joanna. "The Early American Public." *William and Mary Quarterly* 62.1 (2005): 67–92.

Brooks, Peter, and Paul Gewirtz, eds. *Law's Stories: Narrative and Rhetoric in the Law*. New Haven: Yale University Press, 1996.

Burke, Diane Mutti. *On Slavery's Border: Missouri's Small-Slaveholding Households, 1815–1865*. Athens: University of Georgia Press, 2010.

Bush, Barbara. *Slave Women in Caribbean Society, 1650–1838*. Bloomington: Indiana University Press, 1990.

Calloway-Thomas, Carolyn. "Mary Ann Shadd Cary: Crafting Black Culture through Empirical and Moral Arguments." *Howard Journal of Communications* 24 (2013): 239–56.

Camp, Stephanie M. H. *Closer to Freedom: Enslaved Women and Everyday Resistance in the Plantation South*. Chapel Hill: University of North Carolina Press, 2004.

Campbell, Timothy. "'Enough of a Self': Esposito's Impersonal Biopolitics." *Law, Culture, and the Humanities* 8.1 (2012): 31–46.

Carbonella, August, and Sharryn Kasmir. "W.E.B. Du Bois's *Darkwater* and Anti-Colonial, Internationalist Anthropology." *Dialectical Anthropology* 32, nos. 1/2 (2008): 113–21.

Carr, Robert. *Black Nationalism in the New World: Reading the African American and West Indian Experience*. Durham: Duke University Press, 2002.

Cartwright, Keith. *Reading Africa into American Literature: Epics, Fables, and Gothic Tales*. Lexington: University Press of Kentucky, 2002.

Cesareo, Mario. "When the Subaltern Travels: Slave Narrative and Testimonial Erasure in the Contact Zone." *Women at Sea: Travel Writing and the Margins of Caribbean Discourse*. Ed. Lizabeth Paravisini-Gebert and Ivette Romero-Cesareo. New York: Palgrave, 2001. 99–134.

Chinn, Sarah E. *Technology and the Logic of American Racism*. London: Continuum, 2000.

Chrisman, Laura. *Postcolonial Contraventions: Cultural Readings of Race, Imperialism, and Transnationalism*. Manchester: Manchester University Press, 2003.

Clarke, George Elliott. "Must All Blackness Be American? Locating Canada in Borden's 'Tightrope Time,' or Nationalizing Gilroy's *The Black Atlantic*." *Odysseys Home: Mapping African Canadian Literature*. Toronto: University of Toronto Press, 2002. 71–85.

———. "Race and Racism in Canadian Literature." *Encyclopedia of Literature in Canada*. Ed. William H. New. Toronto: University of Toronto Press, 2002. 922–26.

———. "'This Is No Hearsay': Reading the Canadian Slave Narratives." *Papers of the Bibliographical Society of Canada* 43.1 (2005): 7–32.

Clifford, James. "Diaspora." *Routes: Travel and Translation in the Late Twentieth Century*. Cambridge: Harvard University Press, 1988. 244–77.

Clymer, Jeffory A. "Martin Delany's *Blake* and the Transnational Politics of Property." *American Literary History* 15.4 (2003): 709–31.

Cohen, Daniel A. *Pillars of Salt, Monuments of Grace: New England Crime Literature and the Origin of American Popular Culture, 1674–1860*. New York: Oxford University Press, 1993.

———. "Social Injustice, Sexual Violence, Spiritual Transcendence: Constructions of Interracial Rape in Early American Crime Literature, 1767–1817." *William and Mary Quarterly* 56.3 (1999): 481–526.

Coleman, Daniel. *White Civility: The Literary Project of English Canada*. Toronto: University of Toronto Press, 2006.

Cook, William W., and James Tatum. *African American Writers and the Classical Tradition*. Chicago: University of Chicago Press, 2010.

Crane, Gregg D. "The Lexicon of Rights, Power, and Community in *Blake*: Martin R. Delany's Dissent from *Dred Scott*." *American Literature* 68.3 (1996): 527–53.

———. *Race, Citizenship, and Law in American Literature*. Cambridge: Cambridge University Press, 2002.

Crawford, Alison. "Prison Watchdog Probes Spike in Number of Black Inmates." *CBC News*, December 15, 2011. http://www.cbc.ca/news/politics/story/2011/12/14/crawford-black-prison.html.

Dain, Bruce. *A Hideous Monster of the Mind: American Race Theory in the Early Republic*. Cambridge: Harvard University Press, 2002.

Davidson, Adenike Marie. *The Black Nation Novel: Imagining Homeplaces in Early African American Literature*. Chicago: Third World Press, 2008.

DeLombard, Jeannine M. "Adding Her Testimony: Harriet Jacobs's *Incidents* as Testimonial Literature." *Multiculturalism: Roots and Realities*. Ed. C. James Trotman. Bloomington: Indiana University Press, 2002. 30–48.

———. *In the Shadow of the Gallows: Race, Crime, and American Civic Identity*. Philadelphia: University of Pennsylvania Press, 2012.

———. *Slavery on Trial: Law, Abolitionism, and Print Culture*. Chapel Hill: University of North Carolina Press, 2007.

Downes, Paul. *Democracy, Revolution, and Monarchism in Early American Literature*. Cambridge: Cambridge University Press, 2002.

Du Bois, W.E.B. *Darkwater: Voices from within the Veil*. 1920. Rpt. New York: Oxford University Press, 2007.

———. *The Souls of Black Folk: Essays and Sketches*. Chicago: A. C. McClurg, 1903.

Duffy, John. *From Humors to Medical Science: A History of American Medicine*. Urbana: University of Illinois Press, 1993.

Edwards, Brent Hayes. *The Practice of Diaspora: Literature, Translation, and the Rise of Black Internationalism*. Cambridge: Harvard University Press, 2003.

Einstein, Gillian, and Margrit Shildrick. "The Postconventional Body: Retheorising Women's Health." *Social Science & Medicine* 69 (2009): 293–300.

Elmer, Jonathan. *On Lingering and Being Last: Race and Sovereignty in the New World*. New York: Fordham University Press, 2008.

Esposito, Roberto. *Bíos: Biopolitics and Philosophy*. Trans. Timothy Campbell. Minneapolis: University of Minnesota Press, 2008.

———. "The *Dispositif* of the Person." *Law, Culture, and the Humanities* 8.1 (2012): 17–30.

Fabian, Ann. *The Skull Collectors: Race, Science, and America's Unburied Dead*. Chicago: University of Chicago Press, 2010.

Fanon, Frantz. *Black Skin, White Masks*. Trans. Charles Lam Markmann. New York: Grove, 1967.

———. *The Wretched of the Earth*. 1963. Trans. Richard Philcox. New York: Grove, 2004.

Ferguson, Moira. *Subject to Others: British Women Writers and Colonial Slavery, 1670–1834*. New York: Routledge, 1992.

Finkelman, Paul. "Slavery in the United States: Persons or Property?" In *The Legal Understanding of Slavery: From the Historical to the Contemporary. Ed. Jean Allain. Oxford: Oxford University Press, 2012. 105–34.

Fishkin, Shelley, and Carla Peterson. "'We Hold These Truths to Be Self-Evident': The Rhetoric of Frederick Douglass's Journalism." *Frederick Douglass: New Literary and Historical Essays*. Ed. Eric J. Sundquist. Cambridge: Cambridge University Press, 1990.

Foucault, Michel. *Discipline and Punish: The Birth of the Prison*. Trans. Alan Sheridan. New York: Vintage, 1979.

———. *The History of Sexuality: Vol. I*. Trans. Robert Hurley. 1978. New York: Vintage, 1990.

Fraser, John. *America and the Patterns of Chivalry*. New York: Cambridge University Press, 1982.

Fredrickson, George M. *The Black Image in the White Mind: The Debate on Afro-American Character and Destiny*. New York: Harper and Row, 1971.

Gardner, Eric. *Unexpected Places: Relocating Nineteenth-Century African American Literature*. Jackson: University Press of Mississippi, 2009.

Garfield, Deborah. "Earwitness: Female Abolitionism, Sexuality, and *Incidents in the Life of a Slave Girl*." *Harriet Jacobs and* Incidents in the Life of a Slave Girl: *New Critical Essays*. Ed. Deborah Garfield and Rafia Zafar. Cambridge: Cambridge University Press, 1996.

———. "Speech, Listening, and Female Sexuality in *Incidents in the Life of a Slave Girl*." *Arizona Quarterly* 50.2 (1994): 19–49.

Garrison, William Lloyd. Preface. *Narrative of the Life of Frederick Douglass, an American Slave*. By Frederick Douglass. Boston: Anti-Slavery Office, 1845.

Gates, Henry Louis. Introduction. *The Classic Slave Narratives*. New York: Mentor, 1987.

Gates, Henry Louis, and Nellie Y. McKay, eds. *The Norton Anthology of African American Literature*. 2nd ed. New York: Norton, 2004.

Gathuru, Irene M. "The Role of Socioeconomic and Environmental Factors in the Risk of Obstructive Lung Disease and Impaired Lung Function in Urban Nigerian Adults." PhD diss. University of Pittsburgh, 2001.

Gathuru, Irene M., Clareann H. Bunker, Flora A. Ukoli, and Eruke E. Egbagbe. "Differences in Rates of Obstructive Lung Disease between Africans and African Americans." *Ethnicity and Disease* 12.4 (2002): S3 107–13.

Gilroy, Paul. *The Black Atlantic: Modernity and Double Consciousness*. Cambridge: Harvard University Press, 1993.

Glaude, Eddie S., Jr. *Exodus! Religion, Race, and Nation in Early Nineteenth-Century Black America*. Chicago: University of Chicago Press, 2000.

Goddu, Teresa. *Gothic America: Narrative, History, and Nation*. New York: Columbia University Press, 1997.

Gosse, Van. "'As a Nation, the English Are Our Friends': The Emergence of African American Politics in the British Atlantic World, 1772–1861." *American Historical Review* 113.4 (2008): 1003–28.

Greenberg, Kenneth S. *Honor and Slavery: Lies, Duels, Noses, Masks, Dressing as a Woman, Gifts, Strangers, Humanitarianism, Death, Slave Rebellions, the Proslavery*

Argument, Baseball, Hunting, and Gambling in the Old South. Princeton: Princeton University Press, 1996.

Gross, Ariela. *Double Character: Mastery and Slavery in the Antebellum Southern Courtroom*. Princeton: Princeton University Press, 2000.

———. "Pandora's Box: Slave Character on Trial in the Antebellum Deep South." *Slavery and the Law*. Ed. Paul Finkelman. Lanham, Md.: Roman & Littlefield, 2002.

Grosz, Elizabeth. *Becoming Undone: Darwinian Reflections on Life, Politics, and Art*. Durham: Duke University Press, 2011.

Hairston, Eric Ashley. *The Ebony Column: Classics, Civilization, and the African American Reclamation of the West*. Knoxville: University of Tennessee Press, 2013.

Halttunen, Karen. *Murder Most Foul: The Killer and the American Gothic Imagination*. Cambridge: Harvard University Press, 1998.

Harris, Cheryl I. "Whiteness as Property." *Harvard Law Review* 106.8 (1993): 1707–91.

Hartman, Saidiya. *Scenes of Subjection: Terror, Slavery, and Self-Making in Nineteenth-Century America*. New York: Oxford University Press, 1997.

Health Canada. "Healthy Diverse." 2003.

Hegel, Georg Wilhelm Friedrich. *Phenomenology of Spirit*. Trans. A. V. Miller. Oxford: Oxford University Press, 1997.

Held, David, Anthony McGrew, David Goldblatt, and Jonathan Perraton. *Global Transformations: Politics, Economics, and Culture*. Stanford: Stanford University Press, 1999.

Henry, Katherine. "Slavery and Civic Recovery: Gothic Interventions in Whitman and Weld." *The Gothic Other: Racial and Social Constructions in the Literary Imagination*. Ed. Ruth Bienstock Anolik and Douglas L. Howard. Jefferson, N.C.: McFarland, 2000. 32–53.

Hitchcock, Peter. *Imaginary States: Studies in Cultural Transnationalism*. Urbana: University of Illinois Press, 2003.

Holmes, Martha Stoddard. *Fictions of Affliction: Physical Disability in Victorian Culture*. Ann Arbor: University of Michigan, 2004.

Horsman, Reginald. *Josiah Nott of Mobile: Southerner, Physician, and Racial Theorist*. Baton Rouge: Louisiana State University Press, 1987.

Hume, David. "Of National Characters." *Race and the Enlightenment: A Reader*. Ed. Emmanuel Chukwudi Eze. Cambridge: Blackwell, 1997. 30–33.

Jahn, Janheinz. *Muntu*. New York: Grove Press, 1961. 125.

Jordan, Winthrop. *White over Black: American Attitudes toward the Negro, 1550–1812*. New York: Norton, 1968.

Johnson, Walter. *Soul by Soul: Life Inside the Antebellum Slave Market*. Cambridge: Harvard University Press, 1999.

Juvenal. *The Sixteen Satires*. Trans. Peter Green. Harmondsworth: Penguin, 1974.

Kiple, Kenneth. *Another Dimension to the Black Diaspora: Diet, Disease, and Racism*. Cambridge: Cambridge University Press, 1981.

———. *The Caribbean Slave: A Biological History*. Cambridge: Cambridge University Press, 1984.

Korobkin, Laura Hanft. *Criminal Conversations: Sentimentality and Nineteenth-Century Legal Stories of Adultery*. New York: Columbia University Press, 1998.

Krieger, Nancy. "Shades of Difference: Theoretical Underpinnings of the Medical Controversy on Black/White Differences in the United States, 1830-1870." *International Journal of Health Services* 17.2 (1987): 259-72.

Kristeva, Julia. *Powers of Horror: An Essay on Abjection*. Trans. Leon S. Roudiez. New York: Columbia University Press, 1982.

Kyser, Kristina. Interview with George Elliott Clarke. *University of Toronto Quarterly* 76.3 (2007): 861-73.

Lee, Debbie. *Slavery and the Romantic Imagination*. Philadelphia: University of Pennsylvania Press, 2002.

Levin, Susan B. "Eryximachus' Tale: The Symposium's Role in Plato's *Critique of Medicine*." *Apeiron, a Journal for Ancient Philosophy and Science* 42.4 (2011): 275-308.

Levine, Robert S. *Martin Delany, Frederick Douglass, and the Politics of Representative Identity*. Chapel Hill: University of North Carolina Press, 1997.

Long, Edward. *The history of Jamaica; or, General survey of the ancient and modern state of that island with reflections on its situation, settlements, inhabitants, climate products, commerce, laws and government*. London: Lowndes, 1774.

Madison, James. *The Federalist: a collection of essays, written in favour of the new Constitution, as agreed upon by the Federal convention, September 17, 1787, in two volumes*. New York: J. and A. M'Lean, 1788.

Malchow, H. L. *Gothic Images of Race in Nineteenth-Century Britain*. Stanford: Stanford University Press, 1996.

Martensen, Robert L. *The Brain Takes Shape: An Early History*. Oxford: Oxford University Press, 2004.

Mason, H. D., S. C. Cwyfan-Hughes, G. Heinrich, S. Franks, and J. M. Holly. "Insulin-like Growth Factor (IGF) I and II, IGF-Binding Proteins, and IGF-Binding Protein Proteases Are Produced by Theca and Stroma of Normal and Polycystic Human Ovaries." *Journal of Clinical Endocrinology and Metabolism* 81.1 (1996): 276-84.

Matthews, John Pengwyrne. *Tradition in Exile: A Comparative Study of Social Influences on the Development of Australian and Canadian Poetry in the Nineteenth Century*. Toronto: University of Toronto Press, 1962.

Mbanya, Jean-Claude, J. Kennedy Cruickshank, Terrence E. Forrester, B. Balkau, J. Y. Ngogang, Lisa K. Riste, A. Forhan, N. M. Anderson, Franklyn I. Bennett, and Rainford J. Wilks. "Standardized Comparison of Glucose Intolerance in West African-Origin Populations of Rural and Urban Cameroon, Jamaica, and Caribbean Migrants to Britain." *Diabetes Care* 22.3 (1999): 434-40.

McGowen, Randall. "The Body and Punishment in Eighteenth-Century England." *Journal of Modern History* 59 (1987): 651-79.

McLaurin, Melton A. *Celia, a Slave*. New York: Avon, 1991.

Merish, Lori. *Sentimental Materialism: Gender, Commodity Culture, and Nineteenth-Century American Literature*. Durham: Duke University Press, 2000.

Miller, Floyd. "Introduction." *Blake; or, The Huts of America*. By Martin Robison Delany. Boston: Beacon, 1970.

Miller, Keith D., and Kevin Quashie. "Slave Mutiny as Argument, Argument as Fiction,

Fiction as America: The Case of Frederick Douglass's *The Heroic Slave*." *Southern Communication Journal* 63.3 (1998): 199–207.

Mohanty, Chandra. "Under Western Eyes: Feminist Scholarship and Colonial Discourses." *Colonial Discourse and Post-Colonial Theory: A Reader*. Ed. Patrick Williams and Laura Chrisman. Hemel Hampstead: Hertfordshire, 1994. 196–220.

Mohr, James C. *Doctors and the Law: Medical Jurisprudence in Nineteenth-Century America*. New York: Oxford University Press, 1993.

Moody, Joycelyn. "Unsentimental Journeys: Christian Landscapes of Women's Slavery." *Mapping the Sacred: Religion, Geography, and Postcolonial Literatures*. Ed. Jamie S. Scott and Paul Simpson-Housley. Amsterdam: Rodopi, 2001.

Morris, Thomas D. *Southern Slavery and the Law, 1619–1860*. Chapel Hill: University of North Carolina Press, 1996.

Mtubani, V.C.D. "African Slaves and English Law." *PULA Botswana Journal of African Studies* 3.2 (1983): 71–75.

Nelson, Dana D. *National Manhood: Capitalist Citizenship and the Imagined Fraternity of White Men*. Durham: Duke University Press, 1998.

Ngai, Mae. *Impossible Subjects: Illegal Aliens and the Making of Modern America*. Princeton: Princeton University Press, 2004.

NIAID (National Institute of Allergy and Infectious Diseases). *Women's Health*. 2006.

Noble, Marianne. "Sympathetic Listening in Frederick Douglass's 'The Heroic Slave' and *My Bondage and My Freedom*." *Studies in American Fiction* 34.1 (2006): 53–68.

Nowell-Smith, Harriet. "Nineteenth-Century Narrative Case Histories: An Inquiry into Stylistics and History." *Canadian Bulletin of Medical History* 12 (1995): 47–67.

Nwankwo, Ifeoma Kiddoe. *Black Cosmopolitanism: Racial Consciousness and Transnational Identity in the Nineteenth-Century Americas*. Philadelphia: University of Pennsylvania Press, 2005.

Oakes, James. *Ruling Race: A History of American Slaveholders*. New York: Knopf, 1982.

O'Brien, Colleen C. *Race, Romance, and Rebellion: Literatures of the Americas in the Nineteenth Century*. Charlottesville: University of Virginia Press, 2013.

O'Callaghan, Evelyn. "A Hot Place Belonging to Us." *Women Writing the West Indies, 1804–1939*. London: Routledge, 2004.

Peterson, Carla L. *Doers of the Word: African American Women Speakers and Writers in the North (1830–1880)*. New York: Oxford University Press, 1995.

Powell, Timothy. "Postcolonial Theory in an American Context: A Reading of Martin Delany's *Blake*." *The Pre-occupation of Postcolonial Studies*. Ed. Fawzia Afzal-Khan and Kalpana Seshadri-Crooks. Durham: Duke University Press, 2000. 347–65.

Pratt, Mary Louise. *Imperial Eyes: Travel Writing and Transculturation*. London: Routledge, 1992.

Prichard, James Cowles. *Researches into the Physical History of Man*. London: J. and A. Arch, 1813.

Rael, Patrick. *Black Identity and Black Protest in the Antebellum North*. Chapel Hill: University of North Carolina Press, 2002.

Randall, Vernellia R. "Slavery, Segregation, and Racism: Trusting the Health Care System Ain't Always Easy! An African American Perspective on Bioethics." *Saint Louis University Public Law Review* 15 (1996): 191–235.

Rankine, Patrice. *Ulysses in Black: Ralph Ellison, Classicism, and African American Literature*. Madison: University of Wisconsin Press, 2006.

Reed, Henry. *Platform for Change: The Foundations of the Northern Free Black Community, 1775–1865*. East Lansing: Michigan State University Press, 1994.

Reid-Pharr, Robert. *Conjugal Union: The Body, the House, and the Black American*. New York: Oxford University Press, 1999.

Reynolds, Larry J. *Righteous Violence: Revolution, Slavery, and the American Renaissance*. Athens: University of Georgia Press, 2011.

Rhodes, Jane. *Mary Ann Shadd Cary: The Black Press and Protest in the Nineteenth Century*. Bloomington: Indiana University Press, 1998.

Richie, Beth E. *Compelled to Crime: The Gender Entrapment of Battered Black Women*. New York: Routledge, 1996.

Ricoeur, Paul. *Oneself as Another*. Chicago: University of Chicago Press, 1992.

Sabol, William J., Todd D. Minton, and Paige M. Harrison. "Prison and Jail Inmates at Midyear 2006." *Bureau of Justice Statistics Bulletin*. June 2007.

Sale, Maggie Montesinos. "Critiques from Within: Antebellum Projects of Resistance." *American Literature* 64 (1992): 695–718.

———. *Slumbering Volcano: American Slave Ship Revolts and the Production of Rebellious Masculinity*. Durham: Duke University Press, 1997.

Salih, Sara. Introduction. *The History of Mary Prince, a West Indian Slave*. Ed. Sara Salih. London: Penguin, 2000.

Sanchez-Eppler, Karen. *Touching Liberty: Abolition, Feminism, and the Politics of the Body*. Berkeley: University of California Press, 1993.

Savitt, Todd. *Race and Medicine in Nineteenth- and Early Twentieth-Century America*. Kent: Kent State University Press, 2007.

Scarry, Elaine. *The Body in Pain: The Making and Unmaking of the World*. New York: Oxford University Press, 1985.

Schroeder, Janice. "'Narrat[ing] Some Poor Little Fable': Evidence of Bodily Pain in *The History of Mary Prince* and 'Wife-Torture in England.'" *Tulsa Studies in Women's Literature* 23.2 (2004): 261–81.

Schwartz, Marie Jenkins. *Birthing a Slave: Motherhood and Medicine in the Antebellum South*. Cambridge: Harvard University Press, 2006.

Scott, Joan. "The Evidence of Experience." *Critical Inquiry* 17 (1991): 773–97.

Scruggs, Dalila. "'Photographs to Answer Our Purposes': Representations of the Liberian Landscape in Colonization Print Culture." *Early African American Print Culture*. Ed. Lara Langer Cohen and Jordan Alexander Stein. Philadelphia: University of Pennsylvania Press, 2012. 203–30.

Sharpe, Jenny. *Ghosts of Slavery: A Literary Archaeology of Black Women's Lives*. Minneapolis: University of Minnesota Press, 2003.

Shelby, Tommie. "Two Conceptions of Black Nationalism: Martin Delany on the Meaning of Black Political Solidarity." *Political Theory* 31.5 (2003): 664–92.

Shildrick, Margrit. *Embodying the Monster: Encounters with the Vulnerable Self*. London: Sage Publications, 2002.

Shklar, Judith. *American Citizenship: The Quest for Inclusion*. Cambridge: Harvard University Press, 1991.

Siemerling, Winfried. "Slave Narratives and Hemispheric Studies." *Oxford Handbook of the African American Slave Narrative*. Ed. John Ernest. Oxford: Oxford University Press, 2014. 344–61.

Slotkin, Richard. "Narratives of Negro Crime in New England, 1675–1800." *American Quarterly* 25.1 (1973): 3–31.

Smith, Chas. Hamilton, Lieut.-Col. *The Natural History of the Human Species: Its Typical Forms, Primeval Distribution, Filiations, and Migrations. With a Preliminary Abstract of the Views of Blumenbach, Prichard, Bachman, Agassiz, and Other Authors of Repute on the Subject*. By S. Kneeland, Jr., M.D. Boston: Gould and Lincoln, 59 Washington Street. 1851.

Smith, Kimberly K. "Environmental Criticism and the Slave Narratives." *The Oxford Handbook of the African American Slave Narrative*. Ed. John Ernest. Oxford: Oxford University Press, 2014. 315–27.

Smith, Shawn Michelle. *American Archives: Gender, Race, and Class in Visual Culture*. Princeton: Princeton University Press, 1999.

Smith, Valerie. "'Loopholes of Retreat': Architecture and Ideology in Harriet Jacobs's *Incidents in the Life of a Slave Girl*." *Reading Black, Reading Feminist: A Critical Anthology*. Ed. Henry Louis Gates Jr. New York: Meridian, 1990. 212–26.

Smith Foster, Frances. "A Narrative of the Interesting Origins and (Somewhat) Surprising Developments of African American Print Culture." *American Literary History* 17.4 (2005): 714–40.

Sneed, Shamina. "Cary, Mary Ann Shadd." *Dictionary of Early American Philosophers*. Ed. John Shook. New York: Continuum, 2012. 184–86.

Sommerville, Siobhan B. "Notes toward a Queer History of Naturalization." *American Quarterly* 57.3 (2005): 659–75.

Sorisio, Carolyn. *Fleshing Out America: Race, Gender, and the Politics of the Body in American Literature, 1833–1879*. Athens: University of Georgia Press, 2002.

Spillers, Hortense. "Mama's Baby, Papa's Maybe: An American Grammar Book." 1987. *Black, White, and in Color: Essays on American Literature and Culture*. Chicago: University of Chicago Press, 2003. 203–29.

Spivak, Gayatri. "Can the Subaltern Speak?" *Colonial Discourse and Post-Colonial Theory*. Ed. Patrick Williams and Laura Chrisman. New York: Columbia University Press, 1992. 66–111.

———. "Diasporas Old and New: Women in the Transnational World." *Textual Practice* 10.2 (1996): 245–69.

Starling, Kelly. "What's behind the Asthma Epidemic in Black America?" *Ebony* 53.9 (1998): 62–67.

Stepan, Nancy. *The Idea of Race in Science: Great Britain*. London: Macmillan, 1982.

Stepto, Robert B. "Storytelling in Early Afro-American Fiction: Frederick Douglass's 'The Heroic Slave.'" *Georgia Review* 36.2 (1982): 355–68.

Stone, Andrea. "Interracial Sexual Abuse and Legal Subjectivity in Antebellum Law and Literature." *American Literature* 81.1 (2009): 65–92.

Stowe, Harriet Beecher. *Uncle Tom's Cabin: Authoritative Text, Backgrounds and Contexts, Criticism*. Elizabeth Ammons. 1852. New York: Norton, 1994.

Sundquist, Eric. *To Wake the Nations: Race in the Making of American Literature*. Cambridge: Belknap, Harvard University Press, 1993.

Taft, William H. *Missouri Newspapers*. Columbia: University of Missouri Press, 1964.

Taylor, Charles. *Sources of the Self: The Making of the Modern Identity*. Cambridge: Harvard University Press, 1989.

Temple, Kathryn. *Scandal Nation: Law and Authorship in Britain, 1750–1832*. Ithaca: Cornell University Press, 2003.

Thomas, Alexander, and Samuel Sillen. *Racism and Psychiatry*. Secaucus: Citadel Press, 1972.

Todorova, Kremena. "'I Will Say the Truth to the English People': The History of Mary Prince and the Meaning of English History." *Texas Studies in Literature and Language* 43.3 (2001): 285–302.

Tountas, Yannis. "The Historical Origins of the Basic Concepts of Health Promotion and Education: The Role of Ancient Greek Philosophy and Medicine." *Health Promotion International* 24.2 (2009): 185–92.

Tushnet, Mark V. *Slave Law in the American South: State v. Mann in History and Literature*. Lawrence: University Press of Kansas, 2003.

Ullman, Victor. *Martin R. Delany: The Beginnings of Black Nationalism*. Boston: Beacon, 1971.

Virchow, Rudolph. *Post-Mortem Examinations, with Especial Reference to Medico-Legal Practice*. 1846. Trans. Dr. T. Smith. Philadelphia: Presley Blackiston, 1880.

Wade, George N., Jill E. Schneider, and H. Y. Li. "Control of Fertility by Metabolic Cues." *American Journal of Physiology* 270 (1996): E1–19.

Walcott, Rinaldo. "'Who Is She and What Is She to You?' Mary Ann Shadd Cary and the (Im)possibility of Black/Canadian Studies." *Atlantis* 24.2 (2000): 137–46.

Wald, Priscilla. "American Studies and the Politics of Life." *American Quarterly* 64.2 (2012): 85–204.

———. *Constituting Americans: Cultural Anxiety and Narrative Form*. Durham: Duke University Press, 1995.

Waligora-Davis, Nicole. A. *Sanctuary: African Americans and Empire*. Oxford: Oxford University Press, 2011.

Walker, David. *David Walker's Appeal to the Coloured Citizens of the World*. Ed. Peter P. Hinks. 1829. University Park: Pennsylvania State University Press, 2000.

Wallace, Maurice O. *Constructing the Black Masculine: Identity and Ideality in African American Men's Literature and Culture, 1775–1995*. Durham: Duke University Press, 2002.

Walters, Tracey L. *African American Literature and the Classicist Tradition: Black Women Writers from Wheatley to Morrison*. New York: Palgrave Macmillan, 2007.

Warner, John Harley. "A Southern Medical Reform: The Meaning of the Antebellum Argument for Southern Medical Information. *Science and Medicine in the Old South*. Ed.

Ronald L. Numbers and Todd L. Savitt. Baton Rouge: Louisiana State University Press, 1989.

———. "The Idea of Southern Medical Distinctiveness: Medical Knowledge and Practice in the Old South." *Science and Medicine in the Old South*. Ed. Ronald L. Numbers and Todd L. Savitt. Baton Rouge: Louisiana State University Press, 1989. 179–205.

Washington, Harriet A. *Medical Apartheid: The Dark History of Medical Experimentation on Black Americans from Colonial Times to the Present*. New York: Anchor Books, 2008.

Weheliye, Alexander G. *Habeas Viscus: Racializing Assemblages, Biopolitics, and Black Feminist Theories of the Human*. Durham: Duke University Press, 2014.

Weiner, Marli F., with Mazie Hough. *Sex, Sickness, and Slavery: Illness in the Antebellum South*. Urbana: University of Illinois Press, 2012.

White, Charles. *An Account of the Regular Gradation in Man, and in Different Animals and Vegetables*. London: C. Dilly, 1799.

Wilentz, Gay. *Healing Narratives: Women Writers Curing Cultural Dis-ease*. New Brunswick: Rutgers University Press, 2000.

Wilson, Ivy G. "On Native Ground: Transnationalism, Frederick Douglass, and 'The Heroic Slave.'" *PMLA* 121.2 (2006): 453–68.

Winks, Robin. *The Blacks in Canada*. 1971. Montreal and Kingston: McGill-Queens University Press, 1997.

Wood, Marcus. *The Horrible Gift of Freedom: Atlantic Slavery and the Representation of Emancipation*. Athens: University of Georgia Press, 2010.

Wright, Richard, Serin Houston, Mark Ellis, Steven Holloway, and Margaret Hudson. "Crossing Racial Lines: Geographies of Mixed-Race Partnering and Multiraciality in the United States." *Progress in Human Geography* 27.4 (2003): 457–74.

Zahavi, Dan. *Subjectivity and Selfhood: Investigating the First-Person Perspective*. Cambridge: MIT Press, 2008.

Zuck, Rochelle Raineri. "Martin R. Delany and Rhetorics of Divided Sovereignty." In *African American Culture and Legal Discourse*, 39–56. New York: Palgrave Macmillan, 2009.

Index

Page numbers in *italics* indicate illustrations.

Aboriginal remedies, 43–44
Aboriginals, 28, 29; in *Blake*, 181–82; slavery and, 97–98, 106–8, 202n1
Accomando, Christina, 128–29
ACS. *See* American Colonization Society
African American life expectancy, 25
African Canadian population, 25
African colonization, 53, 67, 79
Agamben, Giorgio, 11, 87–88
Agassiz, Louis, 28–29, *37*; polygenism and, 31–32
Allen, Richard, 38
Allewaert, Monique, 10
Almonte, Richard, 203n1
American Colonization Society, 16; Delany on, 74, 79; *A Plea for Emigration* on, 66, 67
Americanism, 42–43
American print culture, 52, 194–95
American School of Ethnology, 28
Andrews, William L., 158–59, 170, 209n2
Antebellum American medicine, 4
Antebellum personhood, 4, 7, 121
Anthropology, 28–29, 182–83
Anti-American sentiments, 42–43
Antigua, 115
Antislavery literature, 95, 108
Antislavery propaganda, 96, 108
Apes, 28, 33–34, *35*, *36*, 185
Arendt, Hannah, 201n3
Aristotle, 81
Autonomy: Delany on, 81–83; Greek ideals on, 70, 81; Shadd on, 81–83; slave narratives on, 86

Bachman, John, 6, 13, 39; on polygenism, 48
The Backwoods of Canada (Traill), 203n1
Baehre, Rainer, 202n4
Ball, Erica, 70
Beavers, Herman, 162
Bederman, Gail, 178
Bhabha, Homi, 87, 116
Bird allusions, 164–65
Black American canon, 3–4
Black Americans, 2
Black exodus, 14
Black health: aboriginal remedies, 43–44; African colonization relating to, 79; black well-being and, 3–4, 14–15, 199–200; Delany on, 62–63, 73–83; "The Heroic Slave" and, 164–66; immigrant sickness, 44; in Liberia, 79; "negro diseases" and, 39–50, 69; *A Plea for Emigration* on, 64, 65–67; political independence and, 14, 63; Shadd on, 15–17, 62–63; slavery relating to, 41, 75
Black inferiority, 6
Black intellectuals, 194–200
Black literature, 3–4, 14–15, 62, 194–200
Black masculinity, 158; black selfhood and, 166–67, 170, 190; in *Blake*, 182, 185–86, 189–90; heroic rebellion and, 20–22; in "The Heroic Slave," 162, 165–67, 170–72
Black migration: British Imperial law and, 5; to Canada, 2, 40; personhood and, 5
Black mobility, 63
Black Nationalism, 74

Black physicality, 199; in *Blake*, 178–79, 183; Delany on, 57–58, 62–63; endurance, 40–41; in "The Heroic Slave," 165–69, 171–75; Shadd on, 57–58

Black selfhood, 2–4, 84–85; black masculinity and, 166–67, 170, 190; black well-being and, 13–22; for black women, 94–96; Delany on, 176–77; harm prevention and, 19; personhood, humanness, and selfhood, 4–13, 16, 47, 196–200; *A Plea for Emigration* on, 64–65; slave narratives and, 85–86; white selfhood compared to, 18; women's selfhood, 18, 19

Black sexuality: in *Blake*, 177–80, 189–93; heroic rebellion and, 20–22, 158; in "The Heroic Slave," 170–71; interracial sexual relations and, 131–32; slave lust, 127–28, 129; vulnerability and, 19–20, 158

Black well-being: black health and, 3–4, 14–15, 199–200; black intellectuals on, 194–200; black selfhood and, 13–22; in Canada, 79; climate relating to, 68–70; Delany on, 59, 62–63; nation-building and, 17; New World slavery and, 24–26; Nott on, 38–39; Shadd on, 62–63, 67–68; in slavery rhetoric, 1–2

Black women: black selfhood for, 94–96; black sexuality, 19–20; fertility rates of, 92–93; for gynecological experiments, 47; personhood for, 6; sexual vulnerability of, 19–20, 158; women's selfhood, 18, 19

Black Women's Health Project, 25

Blake (Delany), 4, 59, 73, 156; aboriginals in, 181–82; background on, 159, 160, 175–76; black masculinity in, 182, 185–86, 189–90; black physicality in, 178–79, 183; black sexuality in, 177–80, 189–93; on Canada, 186–88; on Cuba, 188–90; freedom in, 184–85; health in, 180–81; heroic rebellion and analysis of, 175–93; other in, 183; Plácido and, 188–89, 191, 212n29; women in, 177–80, 185–88, 190–93

Blumenbach, Johann Friedrich, 28, 29

Body: Delany on, 75–76; in "The Heroic Slave," 162–63, 166–68; labor and, 88, 90; mind and, 70, 75–76, 157–58, 162–63, 166–68; *Missouri v. Celia* and, 134–35; in *A Plea for Emigration*, 65; politic, 65; selfhood and, 12–13, 89, 95–96; Shadd on, 70; in slave narratives, 94–97; voice and, 96

Bouvier, John, 7

Brain studies, 30–31

Brant, Joseph, 97, 106–8

British American Journal, 43

British Imperial Act of 1790, 5

British Imperial Act of 1833, 5

British law, 5, 7–8

British propaganda, 71

British Slavery Abolition Act of 1833, 4

Brokenness, 67, 74

Burke, Diane Mutti, 131

Bush, Barbara, 92

Calloway-Thomas, Carolyn, 60, 69

Camp, Stephanie, 141–42

Canada: anti-American sentiments in, 42–43; black migration to, 2, 40; black well-being in, 79; *Blake* on, 186–88; citizenship in, 68; Delany on, 79, 176, 186–87; diseases in, 68; emigration to, 67–69, 79, 82–83; health in, 68, 79; in "The Heroic Slave," 169; map of Canada West, 54–55; medicine in colonial, 42–44; Shadd, on Canada West, 14, 67–68, 82–83; slavery in, 44

Canadian print, 52

Canniff, William, 44

Carey, Matthew, 38

Cartwright, Samuel A., 13, 69; background on, 45–46; on Constitution, 45, 46; criticism of, 49–50; on diseases, 48–49; on labor, 46; in *New Orleans Medical and Surgical Journal*, 45–46, 52; polygenism and, 49; scientific racism by, 45–50; "Slavery in the Light of Ethnology," 45, 52

Celia, a slave. See *Missouri v. Celia*

Cesareo, Mario, 96

Children, 75–76

Citizenship: in Canada, 68; freedom, refugees, and, 87–88; personhood and, 5; of Shadd, 204n14

Civil War, U.S., 4, 49

Clarke, George Elliott, 106, 205n2
Class, 72, 77–79
Clay, Henry, 52
Climate: black well-being relating to, 68–70; diseases relating to, 46–47, 50; emigration relating to, 68–69; energy and, 68–69; Shadd on, 68–70
Cobb, Thomas R. R., 13; on double character, 122; on negroes, 32, 33, 40–41; on sexual abuse, 123–24, 129
Coleman, Daniel, 202n7
Combe, George, 13, 30–31
The Condition, Elevation, Emigration, and Destiny of the Colored People of the United States (Delany), 14, 73–74; on brokenness, 67, 74; Douglass on, 61
Confession: of Celia, 143–49, 152–53; of Jacobs, H., 143–45, 149–50, 152
Consciousness, 12
Constitution: Cartwright on, 45, 46; Martensen on, 202n8; racism and, 45
Cook, Thomas, 87, 101–2, 104, 119
Cook, William, 14–15
Corporeal control, 63
Corporeal physicality, 62–63
Crane, Gregg, 80, 187
Crawford, Alison, 25
Cuba, 188–90
Culture, medicine and, 44

Dain, Bruce, 27, 52; on African colonization, 67
Daniel (slave), 108–10, 111
Davidson, Adenike Marie, 177
De Bow, J. B., 38
De Bow's Review (De Bow), 38
Deception, 102
Degradation, 80
Delany, Martin Robison, 1, 2, 3, 16–17; on American Colonization Society, 74, 79; on Americanism, 42–43; on autonomy, 81–83; background on, 59–60; on black health, 62–63, 73–83; on black physicality, 57–58, 62–63; on black selfhood, 176–77; on black well-being, 59, 62–63; *Blake*, 4, 59, 73, 156, 160, 175–93, 212n29; on body, 75–76; on brokenness, 67, 74; on Canada, 79, 176, 186–87; on class, 77–79; on degradation, 80; Douglass and, 60–62; on education, 78–79; on emigration, 39, 53, 57, 73–83; on Gliddon, 78; on Greek ideals, 74, 77, 78; heroic rebellion relating to, 156–58, 161–62; on Irish immigrants, 76; on mind, 75–76; on nation, 73; on power, 81; *Principia of Ethnology*, 204n18; *Provincial Freeman* and, 61–62; on racism, 81; on revolution, 73; on self-sufficiency, 76–77; on Shadd, 59–62; on slavery, 75, 80–81

De las Casas, Bartolomé, 75, 202n1
DeLombard, Jeannine, 4, 7, 149–50
Democracy, 11–12
Department of Justice, U.S., 25
Dew, Thomas Roderick, 13, 41
Diabetes, 93
Disability, 91
Diseases: in Canada, 68; Cartwright on, 48–49; classification of, 43; climate relating to, 46–47, 50; diabetes, 93; drapetomania, 41, 45; dysesthesia Ethiopia, 41; immunities and, 34, 36, 38; "negro diseases" and black health, 39–50, 69; place relating to, 45–47; yellow fever, 34, 36, 38, 164
Double character, 122–24
Douglass, Frederick, 2, 19–20, 51, 202n9; on *The Condition, Elevation, Emigration, and Destiny of the Colored People of the United States*, 61; Delany and, 60–62; *Frederick Douglass' Paper*, 60–61; heroic rebellion relating to, 156–58, 161–75; "The Heroic Slave," 156, 159–60, 161–75; journalism by, 60–61; *My Bondage and My Freedom*, 104
Drake, Daniel, 43–44
Drapetomania (running away), 41, 45
Drew, Benjamin, 11, 86, 87; Pooley, Sophia, and, 97–98, 106, 118; *The Refugee*, 87, 108
Du Bois, W.E.B., 71, 183
Duffy, John, 45
Dysesthesia Ethiopia (rascality), 41

Early American literature, 59–60, 62
Education, 78–79

Index • 231

Edwards, Brent Hayes, 22
Elmer, Jonathan, 26
Emigration, 51–52; to Canada, 67–69, 79, 82–83; climate relating to, 68–69; Delany on, 39, 53, 57, 73–83; Great Britain relating to, 72; Irish immigrants and, 76; Shadd on, 14, 15, 39, 53, 57, 70–73, 82–83. *See also* *A Plea for Emigration*
Endurance, 40–41
Energy, 68–70
Environmentalism, 42
Escaped slaves, 39–40; fugitives, 52
Esposito, Roberto, 88, 90; on personhood, 8, 91, 198–99
An Essay on the Natural History of History (Nott), 9
Ethical responsibility, 111
Exclusion, 11–12

Fabian, Ann, 31
Facial construction, 31
The Federalist (Madison), 4–5, 19, 122
Fertility rates, 92–93
Fictive voice, 209n2
Finkelman, Paul, 4
Foucault, Michel, 142, 143–44, 208n23
Fourteenth Amendment, 5
Franklin, Benjamin, 53
Frederick Douglass' Paper, 60–61
Frederickson, George, 127
Freedom: in *Blake*, 184–85; citizenship, refugees, and, 87–88; medicine relating to, 39; Prince on, 115–17; scientific racism relating to, 39
Fugitive Slave Act of 1850, 4, 16; overview of, 39–40; scientific racism and, 40–41; Shadd on, 72

Gall, Franz Josef, 30–31
Gardner, Eric, 14
Garfield, Deborah, 151–52
Garrison, William Lloyd, 19
Gender entrapment, 207n10
Gender issues, 21, 121, 156
Genesis, 6
Gilroy, Paul, 160, 164

Gliddon, George, 28–29, 52–53; Delany on, 78; *Types of Mankind*, 31–33, 35, 36, 37, 52–53
Gosse, Van, 68, 108
Gothic literature, 136–38, 149
Gray, Thomas Ruffin, 22
Great Britain: British Imperial Act of 1790, 5; British Imperial Act of 1833, 5; British law, 5, 7–8; British propaganda, 71; British Slavery Abolition Act of 1833, 4; emigration relating to, 72; monarchy of, 65, 72–73; Prince on, 112–17; superiority of, 108
Greek ideals, 46, 50; on autonomy, 70, 81; Delany on, 74, 77, 78; heroic rebellion relating to, 159, 166–67, 179; Shadd on, 62, 64, 69, 70, 72
Greenberg, Kenneth, 102–3
Griffiths, Julia, 159–60
Gross, Ariela, 4, 49, 101; on slave vice, 41
Grosz, Elizabeth, 90, 197–98
Gynecological experiments, 47

Habeas Corpus Act, 7–8, 91–92
Hairston, Eric Ashley, 14–15
Hall (Judge), 136, 138. *See also* *Missouri v. Celia*
Harm prevention, 19
Harper, Frances Watkins, 64
Harper, William, 13, 21, 158; "Memoir on Slavery," 52; on whipping, 40
Hartman, Saidiya, 4, 150–51; on sexual abuse, 85–86, 123, 132
Health: in *Blake*, 180–81; in Canada, 68, 79; of Celia, 135–36, 146–47, 153–54; Jacobs, H., on, 139–41, 153–54; nationalism relating to, 112; Plato on, 66; Prince on, 112–15, 206n18; Pythagorean doctrine on, 69. *See also* Black health
Health Care, 202n8
Henry, Katherine, 136
Henson, Josiah, 86–87
Heroic rebellion, 20–22, 73; Black masculinity and, 20–22; black sexuality and, 20–22, 158; in *Blake*, 175–93; Delany relating to, 156–58, 161–62; Douglass relating to, 156–

58, 161–75; Greek ideals relating to, 159, 166–67, 179; power and, 156, 159; revenge fantasy, 155; ship relating to, 160–61

"The Heroic Slave" (Douglass), 156; analysis of, 161–75; background on, 159–62; bird allusions in, 164–65; black health and, 164–66; black masculinity in, 162, 165–67, 170–72; black physicality in, 165–69, 171–75; black sexuality in, 170–71; Canada in, 169; mind and body in, 162–63, 166–68; moral and social codes in, 172–73; nation in, 168–69, 173–74; ship in, 163–64, 174–75; storytelling technique in, 161–62; white characters in, 172–74; women in, 167–68, 169–71

Herzogenrath, Bernd, 53, 65

Higginbotham, A. Leon, Jr., 33

Hippocrates, 70

History (Prince), 4, 10–11, 86–97, 108–17

History of Jamaica (Long), 29

Hobbes, Thomas, 53

Homicide, 127. See also *Missouri v. Celia*

Homo Sacer (Agamben), 11

Hood, Michael, 197

The Horrible Gift of Freedom (Wood), 204n8

Horsman, Reginald, 31, 48, 128

Hough, Mazie, 43

Humanness, 18; Allewaert on, 10; Esposito on, 8; Grosz on, 90, 197–98; parahumanity, 10; personhood, selfhood, and, 4–13, 16, 47, 196–200; race and, 8–9, 91; sexual abuse relating to, 126; Weheliye on, 91, 113, 198–99

Human origins, 27–28

Human rights, 6. See also Legal rights

Immigrant sickness, 44

Immunities, 202n2; diseases and, 34, 36, 38; race and, 34; slavery relating to, 34, 36, 38, 40, 75

Incidents in the Life of a Slave Girl (Jacobs), 2, 19–20, 125, 139–45, 149–52

Inclusion, 11–12

Indians. See Aboriginals

Interracial sexual relations, 131–32

Irish immigrants, 76

Jacobs, Anne F., 33

Jacobs, Harriet, 2, 19–20; Accomando on, 128–29; background on, 125; confession of, 143–45, 149–50, 152; Garfield on, 151–52; health of, 139–41, 153–54; *Incidents in the Life of a Slave Girl*, 2, 19–20, 125, 139–45, 149–52; law relating to, 142, 150–51; on pregnancy, 139–41; on violence, 151

Jefferson, Thomas, 29–30

Johnson, Walter, 97

Jones, Absalom, 38

Jones, Jefferson, 136, 207n4

Journalism, 60–61

Kiple, Kenneth, 34, 49

Korobkin, Laura Hanft, 135

Krieger, Nancy, 49

Labor: body and, 88, 90; Cartwright on, 46; at salt ponds, 89–91; washing clothes, 93–94

Landownership, 70

Law: British, 5, 7–8; British Slavery Abolition Act of 1833, 4; Fugitive Slave Act of 1850, 4, 16, 39–41, 72; *Habeas Corpus* Act, 7–8, 91–92; on homicide, 127; on interracial sexual relations, 131–32; Jacobs, H., relating to, 142, 150–51; medical licensing laws, 42, 45, 202n4; medicine, personhood, and, 4–5, 95; *Missouri Revised Statute, 1845*, 127; in *Missouri v. Celia*, 127, 131, 134–39; Naturalization Act of 1790, 5; Navigation Acts, 7–8; *Revised Code of North Carolina, 1854*, 127; rule and regulation, medicine, and scientific racism, 30–39; scientific racism and, 32–33; on sexual abuse, 121–33; slavery and, 27; violence and, 104. See also Legal rights

Law Dictionary (Bouvier), 7

Lawrence, William, 41

Leclerc, Georges-Louis, 28

Lectures on Physiology (Lawrence), 41

Legal rights: human rights, 6; personhood and, 4–8, 187; for slaves, 19–20

Leg irons, 105

Levin, Susan, 66
Levine, Robert, 60–62, 176, 203n5
Lewis, Robert Benjamin, 78
Liberia, 79
Light and Truth (Lewis), 78
Linné, Carl von, 28
Literature: antislavery, 95; Black, 3–4, 14–15, 62, 194–200; early American, 59–60, 62; Gothic, 136–38, 149; on slave fugitives, 52
Long, Edward, 29

Madison, James, 4–5, 19, 122, 161
Malchow, H. L., 138
Manifest Destiny imperialism, 183–84
Martensen, Robert, 202n8
Matthews, John Pengwyrne, 42
McGowen, Randall, 131
McLaurin, Melton, 131, 207n4
Medical assistance, 202n6
Medical case histories, 100–101
Medical examinations: interpretation, of scars, 101; of Pooley, Sophia, 97–98; of Prince, 96–97; of Wormeny, 99–102
Medical research and experimentation, 47
Medicine: aboriginal remedies, 43–44; Antebellum American, 4; *British American Journal* on, 43; Civil War relating to, 49; in colonial Canada, 42–44; freedom relating to, 39; immigrant sickness, 44; law, personhood, and, 4–5, 95; licensing laws for, 42, 45, 202n4; nationalism, culture, and, 44; *New Orleans Medical and Surgical Journal* on, 43, 45–46, 52; paternalistic rhetoric in, 49; place relating to, 45–48, 50; pregnancy and, 140; racial categorization in, 39–50, 203n13; rule and regulation, scientific racism, and, 30–39; slavery and, 27, 41; on slave vice, 41; southern American medical sectionalism, 41, 44, 46–48
Medico-political theory, 13–14
Meigs, J. Aitken, 13
"Memoir on Slavery" (Harper, William), 52
Merish, Lori, 189–90
Mind: body and, 70, 75–76, 157–58, 162–63, 166–68; Delany on, 75–76; in "The Heroic Slave," 162–63, 166–68; Shadd on, 70

Missouri Revised Statute, 1845, 127
Missouri v. Celia, 19–20; addenda to trial summary, 137, 139; background on, 124–25, 130–31; body and, 134–35; confession, of Celia, 143–49, 152–53; deposition, bearing Celia's Mark, 146; Gothic literature relating to, 136–38, 149; health, of Celia, 135–36, 146–47, 153–54; law in, 127, 131, 134–39; newspaper coverage on, 133–34, 143, 146–49, 152–53, 208n17, 208n26; questions for testifying physicians, 147; sentimentality in, 134–36; witness accounts and testimony, 135–39, 207n4
Monaghan, Jennifer, 195
Monarchy, 65, 72–73
Monogenism, 27–30
Monster imagery, 10
Moodie, Susanna, 52, 203n1
Morris, Thomas D., 32
Morrissey, Marietta, 92
Morton, Samuel George, 13, 28–31, 52; scientific racism relating to, 31–34
Mtubani, V.C.D., 7
My Bondage and My Freedom (Douglass), 104

Nation: Delany on, 73; in "The Heroic Slave," 168–69, 173–74; race relating to, 73
Nation-building, 17
Nationalism: Black, 74; health relating to, 112; medicine and, 44; Pooley, Sophia, and, 118; Prince relating to, 112–17; slave narratives on, 88–89, 112–20; Wormeny and, 118–20
Naturalization Act of 1790, 5
Natural order, 27–28, 186–87
Navigation Acts, 7–8
Negroes, 6; Cobb on, 32, 33, 40–41; "negro diseases" and black health, 39–50, 69; Nott on, 33, 36, 50; portrait of, in *Types of Mankind*, 35, 36, 37; White on, 28
New Orleans Medical and Surgical Journal, 43; Cartwright in, 45–46, 52; "Slavery in the Light of Ethnology," 45, 52
Newsom, Robert, 130. See also *Missouri v. Celia*

New World slavery, 22, 24–26
Noble, Marianne, 162
Noses, 102–3
Notes on Canada West (Shadd), 14
Notes on the State of Virginia (Jefferson), 29–30
Nott, Josiah, 9–10, 13, 28–29; background on, 31–32; on black well-being, 38–39; on Negroes, 33, 36, 50; polygenism and, 32; on race, 30–33; scientific racism and, 31–32; Shadd and, 68–69; on southern American medical sectionalism, 48; *Types of Mankind*, 31–33, 35, 36, 37, 52–53
Nowell-Smith, Harriet, 100–101

Obama, Barack, 25
Ostend Manifesto, 183–84
Other: in *Blake*, 183; selfhood and, 9–11, 23, 198

Pain: Prince on, 108–10; suffering and, 94; tolerance, 40
Parahumanity, 10
Parker, Daniel McNeil, 42
Parker, Theodore, 17
Paternalistic rhetoric, 6; in medicine, 49; on sexual abuse, 121, 124, 128, 129
Patterson, Henry, 41
Personhood: antebellum, 4, 7, 121; black migration and, 5; for black women, 6; citizenship and, 5; Esposito on, 8, 91, 198–99; humanness, selfhood, and, 4–13, 16, 47, 196–200; legal rights and, 4–8, 187; medicine, law, and, 4–5, 95; Naturalization Act on, 5; property and, 19, 63, 121
Peterson, Carla, 177, 199
Place, 22–23, 42; diseases relating to, 45–47; medicine relating to, 45–48, 50; Shadd on, 68–69; slavery relating to, 47
Plácido (poet), 188–89, 191, 212n29
Plato, 57; on health, 66; Levin on, 66; Shadd and, 65–66, 70
A Plea for Emigration (Shadd), 14; Almonte on, 203n1; on American Colonization Society, 66, 67; background on, 64; on black health, 64, 65–67; on black selfhood, 64–65; body politic in, 65; as British propaganda, 71; first edition, 56; on Great Britain and monarchial head, 65; "Introductory Remarks," on colonization, 67; Plato relating to, 65–66; on property, 71
Political independence: black health and, 14, 63; race relating to, 71–72
Polygenism, 6; Agassiz and, 31–32; Bachman on, 48; Cartwright and, 49; monogenism and, 27–30; Nott and, 32; slavery and, 29–30
Pooley, Sophia, 2; Drew and, 97–98, 106, 118; Medical examination of, 97–98; nationalism and, 118; slave narrative of, 17–18, 86–87, 97–98, 106–8, 117–18
Post-Mortem Examinations (Virchow), 100
Powell, Timothy, 188
Powell, William, 135
Power, 80, 208n23; Delany on, 81; heroic rebellion and, 156, 159; racism and, 81
Pregnancy, 138, 139–41, 147
Prichard, James Cowles, 29
Prince, Mary, 2; on Daniel, 108–10, 111; on disability, 91; on freedom, 115–17; on Great Britain, 112–17; Grosz on, 90; on health, 112–15, 206n18; *History*, 4, 10–11, 86–97, 108–17; medical examination of, 96–97; nationalism relating to, 112–17; on pain, 108–10; as property, 91–92; on salt ponds, 89–91; on selfhood, 10–11; slave narrative of, 17–18, 86–97, 108–17; on slavery, 116–17; on suffering, 110–11; in Turks Island, 88–89; on vulnerability, 108–10; on washing clothes, 93–94; on West Indies, 115–17
Principia of Ethnology (Delany), 204n18
Prison inmates, 25
Professionalization, 202n4
Property: landownership, 70; personhood and, 19, 63, 121; *A Plea for Emigration* on, 71; Prince as, 91–92
Proslavery medical writers, 6
Provincial Freeman, 203n4; Delany and, 61–62; Shadd and, 58–59
Pythagorean doctrine, 69

Race: anthropology and, 28–29; conceptualization of, 24; humanness and, 8–9, 91; immunities and, 34; nation relating to, 73; Nott on, 30–33; political independence relating to, 71–72; racial categorization, in medicine, 39–50, 203n13; skull size, facial construction, and, 31; theorizing, 24; transcolonial African diasporas relating to, 23–24

Racism: Constitution and, 45; Delany on, 81; power and, 81. *See also* Scientific racism

Rael, Patrick, 47

Rankine, Patrice, 14–15

Rascality, 41

Reddy (Doctor), 99–100, 101, 119

The Refugee (Drew), 87, 108

Refugee Home Society, 58

Refugees: Agamben on, 87–88; citizenship, freedom, and, 87–88; slaves as, 11

Researches into the Physical History of Man (Prichard), 29

Revenge fantasy, 155

Revised Code of North Carolina, 1854, 127

Revolution, 73. *See also* Heroic rebellion

Rhodes, Jane, 53

Richie, Beth E., 207n10

Ricoeur, Paul, 9, 111

Romantic racialism, 167

Roughing It in the Bush (Moodie), 52, 203n1

Running away: without cause, 129–30; as drapetomania, 41, 45

Salt ponds, 89–91

Sanchez-Eppler, Karen, 151

Savitt, Todd, 43–44, 46–47

Scarry, Elaine, 94

Scars, 101

Schroeder, Janice, 95–96

Scientific racism: by Cartwright, 45–50; freedom relating to, 39; Fugitive Slave Act and, 40–41; law and, 32–33; Morton relating to, 31–34; Nott and, 31–32; rule and regulation, medicine, and, 30–39; slavery relating to, 33

Selfhood: Agamben on, 11; body and, 12–13, 89, 95–96; consciousness and, 12; humanness, personhood, and, 4–13, 16, 47, 196–200; other and, 9–11, 23, 198; Prince on, 10–11; Ricoeur on, 9, 111. *See also* Black selfhood

Self-sufficiency, 76–77

Sentimentality, 134–36

Sexual abuse: Cobb on, 123–24, 129; double character relating to, 122–24; Hartman on, 85–86, 123, 132; humanness relating to, 126; in *Incidents in the Life of a Slave Girl*, 19–20, 125, 139–45, 149–52; law on, 121–33; paternalistic rhetoric on, 121, 124, 128, 129; reports of, 128; slave lust relating to, 127–28, 129. *See also Missouri v. Celia*

Shadd, Mary Ann, 2; on autonomy, 81–83; background on, 58–60; on black health, 15–17, 62–63; on black physicality, 57–58; on black well-being, 62–63, 67–68; Calloway-Thomas on, 60, 69; on Canada West, 14, 67–68, 82–83; citizenship of, 204n14; on class, 72, 77; on climate, 68–70; Delany on, 59–62; on emigration, 14, 15, 39, 53, 57, 70–73, 82–83; on energy, 68–70; on Fugitive Slave Act, 72; on Greek ideals, 62, 64, 69, 70, 72; in journalism, 60; on mind and body, 70; on monarchy, 65, 72–73; *Notes on Canada West*, 14; Nott and, 68–69; on place, 68–69; Plato and, 65–66, 70; *Provincial Freeman* and, 58–59; on slavery, 80–81; on vice, 65, 69, 70. *See also A Plea for Emigration*

Sharpe, Jenny, 85, 92

Shildrick, Margrit, 9, 10, 109–10

Ship, 160–61, 210n7; in "The Heroic Slave," 163–64, 174–75

Shootman, Thomas, 138

Sims, J. Marion, 47

Sitze, Adam, 196

Skull proportions, 31

Slave codes, 10, 172

Slave fugitives, 52

Slave narratives: on autonomy, 86; black selfhood and, 85–86; body in, 94–97; contesting testimonies of, 94–111; functions of, 87–88; of Jacobs, H., 19–20, 125, 128–29, 139–52; on nationalism,

88–89, 112–20; of Pooley, 17–18, 86–87, 97–98, 106–8, 117–18; of Prince, 17–18, 86–97, 108–17; suffering in, 85, 94, 104–5; testimony and, 95–97, 104–5; *Uncle Tom's Cabin* as, 86–87; white authentication of, 85, 94–102, 104–6; of Wormeny, 17–18, 86–87, 98–106, 118–20

Slavery: aboriginals and, 97–98, 106–8, 202n1; black health relating to, 41, 75; in Canada, 44; Delany on, 75, 80–81; immunities relating to, 34, 36, 38, 40, 75; law and, 27; medicine and, 27, 41; New World, 22, 24–26; origins of, 75; place relating to, 47; polygenism and, 29–30; Prince on, 116–17; rhetoric of, 1–2; scientific racism relating to, 33; Shadd on, 80–81

"Slavery in the Light of Ethnology" (Cartwright), 45, 52

Slaves: character of, 94; children of, 75–76; executions of, 128; legal rights for, 19–20; lust of, 127–28, 129; as refugees, 11

Slave vice, 41, 102

Smith, Samuel Stanhope, 29–30

Socrates, 77, 78

Sommerville, Siobhan, 5

Southern American medical sectionalism, 41, 44, 46–48

Spillers, Hortense, 127

Spurzheim, Johann Gaspar, 30–31

Stepan, Nancy, 28

Stewart, Maria, 15

Stowe, Harriet Beecher, 22, 52, 61, 86–87

Suffering: pain and, 94; Prince on, 110–11; in slave narratives, 85, 94, 104–5

Sugar colonies, 92–93

Sundquist, Eric, 162, 176

Surveillance, 142

Tatum, James, 14–15

Taylor, Charles, 12

Technology, 196–97

Testimony: in *Missouri v. Celia*, 135–39, 207n4; slave narratives and, 95–97, 104–5; white authentication, of slave narratives, 85, 94–102, 104–6

Therapeutic rhetoric, 24–25

Traill, Catherine Parr, 203n1

Transcolonial African diasporas, 22–24

Turks Island, 88–89

Turner, Nat, 22

Types of Mankind (Nott and Gliddon), 31–33, 52–53; negro portraits in, 35, 36, 37

Uncle Tom's Cabin (Stowe), 52, 61, 86–87

Vice: Shadd on, 65, 69, 70; slave, 41, 102

Violence: Jacobs, H., on, 151; law and, 104; transcolonial African diasporas relating to, 22–23

Virchow, Rudolph, 100

Virginia rebellion, 22

Voice, 96, 210n9

Vulnerability: black sexuality and, 19–20, 158; Prince on, 108–10

Walcott, Rinaldo, 71–72, 204n14, 204n16

Wald, Priscilla, 5

Waligora-Davis, Nicole, 11, 87

Walker, David, 157

Wallace, Maurice, 53, 210n7

Walters, Tracey, 14–15

Ward, Samuel Ringgold, 58

Warner, John Harley, 45, 47

Washing clothes, 93–94

Washington, George, 161

Washington, Harriet, 25, 202n2

Weheliye, Alexander, 8, 22–23, 201n5; on humanness, 91, 113, 198–99

Weiner, Marli F., 43

West Indies, 115–17

Whipping, 40

White, Charles, 28

White authentication, 85, 94–102, 104–6

White ethical responsibility, 111

White European thinkers, 201n5

White selfhood, 18

White women's virtue, 128

Wilson, Ivy, 168

Winder, William, 43

Winthrop, John, 53

Women, 7, 195; in *Blake*, 177–80, 185–88, 190–93; gender entrapment and, 207n10;

in "The Heroic Slave," 167–68, 169–71; white women's virtue, 128. *See also* Black women

Wong, Shelley, 87

Wood, Marcus, 63, 73; *The Horrible Gift of Freedom*, 204n8

Wormeny, Lavina, 2; on biting owners' nose, 102–3; on husband, 105–6; medical examination of, 99–102; nationalism and, 118–20; slave narrative of, 17–18, 86–87, 98–106, 118–20

Wyman, Jeffries, 33

Yellow fever, 34, 36, 38, 164

Zahavi, Dan, 12, 111

Andrea Stone is associate professor of English language and literature at Smith College.

www.ingramcontent.com/pod-product-compliance
Lightning Source LLC
Chambersburg PA
CBHW031807220426
43662CB00007B/559